# Adapting Canonical Texts in Children's Literature

Also available from Bloomsbury

*Children's Literature in Context* Fiona McCulloch
*Children's Literature in Second Language Education,*
edited by Janice Bland and Christiane Lütge
*Continuum Encyclopedia of Children's Literature,*
Berenice E. Cullinan and Diane Goetz Person
*Continuum Encyclopedia of Young Adult Literature,*
edited by Berenice E. Cullinan, Bonnie Kunzel and Deborah Wooten
*Language, Gender and Children's Fiction,* Jane Sunderland
*Shakespeare for Young People* Abigail Rokison

# Adapting Canonical Texts in Children's Literature

Edited by Anja Müller

B L O O M S B U R Y

LONDON · NEW DELHI · NEW YORK · SYDNEY

**Bloomsbury Academic**

An imprint of Bloomsbury Publishing Plc

| 50 Bedford Square | 1385 Broadway |
| London | New York |
| WC1B 3DP | NY 10018 |
| UK | USA |

**www.bloomsbury.com**

**Bloomsbury is a registered trade mark of Bloomsbury Publishing Plc**

First published 2013
Paperback edition first published 2014

**British Library Cataloguing-in-Publication Data**

ISBN: HB:   978-1-4411-7877-0
PB:   978-1-4725-7888-4
EPDF:  978-1-4411-6427-8
ePUB:  978-1-4411-5281-7

**Library of Congress Cataloging-in-Publication Data**
Adapting Canonical Texts in Children's Literature / Edited by Anja Müller.
pages cm Includes index.
ISBN 978-1-4411-7877-0 (hardcover) – ISBN 978-1-4411-6427-8 (ebook) –
ISBN 978-1-4411-5281-7 (ebook) 1. Children's literature–Study and teaching.
2. Literature–Adaptations–History and criticism. 3. Canon (Literature)–
Cross-cultural studies. I. Müller, Anja, 1969 Sept. 24–
PN1008.8.A34 2013
809'.89282--dc23
2012041380

Typeset by Deanta Global Publishing Services, Chennai, India

# Contents

# List of Illustrations

# List of Contributors

**Lisa Rowe Fraustino** is a Professor of English at Eastern Connecticut State University, USA, and a Visiting Associate Professor in the Graduate Program in Children's Literature at Hollins University, USA. She is a Past President of the Children's Literature Association and a former Fulbright Scholar to Mahasarakham, Thailand, where she helped to develop a graduate program in children's literature. Her interest in Disney's film adaptations grew from a study of mothering ideology in children's literature, an area in which she has published several essays. She has also authored a number of books for young readers. Her most recent novel, *The Hole in the Wall*, won the 2010 Milkweed Prize for Children's Literature.

**Iain Halliday** teaches English at the University of Catania, Sicily, and he has also worked as a professional literary translator from Italian into English. His research interests include Translation Studies and Children's Literature. In 2009, Fairleigh Dickinson University Press published his *Huck Finn in Italian, Pinocchio in English: Theory and Praxis of Literary Translation*.

**Jan Keane** is an Economic and Social Research Council (ESRC) scholar in the School of Education at the University of Nottingham, where she received her PhD for work on representations of national identity in educational texts read by children. She is also interested more generally in Australian colonial and nationalist literature. In her previous career, she was author and co-author of Teachers of English to Speakers of Other Languages (TESOL) text books for the publishers Collins and Macmillan/EDICEF widely used in Francophone Africa.

**Anne Klaus** received her first state examination as a teacher of English and German in 2008 and was a research assistant at the University of Osnabrück, Germany, from 2008 until 2011. She is working on a doctoral thesis on saviour figures in fantasy fiction for children and young adults while finishing her teacher training to receive her second state examination as a teacher in January 2013. Her publications and research interests are in the fields of children's fantasy fiction, the Victorian era, Shakespeare and Arthurian romance.

**Mark Macleod** is a Senior Lecturer in English at Charles Sturt University, Australia, where he teaches Children's Literature and Creative Writing. He co-ordinated courses in Children's Literature and Australian Literature at Macquarie University, Australia, before becoming Children's Publishing Director at Random House Australia for ten years. He published books for young readers and for adults under his own name imprint, Mark Macleod Books, at Hodder Headline for five years and has worked for the ABC and the Nine and Seven Networks as a television and radio arts presenter. A former New South Wales state president and then national president of the Children's Book Council of Australia, in 2001 he won the Children's Books Council of Australia Lady Cutler Award and in 2003 the Australian Publishers Association Pixie O'Harris Award for distinguished services to children's literature.

**Jana Mikota** is a tenured lecturer of German literature, with special focus on children's literature and literary didactics, at the University of Siegen, Germany. Her research interests and her publications concentrate on literature for children and young adults, on female writers of the nineteenth and early twentieth century, as well as on the development of canonicity and literacy. She is currently preparing a monograph on German reading curricula at secondary schools for girls between 1870 and 1933.

**Anja Müller** is Professor of English Literature and Culture at the University of Siegen, Germany, Vice-President of the Society for Contemporary Theatre and Drama in English and co-editor of the forthcoming monograph series 'Studies in European Literature for Children and Young Adults' (Heidelberg: Winter). Her publications include *Fashioning Childhood in the Eighteenth Century* (ed., Ashgate, 2006) and *Framing Childhood in Eighteenth-Century English Periodicals and Prints, 1689-1789* (Ashgate, 2009; ChLA Honor Book 2009). Other books and articles deal with European children's literature, British contemporary drama and eighteenth-century literature and culture. Her current research project investigates canon formation and the social imaginary in British literature for children and young adults.

**Łukasz Neubauer** is a Senior Lecturer in the Institute of Neophilology and Social Communications at the Technical University of Koszalin, Poland. He specialises in early medieval history and Old Germanic literatures, in particular English poetry and Norse sagas. His publications include academic papers on the metrical structure of Anglo-Saxon verse and animal imagery in Old English battle poems. He is also interested in the Icelandic language and onomastics and so has written a number of articles on place as well as proper names in Iceland.

**Eva Oppermann** wrote her PhD dissertation about the First Golden Age of English Children's Literature (1865–1914). She was Assistant Professor at the Universities of Kassel and Rostock, Germany, and is currently finishing her Second Book about Milton's *Paradise Lost* and its intertexts in Kassel. She has published various contributions concerning the Animal Novel, *The Wind in the Willows*, Walter Moers' Zamonian Novels, Aldous Huxley's works, Helen Dunmore's novels and C. S. Lewis' Ransom-books. Her main research interests are intertextuality and narratology.

**Maddalena Pennacchia** is Tenured Researcher of English Literature at Roma Tre University, Italy. She is the author of *Il mito di Corinne. Viaggio in Italia e genio femminile nella scrittura di Anna Jameson, Margaret Fuller e George Eliot* (2001), and *Tracce del moderno nel teatro di Shakespeare* (ESI, 2008). She has edited *Literary Intermediality. The Transit of Literature through the Media Circuit* (2007) and co-edited (together with Maria Del Sapio Garbero and Nancy Isenberg) *Questioning Bodies in Shakespeare's Rome* (2010). She has published extensively but mainly in Italian on the interaction between written literature and audio-visual media. She is also the author of a short bio-fiction for children, *Shakespeare e il sogno di un'estate* (2008).

**Elizabeth Thiel** has worked as a Senior Lecturer at the University of Roehampton, UK, teaching Children's Literature at both undergraduate and postgraduate levels. Her academic interests are varied, ranging from contemporary children's literature to visual texts and critical theory, but her most recent research activities have centred on nineteenth-century children's literature by women writers. She is the author of *The Fantasy of Family: Nineteenth-century Children's Literature and the Myth of the Domestic Ideal* (Routledge, October 2008). Publications also include 'Degenerate "Innocents": Childhood, Deviance and Criminality in Nineteenth-Century Texts' in A. Gavin, ed., *The Child in British Literature: Literary Constructions of Childhood Medieval to Contemporary* (Palgrave, 2012) and a forthcoming edited volume on two nineteenth-century 'street arab' tales.

**Laura Tosi** is Associate Professor of English Literature at the University Ca' Foscari in Venice, Italy. Her research spans the areas of Elizabethan and Jacobean drama, women's studies, postmodernist fiction and children's literature. She has written monographs on Ben Jonson (Milan 1998) and John Webster (Pisa, 2001) and has edited, with S. Bassi, the collection *Visions of Venice in Shakespeare* (Ashgate, 2011) and with A. Petrina, *Representations of Elizabeth I* (Palgrave Macmillan, 2011). In the area of children's literature, she has edited a collection of essays (*Hearts of Lightness. The Magic of Children's Literature*, Venice 2001) and edited and translated a collection of Victorian fairy tales (Venice, 2003). Her latest monograph study is on the literary fairy tale in England (Venice, 2007) while her current research is focused on Victorian and contemporary adaptations of Shakespeare's plays for children.

**Monika Wozniak** is Associate Professor of Polish Literature and Language at the 'Sapienza' University of Rome, Italy. Her research has addressed several topics in Literary Translation; more recently it has focused on Children's Literature and Translation as well as Audiovisual Translation. She has been guest editor of the special issues of 'Przekładaniec. Journal of Literary Translation' (Cracow) on Audiovisual Translation (2008) and on the Fairy Tales in Translation (2010). She has also translated works of Moravia, Eco and Calvino in Polish and Polish Children's classics in Italian.

# Introduction: Adapting Canonical Texts in and for Children's Literature

## Anja Müller

Adaptations of canonical texts have always played an important role in the history of children's literature. Arguably the first European children's classic, Joachim Heinrich Campe's *Robinson the Younger* (*Robinson der Jüngere* 1779/80), was an adaptation of Daniel Defoe's *Robinson Crusoe* (1717) and triggered off a wave of Robinsonades. Adaptations of originally 'adult' texts for children are intended to initiate young readers to a literary canon that is deemed essential for sharing a common cultural heritage. As such, they follow an aesthetic as well as an educational agenda. Children's classics, in turn, have also been adapted through the ages, either to meet changing tastes, shifts in the conceptualization of childhood or to take cognizance of the possibilities offered by new media, such as television, film, graphic novels or, more recently, computer games. During this process, children's classics sometimes cross borders via translation or intercultural adaptation. The resulting transcultural literary and cultural heritage can provide common ground for intercultural communication in a globalized world. This volume seeks to explore the range of these different directions which adaptations of canonical texts can take in children's literature.[1] It brings together chapters looking at various adaptations of English classics (works by Shakespeare and Dickens as well as *Beowulf* and Arthuriana) with contributions that examine how children's classics move across European borders or the Atlantic, and in how far these 'traveling tales' (cf. Appiah 2005, pp. 256–9) might establish a literary and cultural knowledge shared among generations and, sometimes, even across national borders.

Theoretically, the volume takes its cue from recent adaptation studies, as forwarded in the wake of Linda Hutcheon's *Theory of Adaptation*. Tantamount to this approach is the endeavour to jettison fidelity as a main criterion to evaluate adaptations in order to embrace postmodern and poststructuralist notions of intertextuality or intermediality. As a result, the 'paragone' between adapted work and adaptation, as Cartmell puts it (see Cartmell 2007, p. 167), does not grant the adapted work a higher authority or legitimacy, nor is it the residue of the true meaning the adaptation ought to convey. Instead, it is important to appreciate adaptations as artistic creations in their own right. Their success or artistic value solely depends on their own intrinsic merits and is governed by the rules of the genre or medium of the adaptation.

If one looks at the most investigated mode of adaptation, adaptations of literature into film, one can assume that the reassertion of the artistic value of adaptations was to a certain extent motivated by the attempt to raise the status of film vis-à-vis literature. The surge of cultural studies and media studies certainly have paved the way for film, video, television, pop songs, computer games or even theme parks becoming acceptable cultural material for serious academic research. It is interesting to note that the cases of adaptation addressed in the key texts of adaptation studies or in the conferences and journals of the Association of Adaptation Studies hardly consider adaptations that also involve a shift in the age group of the audience. I would argue, however, that the claims made for adaptations across genres and media must also apply to adaptations for different audience groups. In this respect, adaptations of canonical texts in children's literature are an important test case where an 'original' certified as belonging to a so-called 'high culture' is transported to a genre or medium with a still highly contested cultural status. Looking at the existing critical studies on adaptations of (adult) canonical texts for children, one soon realizes that one is still far from acknowledging equal artistic status in this case. Fears of 'downsizing', 'dumbing down', oversimplifying, bowdlerizing or even only abridging venerable canonical artefacts still inform the evaluations. Even if the adaptation itself is appreciated, the underlying hope seems to be to guide the young reader 'home', that is to the original, which alone can guarantee full aesthetic enjoyment. Such subtexts can even be found in the adaptations themselves, as some chapters in this volume reveal (so Oppermann, Penacchia, MacLeod or Müller on Shakespeare, Neubauer on *Beowulf* or Thiel on Dickens). Adaptations like, for instance, the Animated Shakespeare series, several editions of the Classics Illustrated or Classical Comics series, Marcia Williams' picture books or Rosemary Sutcliff *Beowulf Dragonslayer*, explicitly pursue such an educational agenda. Behind all this lies, of course, a low estimation of the young readers' literacy and aesthetic capacities. The concept of the vulnerable child who must be protected from morally harmful or traumatic material (like sex, violence, crime, extreme suffering) additionally may lead to a call for sanitizing texts before offering them to children; the very term 'bowdlerizing' goes back to the name of Thomas Bowdler whose *Family Shakespeare* (1807) was such an endeavour to create an expurgated version of Shakespeare's plays for children.

At present, the artistic merits of children's literature have become acknowledged through a number of prestigious book prizes, and children's literature studies is affirming its position in academia; hence the claim of the genre for serious treatment by literary (and not only didactic) scholars. Nevertheless, when preparing this volume, I have realized that when it comes to investigate adaptations of canonical texts in children's literature, it seems particularly difficult to apply Hutcheon's formula. Children's literature scholars largely tend to circumnavigate the problem of adaptation by evading more theoretical considerations in favour of case studies, mostly on adaptations of Shakespeare.[2] The only article that seems to engage theoretically with the problem, Deborah Cartmell's 'Adapting Children's Literature', addresses the second concern of the present volume: adaptations of children's classics. Cartmell's essay is remarkable for a number of reasons. First, it remains within the conventional field of film adaptations by exclusively dealing with Disney movies, which are known for sanitizing their products according to the company's ideology. Disney is undeniably the most prolific adaptor for children's audiences, but it is by far not the only adaptive mode available (as the article could make believe). Second, the essay appears to be largely uninformed about the canonical status of the children's books it discusses. *The Wizard of Oz, Mary Poppins* or *The Neverending Story* are hardly 'lesser known' or 'obscure' texts (Cartmell 2007, p. 168 and pp. 172–3) but form part of the children's literary canon in the respective countries of origin. Who would, in turn, doubt the 'classic' or canonical status of *Robinson Crusoe, Frankenstein, David Copperfield, Dracula* or *Moby Dick*, even though adult readers may 'know' these novels only through film adaptations? Third, it is surprising to see how freely the essay chastises Disney for 'usurp[ing] its source ... so that the film adaptation triumphs over its literary original' (Cartmell 2007, p. 169). Such a statement exemplifies the powerful impact adaptations can have; yet in the context of children's literature, such usurpation is presented as problematic. Significantly, Cartmell opines that the paragone of film and literature is at its 'most ferocious' when it comes to children's literature because of 'concerns over film's moral influence and threat to literacy' (2007, p. 167). Adaptations of children's literature are, therefore, said to be subject to 'higher demands on fidelity' (Cartmell 2007, p. 168) because children's literature is generally better known and there is closer intimacy between the reader and the original. Such remarks express two clichés about childhood and children's literature, which cannot remain entirely uncontested.

One cliché concerns the supposed morality of children's literature. Whereas moral and didactic aims have been an essential feature of the genre throughout the ages, the insistence on the entertaining and subversive potential of children's literature has since become at least as important for definitions of the genre. Second, suggesting a closer intimacy between the child reader and the text, which should not be disrupted, implies a view of the child whose world must remain safe and whole; nothing in it – not even the child's books – is to be violated or corrupted. This legacy of a Romantic concept of childhood that should be protected can apparently become a powerful discourse that also protects the child, childhood and children's literature or culture from closer scrutiny, or, in other words, from being submitted to analytical techniques that might deconstruct the alleged wholeness of the child's world. As a result, children's literature comes to be seen as a monolithic genre, a residue of wholeness that is not to be corrupted by adaptations, especially not in media of less esteem, such as film, comics or other visualizations. This attitude, however, is more detrimental to children's literature than beneficial, as it tends to deprive a versatile, artistically complex and highly creative genre of the serious critical investigation with the available theoretical tools it deserves. When dealing with adaptation in children's literature, it is, therefore, important to eschew concerns about fidelity, to analyse the adaptations in their own right and to explore how they make use of the new genre conventions or how they respond to cultural changes or cultural contact. For this purpose, it may be worthwhile to shift one's attention from the 'what' to the 'how'.

The present volume attempts to undertake some tentative steps on this way. In 'Shakespeare for Girls', Laura Tosi highlights the cultural work of Shakespeare adaptations for an audience that is defined by its gender and age. By highlighting 'the cultural relationship that girls or young women establish with the Bard', Tosi does not simply perceive Shakespeare adaptations for young female readers as instruments of indoctrination, but she emphasizes the readers' agency as a determining factor for Victorian, Edwardian and contemporary meddlings with the Bard. In a similar vein, Jana Mikota presents how German author Mirjam Pressler creatively rewrites European classics such as *The Merchant of Venice* or *Nathan the Wise*. Pressler's concern is with the Jewish or anti-Semitic subtexts of the canonical texts, and her adaptations offer to her young readers reinterpretations of the canon informed by critical reconsiderations of the text after the Shoa. Eva Oppermann's close reading of Tad Williams' *Caliban's Hour* (1993) and Susan Cooper's *King of Shadows* (1999) reveals in a detailed manner the different modes of adaptation employed by the respective writers, such as change of perspective or creative experiment with the adapted text(s).

The chapters by Maddalena Pennacchia, Mark MacLeod and Anja Müller examine Shakespeare adaptations in popular media that also take cognizance of the importance of visual literacy among contemporary young audiences. As a result, adaptations may come in the form of TV series (see Pennacchia), illustrated books (see MacLeod) or graphic novels (see Müller). As the chapters show, all these adaptations share the agenda of not simply introducing literary texts of canonical status to young readers, but also of ensuring the position of Shakespeare as a cultural icon in today's culture. Whereas the comic book adaptations of *Macbeth* introduced by Müller are largely British endeavours that may or may not appeal to an international market, the contributions by Pennacchia and MacLeod illustrate the intercultural dimension which adaptation processes can take. The Animated Shakespeare series discussed by Pennacchia was a joint effort of Welsh and Russian studios and presented itself as a contribution to the cultural collaboration of Western and Eastern Europe, establishing Shakespeare as their common cultural heritage. Mark MacLeod positions John Marsden's novel *Hamlet* and Andy Griffiths' satirical illustrated book *Just Macbeth!* within Australian 'culture wars' and the concomitant discussion on the status of the English Bard Down Under.

Of course, adapting canonical texts in children's literature is not exclusively restricted to Shakespeare adaptations. Łukasz Neubauer and Anne Klaus show how an interest in medieval culture is reflected in contemporary adaptations of *Beowulf* (Neubauer) or Thomas Malory's *Le Morte D'Arthur* (Klaus). Whereas Neubauer highlights various levels of philological creativity in Rosemary Sutcliff's *Beowulf Dragonslayer*, Klaus expounds on the importance of Arthurian adaptations for the development of contemporary children's fantasy literature and suggests a typology for the different modes of adaptation she discovered. In 'Downsizing Dickens', Liz Thiel focuses on graphic novel adaptations of *Oliver Twist*, a novel with canonical status for both adult and child readers. This situation renders adaptations of *Oliver Twist* an ideal case for examining the issue of supposed 'downsizing' if young readers are not offered the original text but an abridged or, even more challenging, a graphic novel version. In her meticulous analysis, Thiel arrives at a balanced conclusion: whereas adaptations may 'diminish the source text and invalidate the historicity of the work', they 'can also invite extensive contemplation of the past, the present and the importance of the written word' and guarantee a text's survival.

The final four chapters of the volume shed light on various manifestations of intercultural adaptations of children's classics. Tracing adaptations of '*The Nutcracker* from ETA Hoffmann to Matthew Bourne', Jan Keane provides close readings of the cross-media transformations which ETA Hoffmann's literary fairy tale undertook while travelling across different European borders (to France, Russia and the United Kingdom) and simultaneously metamorphosing from fantastic prose tale to ballet script and performance. Like *Oliver Twist*, *The Nutcracker* can be regarded as canonical for both adult and children's literature, and Keane's assessment demonstrates how the different adaptations retain this double address. Ian Halliday and Monika Wozniak both look at adaptation from the perspective of translation studies. Carefully scrutinizing translations of Carlo Collodi's *Pinocchio* into English, Halliday suggests regarding any republication of *Pinocchio* as an adaptation, especially since the expiry of copyright of the source text legally allows free reign for the editor or translator. Besides, he argues that the inherent ambivalence of texts that address a double audience like *Pinocchio* often lies 'behind the motivations for the various adaptations and abridgements' of a text. 'To Be or Not to Be a Canonical Text of Children's Literature' is the question Monika Wozniak ponders about with regard to *Winnie-the-Pooh*. Whereas Milne's bear with little brain is undoubtedly part of the English canon of children's literature, this does not automatically render him canonical once Milne's books are translated into other languages. Nor is the number of translations reliable evidence of a text's popularity in a particular country. As it compares the case of Poland, where *Kubuś Puchatek* is a veritable cultural icon, with that of Italy, where this elevated status has not been achieved despite a higher number of translations, Wozniak's chapter proves how little the success of an intercultural adaptation depends on literary qualities and how much on its absorption into the new cultural context. Lisa Fraustino's concluding chapter finally sheds light on the dark side of the power of adaptation. In her provocative account of Disney's campaign for a new Tinkerbell, Fraustino reveals the extension and pervasiveness which adaptations in children's literature can acquire: here, it does not suffice to look at individual texts, at media change or crossing borders. As remediation may end up linking children's literature with global players in economy and politics, adaptation ceases to be merely a literary concern. It clearly betrays its concerns about power – even, and maybe particularly in adaptations of children's literature.

As is reflected in this short summary of its respective contributions, this volume deliberately assembles chapters that represent a variety of positions with regard to their approach to adaptation. Studies of intercultural and, especially, interlingual translation can hardly avoid commenting on the relationship between the original and the translation if they want to appreciate fully the work performed by the adaptation. Yet the achievement of the translation is as much determined by its success in the target language and culture as by its relation to the source text. Equally, when examining adaptations of Shakespeare or other canonical texts, one can hardly eschew comments on the educational purposes some of the adaptations explicitly mention. Nor can a study on the global impact of Disney ignore the company's concerns over its own economic and cultural hegemony. All chapters have in common, however, their focus on the adaptation process and on the creative potential set free by the respective adaptations in children's literature. They all show what adaptations can perform – and that it is, therefore, important to appreciate these adaptations in their own right: in children's literature as much as in any other genre or medium.

## Notes

1  This volume originated in a seminar of the ESSE conference in Torino in August 2012. I wish to thank my co-convenor, Laura Tosi, who helped to organize a fascinating panel. Special thanks are also due to Simone Herrmann for her invaluable help with the manuscript.

2  Among them are Megan Lynn Isaac's *Heirs to Shakespeare*, Erica Hateley's *Shakespeare in Children's Literature*, Jennifer Hulbert and Robert York's *Shakespeare in Youth Culture* and Naomi J. Miller's edited volume *Reimagining Shakespeare*. One may also add Barbara Tepa Lupak's edited collection on *Adapting the Arthurian Legends for Children*.

## List of works cited

Appiah, Kwame Anthony (2005), *The Ethics of Identity*. Princeton, NJ: Princeton University Press.

Cartmell, Deborah (2007), 'Adapting Children's Literature', in D. Cartmell and I. Whelehan (eds), *The Cambridge Companion to Literature on Screen*. Cambridge: Cambridge University Press, pp. 166–80.

Hateley, Erica (2009), *Shakespeare in Children's Literature.* London: Routledge.

Hulbert, Jennifer and York, Robert (eds) (2006), *Shakespeare and Youth Culture.* Basingstoke: Palgrave.

Hutcheon, Linda (2006), *A Theory of Adaptation.* London: Routledge.

Isaac, Megan Lynn (2000), *Heirs to Shakespeare.* Portsmouth, NH: Heinemann Educational Books.

Lupak, Barbara Tepa (ed.) (2004), *Adapting the Arthurian Legends for Children.* Basingstoke: Palgrave.

Miller Naomi Johnson, (ed.) (2003), *Reimagining Shakespeare for Children and Young Adults.* London: Routledge.

# 1

# Shakespeare for Girls: Victorian versus Contemporary Prose Versions of *Hamlet* and *The Merchant of Venice*

Laura Tosi

One of the main concerns of this chapter is the female readership of Shakespeare's plays and the way abridgements, adaptations and appropriations have mediated and still mediate the cultural relationship that girls or young women establish with the Bard. I hope to show that despite differences in their respective socio-historical contexts, Victorian and Edwardian versions of Shakespeare's plays for a female audience share a number of stylistic and ideological features with contemporary novels based on Shakespeare's plays, such as the choice to focus on a traditionally undeserving or marginalized female character, the construction of a fictional sequel within the narrative and the investigation of the (formal, emotional, religious) education, or lack of it, received by the heroines. It would be impossible to discuss the early appropriations without taking into account the fact that in the nineteenth century, when prose versions of Shakespeare started to appear, female critics in particular were developing ways to discuss Shakespeare's female characters as if they were idealized models of real human beings (see Marshall 2009) with which girl readers could identify: 'Long before a feminist sisterhood was born in the 1960s, nineteenth-century women writers appealed to an audience of fellow women among whom they expected to find sympathetic readers' (Ziegler et al. 1997, p. 19).

The emergence of feminist criticism in the last decades has contributed to transferring general critical attention onto Shakespeare's female characters, exploring in a more theoretically nuanced way gender constructions of identity and the way they interacted in early modern England. It is very tempting to paraphrase Ian Kott's old 'adage' and declare that 'every historical period finds in

Shakespeare's heroines what it is looking for and what it wants to see' (Kott 1996, p. 5), as for most of the nineteenth- and twentieth-century heroines have acted as sites of not only projection but also of negotiation, for different constructions of femininity.

## Female readers of Shakespeare

Ever since the Lambs' *Tales from Shakespeare* (1807), young female audiences have always been an essential part of the history of children's adaptations of Shakespeare. In the 'Preface' to the Lambs' *Tales*, we learn that the intention was to 'make these tales easy reading for very young children' (Lamb 2007, p. 3). Immediately after, though, the author of the 'Preface' (presumably Mary who, because of her lack of formal education, may have been sensitive to the issue of giving girls the chance to read Shakespeare), added that

> For young ladies too it has been my intention chiefly to write, because boys are generally permitted the use of their fathers' libraries at a much earlier age than girls are, they frequently having the best scenes of Shakespeare by heart, before their sisters are permitted to look into this manly book. (Lamb 2007, p. 4)

Access to Shakespeare, Mary suggested, had to be provided with brothers acting as intermediaries, and in the 'Preface' she begs 'their kind assistance in explaining to their sisters such parts as are hardest for them to understand' (Lamb 2007, p. 4).

In the second edition of the *Tales* (1809), an 'Advertisement' identifies a less wide readership than the 1807 edition:

> The Proprietors of this work willingly pay obedience to the voice of the public. It has been the general sentiment that the style in which these tales were written, is not so precisely adapted for the amusement of mere children, as for an acceptable and improving present to young ladies advancing to the state of womanhood. (Lamb 1809, p. iii)

This edition clearly posits the original reference to young children as no longer applicable. A relationship between prose adaptations of Shakespeare and girls (possibly still with the required assistance of a male family member) is, therefore, established very early and is crucial in the construction of a Shakespearean canon for children (a number of studies of the Lambs' *Tales* have discussed in various ways the tensions between representations of gender within the patriarchal order of the plays, see Marsden; James; Wolfson). Both Gary Taylor's *Reinventing Shakespeare* (1989) and the anthology *Women Reading Shakespeare* (1997), among others, have also made it clear that popular dissemination of Shakespeare's plays was never an all-male phenomenon – in the nineteenth century, in particular, women studied Shakespeare in large numbers (Taylor 1989, p. 205) and popularized Shakespeare's plays through children's and adult editions and by contributing articles to journals (Thompson and Roberts 1997, pp. 3–4). As Thompson and Roberts have put it succinctly, 'women's writing on Shakespeare flourished in the nineteenth century' (1997, p. 2). Mary Cowden Clarke was one of these quite exceptional female scholars of Shakespeare and had already an established career as editor and philologist (she published the first *Full Concordance to Shakespeare* in 1845, a work that had taken 16 years to complete; Thompson and Roberts 1993, p. 175) when she wrote *The Girlhood of Shakespeare's Heroines* (1850–52), a collection of 15 novellas that reconstruct the childhood and teenage years of a number of Shakespeare's female characters. Cowden Clarke was persuaded that 'himself possessing keener insight than any other man-writer into womanly nature – Shakespeare may well be esteemed a valuable friend of woman-kind' (1887, p. 355).

Cowden Clarke's novellas can be considered as part of the tradition of character criticism of Shakespeare's heroines that had become prominent in the nineteenth century, especially thanks to the hugely popular *Characteristics of Women, Moral, Poetical and Historical* (1832), by Anna Jameson. As Julie Hankey notes, 'After Jameson it became commonplace to describe Shakespeare as the "champion" of women' (1994, p. 427). Ruskin's lecture 'Sesame and Lilies' (1864), later converted into an essay, in the section 'Of Queen's Gardens' appears to be affected by this critical tradition when he writes that 'Shakespeare has no heroes; only heroines' and that Shakespeare's women are agents of redemption and guides – except 'weak' Ophelia, 'because she fails Hamlet at the critical moment' (see Ruskin 1905, p. 114).

By moving female characters from the margins to the centre and validating their perceptions and experiences, Clarke's novellas inevitably change the reader's perception of the heroines' contributions to the original plays. The protofeminist agenda that was at work in many Victorian fairy tale writers can also be perceived, although in a more subtle way, in *The Girlhood*. Cowden Clarke recognizes a bond with Mary Lamb (she claimed that Mary had taught her Latin):

> Happy is she who at eight or nine years old has a copy of Lamb's *Tales from Shakespeare* given to her, opening a vista of even then understandable interest

and enjoyment! Happy she who at twelve or thirteen has Shakespeare's works themselves read to her by her mother, with loving selection of fittest plays and passages! (Clarke 1887, p. 369)

Mothers are indeed the co-protagonists of many novellas of Clarke's collection where, unlike what happens in most Shakespearean plays, the reader can see their formative (both for good and bad) influence at work and ponder on the way this relationship affects the future behaviour of the heroine. We should not forget that mothers were also the recipients of these tales which were suitable for family reading (in their own very peculiar way, these tales can be considered an early example of crossover fiction). The theme of education in these tales is central, as we follow in detail the heroines' emotional, intellectual and sentimental education (or lack of it – as in the case of Lady Macbeth). The heroines' future choices appear to be determined primarily by the kind of family environments they were born into, from what they learnt (or rather, by what they did not learn) first from their mothers and secondly from their masters, friends, nurses and mentors. Everything that happens in the plays appears to be accounted for in the tales, and everything the girls say or do in Shakespeare fits in with the kind of education they receive in these fictional speculations. What is most noticeable about Clarke's endeavour is the attempt to provide motivation (see Brown 2005, p. 95): her tales give space to minor or absent characters and provide causal connections as well as substantial additional information which ultimately point to a new interpretation of Shakespeare's plays.

In this chapter, I will concentrate on Clarke's prequels (especially *The Merchant of Venice* and *Hamlet*, which centre on the characters of Portia and Ophelia) in order to contrast them with a number of recent novels for a girl/young adult audience based on a fictional biography of a number of Shakespeare's heroines: *Hamlet*'s Ophelia and Portia and Jessica in *The Merchant of Venice*. The last 50 years have seen a spate of novels about Elizabethan theatre – some contemporary juvenile novels are set in the Elizabethan age with witches and spirits, while a number of historical novels for young adults feature Shakespeare as a character who interacts with the adolescent protagonists.[1] In very recent years, no less than three novels[2] have reformulated and expanded on *Hamlet* as a teenage story. The female perspective is also present in teenage novels about Shakespeare's daughters.[3] These operations of centring around Shakespeare as a romantic lover or father, the Bard as seen through the eyes of doting female relations or would-be relations, are not entirely new, as is evidenced by such works as William Black's *Judith Shakespeare* (1884) and Sara Hawks Sterling's

*Shakespeare's Sweetheart* (1905). Turning Shakespeare's life into romance appears to be a component of the larger (and continuing) process of idealizing the Bard which continues well into our days and blends in with our contemporary fixation with fictional biography and postmodernist rewriting of history (see Hateley 2009, pp. 49–81).

## Portia and Jessica in Victorian and Edwardian prose revisions of *The Merchant of Venice*

Both Clarke's tales and many contemporary teenage retellings of Shakespeare can be considered appropriations rather than adaptations – my working definition of appropriation being that provided by Julie Sanders:

> Appropriation frequently affects a more decisive journey away from the informing source into a wholly new cultural product and domain. This may or may not involve a generic shift, and it may still require the intellectual juxtaposition of (at least) one text against another that we have suggested is central to the reading and spectating experience of adaptations. (Sanders 2006, p. 26)

Like collections of prose retellings from Shakespeare for children (notably, the Lambs' *Tales*), Clarke's tales and contemporary novels are characterized, roughly speaking, by the transposition of one genre (drama) into another (prose fiction), by excision of plot lines, scenes and characters, and by simplification of style. Shakespeare's own words are generally summarized or quoted or intercalated in the rest of the prose (although, often, some linguistic archaisms are retained). However, unlike the Lambs' *Tales* and many other children's Shakespeares, Clarke and the novels in question are defined by their massive use of addition and expansion devices: new characters and new incidents or episodes (including new endings, as far as the contemporary novels are concerned) are interpolated into the familiar world of the plays. A trait shared by these texts, despite the time gap, is narrative amplification in the sense used by Genette: 'amplification proceeds chiefly through diegetic development (that is the role of expansion: distension of details, descriptions, multiplication of episodes and secondary characters)' (1997, p. 264). Characters whose mere names are mentioned in Shakespeare's plays become fully developed characters in Clarke and the novels, and they are involved in a story line. Through the use of doubles (generally invented female characters who interact closely with heroines and often mirror their destiny), Clarke's narrator points out the dangers girls must identify and escape, while contemporary authors enlist a number of female helpers that do not necessarily mirror the fate of the heroine. Clarke's focus is on the heroines' 'past' where we find the female characters coming to terms with serious childhood traumas caused by bereavement, parental neglect (generally male), dysfunctional families and sexual threats. While all these narrations tend to expose the double standard between men's and women's sexual conduct and the strictures of the patriarchal world, the contemporary novels emphasize more clearly the importance of romance as well as the value of female independence.

Clarke's Portia was at the same time a Victorian favourite (see Hankey 1994, p. 442) and a 'site of political struggle' (Rozmovitz 1998, p. 57) for her combination of New Woman's capacity to speak up in the public sphere and her readiness to give it all up for love as a true romantic heroine. The novella 'Portia: The Heiress of Belmont' concentrates on the relationship between Portia and the patriarchal world of her uncle Bellario, who instructs her in the secluded domesticity of Belmont but appears to underestimate his niece's intelligence. Bellario's final advice to Portia ('your intellectual accomplishments will draw the accusation of pedantry and unfeminine pre-eminence'; Clarke 2009, pp. 107–8) appears to voice Victorian ambivalence towards this paragon of a Shakespearean woman who ultimately had to balance her exceptional intelligence (most of the novella is about Portia learning from Bellario) and wealth with her more womanly qualities.

M. Leigh-Noel in *Shakespeare's Garden of Girls* (1885) believes Portia to be 'the most wonderful of all Shakespeare's feminine creations' (quoted in Thompson and Roberts 1997, p. 180). Portia's intellectual accomplishments are emphasized by Abbey Sage Richardson's 'The Witty Portia', a retelling of *The Merchant* in *Stories from Old English Poetry*, in which she is described as 'one of the most intellectual women of the age ... an accomplished scholar, learnt in the arts and sciences, and well-read in Venetian laws and history' (Richardson 1871, p. 189). In Carter's Edwardian retelling of *The Merchant of Venice*, Portia 'had been taught by the best of masters ... she was brave and ready, quick-witted and clever' (1910, p. 3). An interesting exception to this panorama of intellectual excellence is provided by Fay Adams Britton's representation of Portia in *Shakespearean Fairy Tales* where a fairy godmother whispers in her ears what to say at the trial – the scene is reminiscent of Cinderella at a loss before the ball: 'Waving her wand over Portia's head, the fair Portia appeared to be dressed like a doctor of Laws' (Britton 1907, p. 26). It is always the warning voice of the fairy that directs Portia: an interesting example of drastic disempowering of the character, reduced to little more than a puppet that lends her voice to somebody else's thoughts and words.

Interestingly enough, Portia is not the undisputed protagonist of contemporary novel versions of the play – she features in *The Turquoise Ring* by Grace Tiffany (2005), a novel that revisits *The Merchant* from the perspective of five characters but cannot be found in Mirjam Pressler's *Shylock's Daughter* (1999). The protagonist of the latter book and an important character of *The Turquoise Ring* is Jessica, the disobedient daughter and not a general favourite in the nineteenth century. Although she is not listed in Anna Jameson's *Characteristics of Women* (1832), she is briefly discussed, in unusually favourable terms, in conjunction with Portia: 'in any other play, and in many other companionship than that of the matchless Portia, Jessica would make a very beautiful heroine of herself' (Jameson 1858, p. 105). In contrast, Henrietta Lee Palmer's *Stratford Gallery or the Shakespeare Sisterhood*, comprising 'forty–five ideal portraits', gives a less-than-ideal character – Jessica has obviously failed in her duty as a daughter for her duplicity and stealing: 'Fancy Juliet, Silvia . . . damaging their father's coffers as well as his authority' (Palmer 1859, p. 126). It is Lorenzo's love that redeems her and makes her more tolerable to Palmer: 'She assumes a more amiable aspect' when she is married: 'Lorenzo is the most poetic of lovers, and for his sake we can almost pardon the episode of the ducats' (1859, p. 126).

Jessica is more frequently perceived as the negative foil of Portia: where Portia is obedient, noble and generous, Jessica is defiant, duplicitous and unruly. In Leigh-Noel's remark (1885):

> How different is the tie between Portia's father and herself, and Jessica and her father. In the latter case there is an utter want of mutual love, confidence, and loyalty, whilst in the former there is the most steadfast observance of respect to the will of one no longer present to enforce its fulfilment. (quoted in Thompson and Roberts 1997, p. 178)

In Carter's *Stories from Shakespeare*, Jessica is described as 'treacherous and unworthy' (1910, p. 24). Ada Stidolph, in *The Children's Shakespeare*, is quite an exception to this chorus of disapproval in that her narrator asks child readers to sympathize with Jessica's plight: 'Poor Jessica! Do you not feel sorry for her? Little boys and girls, who have good kind fathers who do all they can to make you happy?' (1902, p. 18). Spencer Hoffman attempts to justify Jessica's behaviour on the grounds of her dismal childhood without a mother and in the company of a hardened father ('her life with the grasping, grumbling Jew had been a very lonely one'; 1911, p. 84) who has not been able to instil any loving feeling for him so that when they know about his sentence and the inheritance, the reaction is simply and unambiguously 'a moment of perfect happiness' (1911, p. 105).

## Jessica and Portia in contemporary teenage novels based on *The Merchant of Venice*

Jessica, the unruly daughter who can take care of her marriage plans (see Holmer), appears in two novels for a female teenage readership as a protagonist or a co-protagonist. Both *Shylock's Daughter* by the German author Mirjam Pressler (1999) and American Grace Tiffany's *The Turquoise Ring* (2005) centre less on the single character of Jessica than on a multiplicity of female voices and viewpoints that supplement one another and, like Clarke's novellas, provide new motivations and unexpected causal connections for the behaviour of (mainly) female and male characters in Shakespeare's *The Merchant*. This novel, specifically addressed to teenage readers, provides a powerful depiction of sixteenth-century Venice and its Jewish community as well as the restrictions and discrimination that the Jews had to bear.[4] The novel is built on the alternation of third-person narration and the voice of a character who is not present in Shakespeare's play, the ugly and motherless Dalilah, who has lived as a companion and a servant with Jessica and the housekeeper Amalia, since she was a little girl. Through Dalilah's eyes, we see Jessica's love for extravagance and her restlessness in having to obey her father's rules as well as those that regulate the Jewish presence in Venice. Dalilah's perceptions notwithstanding, Jessica's character remains ambivalent. Although the young readers may sympathize with her about her desire to evade from the prison of the ghetto and her motherless state, her rude behaviour towards Dalilah and her emotional detachment from her father and his culture and religion ('It is only an accident that I was born a Jew's daughter'; Pressler 2000, p. 19) do not make her an easy character to identify with. In the end, she experiences the same feeling of rejection and alienation/alienness as her father does: 'Even to him [Lorenzo] she was still the outsider, the stranger' (Pressler 2000, p. 166). Education, once again, is to blame for Jessica's superficiality, as recognized by Shylock's housekeeper Amalia: 'It should have been our task to develop in her an inner beauty. Instead of that, we made her vain' (Pressler 2000, p. 78).

The question of female identity is pivotal in this novel which plays with Shakespeare's favourite device of cross-dressing. Jessica often thinks of (cultural, religious) identity as something that can be played as a role and discarded at will:

> "My sons will never ... know their grandfather ... perhaps they'll never even find out that their mother has always been, in her heart of hearts, a girl from the Ghetto. ..."

> She thought again, as she had done so often, about how young she was, and how many parts she would have to play between now and the end of her days, now that she had cast off so violently the role that had been given to her when she was born, and the thought chilled her, as it always did. (Pressler 2000, p. 266)

It will be Dalilah, the plain but good-hearted foil for Jessica, Amalia's and Shylock's unrecognized and neglected 'good daughter' in this 'family', who will be able to use cross-dressing very much like Shakespeare's heroines in Shakespeare's happier comedies, not to deceive and steal, but as a protective as well as a liberating device, which will enable her to practice her faith beyond the confines of the ghetto, in faraway lands. Unlike Jessica, who will not be able to pass on her heritage and culture to future generations, Dalilah sees herself as the narrator of a story about two girls:

> One of them was rich and one was poor and ugly. But they had one thing in common – they were both motherless. . . . And when they grew up they both left the Ghetto. You ask me why? Children, children, that is a long story, a very long and very Jewish story. (Pressler 2000, p. 277)

*The Turquoise Ring* also revisits *The Merchant of Venice* – this is definitely a crossover novel which may be enjoyed by an adult audience as well as by a teenage one. Jessica here must share the spotlight with four other female characters, two of whom (Leah and Xanthe) are not Shakespeare's characters (although Leah is mentioned by Shylock in the play, in connection with the turquoise ring which she gave him when he was a bachelor and was later sold by Jessica). Leah, the matriarch and martyr figure whose brief life in Toledo ends prematurely through torture by the Inquisition, is connected with the other characters, thanks to the ubiquitous ring which passes into the hands of all the main female characters in the novel.

Even more remarkably than the novels based on *Hamlet* which I will consider shortly, *The Turquoise Ring*, which starts with a prequel to the play which features Leah's parents, relies on an interesting web of intertextual relations with Shakespeare's macrotext: the little boy who turns Leah into the Inquisition (and will reappear launching a mysogynistic tirade in Nerissa's bed much later), for example, is none other than Iago, while one of Portia's suitors is Petruchio, advised by Nerissa to try his amorous fortunes with a certain shrew of Padua. Of all the female characters, Jessica is possibly the closest to nineteenth-century interpretations and prose retellings in her superficiality and absence of scruples. Despite her belated realization that Lorenzo has married her in the vain hope of clearing all his debts, and starved of friends, she appears surprisingly shrewd in her advice to Portia: 'Lady Portia, you must prevent Antonio's sacrifice, and win control of our wealth some other way' (Tiffany 2005, p. 283).

In the novel, Jessica seems condemned, unknowingly, to repeat the unhappy marital fate of other women in her family: like her grandmother, she rejects her Jewish identity for marriage, but unlike her mother, she does not inspire true love in a husband. These female ancestors, with whom the reader has become familiar, have no meaning for Jessica, who has grown up with no female model to look up to for inspiration. Her only acquaintance is Nerissa, a common courtesan. The representation of Nerissa and Portia are examples of a typical device in the novel, which Genette would call 'transvaluation ... a double movement of devaluation and (counter) valuation bearing on the same characters' (Genette 1997, p. 367): in other words, when values traditionally attributed to a character change more or less dramatically. This is the case of Nerissa, a woman 'with a past', who is possibly the most self-reliant, confident, commonsensical and least prejudiced female in the novel, especially if compared to Portia, an exceptionally intelligent but also conceited and unfeeling woman. An expert in legal matters and determined not to let Bassanio squander her fortune on his ventures, Portia has Bassanio sign a contract that says that should he lose the (turquoise) ring that Portia has given him, all substance will revert to Portia. So the play anticipates future annulment of the marriage and no wedding for Nerissa and Graziano.

The end conflates, again, the destinies of two characters, Shylock and the pregnant Moorish servant, who are about to leave Venice for a new life abroad. Xanthe finally returns the turquoise ring to the first and rightful owner and promises to tell him 'a story'. In a way, the novel comes full circle as it was Xanthe who had met Leah in Toledo and had given her the ring as a gift. It appears that Xanthe's multilayered 'survivor' identity (half Jew from her mother, half Moor from her father and carrying the child of a white Christian, Lancelot Gobbo) is the ideal receptacle for Leah's legacy of mixed bloods and religions, and extraordinary female strength.

## Victorian and Edwardian Ophelias

Clarke's 'Rose of Elsinore' is left by her mother in the care of her old nurse's family, in order to further Polonius' political ambitions in Paris, under the mistaken assumption that 'health of body, vigour of frame, activity of limb' would be 'the main things to be secured for her child' (Clarke 2009, p. 187). The mother figure for young Ophelia is, therefore, Jutha, the adolescent daughter of the peasant couple, who takes good care of her (and protects her from the unwanted albeit insistent attentions of an idiot brother) at least until she falls in love with Lord Eric. Abandoned by her noble lover, Jutha is found dead by Ophelia with her stillborn child. Even before Jutha's untimely death, though, life in the cottage does not seem to suit Ophelia's disposition: 'among these rough cottage people, more and more did the child feel herself alone and apart' (Clarke 2009, p. 205). Years later, the unhappiness and loneliness experienced in childhood causes Ophelia's mother to regret 'that she had ever been compelled to leave her little one in what had evidently been so uncongenial a home' (Clarke 2009, p. 220). At court and re-united with her family, Ophelia relives this vicarious experience of abandonment when she finds the lifeless body of her friend, Lady Thyra, who has hanged herself after being abandoned by the same seducer Lord Eric. This cautionary tale of male seduction and female suicide ends with Ophelia dreaming of the two girls' spirits and the armoured ghost of the king who points ominously at a third mysterious girl (obviously, Ophelia herself): 'the white figure moved on, impelled towards the water. I saw her glide on, floating upon the surface' (Clarke 2009, pp. 248–9). Cowden Clarke is quite unique in providing a mother figure and a generally positive Polonius (who 'became dotingly fond of his little girl'; Clarke 2009, p. 220), although underestimation of the absence of a competent guide in her early formative years will have serious consequences. An overview of the characterization of Ophelia in a number of other Victorian and Edwardian retellings parallels nineteenth-century critical interpretations of the character as generally weak and incapable of taking her destiny into her own hands. Grace Latham, in an address read at a meeting of the New Shakespeare Society in 1884, blames education: 'for a weak woman who has been thoroughly cowed, a kind of paralysis of the will takes place, and her acts come not from her own volition, but from that of the stronger nature, under whose domination she lives' (quoted in Thompson and Roberts 1997, p. 167). The double standard in education is also noticed by Jameson who holds Polonius responsible: 'have we not the very man who would send his son to see all . . . but keep his only daughter as far as possible from every taint of the world he knew so well?' (1858, p. 260). Other female critics, not unlike Ruskin, stress the fact that Ophelia was no match for Hamlet: 'Ophelia was weak and timid . . . when Hamlet most needed a friend – most needed her – she miserably failed him' (Jessie Fremont O'Donnell 1897, quoted in Thompson and Roberts 1997, p. 242). The nineteenth-century Ophelia is unprepared, lonely and motherless, almost too ethereal a character to be grasped, 'a mere puppet' (Palmer 1859,

p. 33). While Clarke highlights her emotional instability as the consequence of education and trauma, Mary Macleod's retelling of *Hamlet* (1902) insists on her powerlessness and fragility: 'when the tempest came, she bent her head before it, like a frail reed, and was swept resistlessly away' (1944, p. 195), echoed by Hoffman: 'he seemed a lovely, fragile flower . . . his words [Hamlet's] had been as blows on her fragile body' (1911, p. 254).

## Ophelia in contemporary teenage novels based on *Hamlet*

Contemporary versions of Ophelia's story radically deconstruct the character traits that were outlined by many nineteenth-century critics (and beyond: see, e.g. Bamber 1982, pp. 77, 182) and versions of *Hamlet* for the young: inadequacy, blind obedience, incapacity to react and incapability of having strong feelings are replaced by initiative, emotional and (physical) strength, resistance to the patriarchal world, independence of mind. Fiedler's *Dating Hamlet* (2002) and Klein's *Ophelia* (2006), based on *Hamlet*'s plot and centring on Ophelia, draw attention to the similarity of experiences between early modern girls and the girls of today, starting from the paratext. The book covers feature photos of girls who, in the case of *Dating Hamlet*, for example, emphasize the contemporary appearance of the heroine. Broadly speaking, Klein's and Fiedler's novels portray more 'feminist', more empowered and less obedient Ophelias than their Victorian counterparts ('You cannot control me' Klein's Ophelia tells Laertes 2006, p. 106), although they explore similar issues, turning Ophelia from a marginal character into a central one, a generally friendless woman trying to survive at a patriarchal court where women do not enjoy the same freedom as men.

Like Clarke's 'Rose of Elsinore', these novels provide a prequel to the play and give us information about Ophelia's childhood and teenage years. Ophelia is given a voice and perspective on the events at Elsinore (which also gives us a hint that she has survived). Both novels focus on the love story of Ophelia and Hamlet and its aftermath – they especially expand on the courting period that the play does not show, so the romantic element is emphasized. While Clarke provides doubles for Ophelia as examples of the unhappy outcome of yielding to sexual passion before marriage (hinting that Ophelia will follow the same path later in the play) and other nineteenth-century retellings take great care to dispel the notion that Ophelia is less than chaste, in both novels Ophelia loses her chastity to Hamlet. However, in both novels the heroine's sexual initiation is not followed by unhappiness – the inevitable result of the fallen woman script in Victorian times. In Klein, Ophelia gets pregnant and after Hamlet's death finds shelter in a convent in France (taking Hamlet's suggestion in the nunnery scene quite literally). In this substantial sequel to the play, we follow Ophelia giving birth to Hamlet III and working as a physician/healer in a cottage in the convent grounds until in 1605 Horatio finds her and they fall in love.

In both novels, the court of Elsinore is described as a stifling place, 'Still I am beating my wings against the walls of my cage', says Ophelia, 'for Elsinore sometimes seems a prison to me' (Klein 2006, p. 59), echoing Hamlet who describes Denmark as a prison to Rosencrantz and Guilderstern. In the court, women are never safe from men's predatory instincts: in Fiedler, Barnardo tries to rape Ophelia and her servant Anne, while King Claudius is coldly planning to seduce her when she is mad.

Both Ophelias are very happy to wear breeches – a sign of freedom. Cross-dressing, which is experienced by Shakespeare's heroines in comedies, transmigrates intertextually into the dramatic world of *Hamlet*. Left to their own devices, these Ophelias have turned into tomboys and have learnt to appreciate books.[5] Of course, the construction of the character of Ophelia depends considerably on Hamlet, whose personality is rather different in the two novels: he is very playful and affectionate to Ophelia in Fiedler. They discuss and plan events together – Ophelia is even willing to assist him in his revenge and the nunnery scene is a consummated piece of acting on the part of the lovers. And he is more aloof and a tormented soul in Klein: an ambiguous figure, as in the play. While Cowden Clarke's character criticism is centred on Ophelia, Fiedler's and Klein's novels rely more on the interactions among the characters.

The novels carry out an extensive exploration of the metaphor of acting. Ophelia is as skilful an actor as Hamlet. In both novels, she only pretends to be mad and stages her own fake death (she can swim) very efficiently with the aid of a sleeping potion as she is very adept at recognizing and using herbs in potions and medicines. Like Jessica in *The Turquoise Ring*, the metatheatricality of the play is somewhat reflected by Ophelia's consciousness of playing many roles in life:

> I had been my father's rowdy daughter, then the queen's favoured lady-in-waiting. Later, a shepherd girl in a homespun frock, weaving garlands for her lover. Then a secret wife. Too soon a grieving one, wearing rags like a madwoman. For a time, a free young man striding in breeches and travelling alone. These were but

roles I acted. Who was the true Ophelia? I had wanted to be the author of my tale, not merely a player in Hamlet's drama or a pawn in Claudius's deadly game. (Klein 2006, p. 241)

Unlike Clarke's novella, these contemporary appropriations release Ophelia from her fixed, tragic part in Shakespeare's play, often by showing the reader what happens 'offstage' (like Fiedler's Ophelia and Hamlet planning 'The Mousetrap' together, for example). Both novels engage playfully with the Shakespearean intertext and borrow motives from other Shakespearean plays, like the fake death. The plot of *Romeo and Juliet* is an essential subtext which often works as shorthand for romance – both novels adopt incidents from the tragedy and rework them into the novel. Fiedler's ending suggests a humorous conflation between a version of *Hamlet* and *Romeo and Juliet* where almost everybody stays alive: in the last act, the poison is only a sleeping potion so they all wake up – except for Claudius, as Fortinbras decides not to give him the antidote. After all the sad events of the play, Hamlet only wishes to start a new life in Italy with Ophelia:

> "Where exactly will we go? To some sweet-scented isle of flowers, where we may spend our midsummer nights among fairies?"
>
> I smile. . . . "What think thee of Italy? In particular, the city of Verona."
>
> "Pray, why there?"
>
> I toss a dainty shrug. "Something I read in my mother's journal. You see, she often corresponded with an apothecary there. His letters lead me to believe our sleeping poison would interest me greatly."
>
> "Verona." Hamlet strokes his chin, considering. "At Wittenberg I made the acquaintance of an impetuous fellow from that place. His name, I recall, was. . . Romeo."
>
> . . . I reach for his hand, and the journey begins. (Fiedler 2003, p. 191)

What is interesting here is the fact that *Hamlet*'s fictional world has apparently collided and is about to collide again with that of *Romeo and Juliet*, producing a form of intertextual surprise which derives from the quite unexpected discovery of a breach in the seams that divide one self-contained dramatic world from another: in the world of *Dating Hamlet*, the fictional worlds of *Hamlet* and *Romeo and Juliet* are perceived simultaneously. As these adaptations of *Hamlet* veer towards romance and a happy ending, allusions to *Romeo and Juliet* as the archetypical Shakespearean love story highlight the similarity between the lovers' plots in the two tragedies so that the young readers' knowledge of the Shakespeare intertext is activated.

# Conclusion

In the last 20 years, a number of best-selling social inquiries about the troubles of female adolescence (such as *Reviving Ophelia* 1994 and *Ophelia Speaks* 1999) have used the character of Ophelia as the spokesperson for the American teenage girl. Like Klein's and Fiedler's novels, these studies have given a voice and something to say to this typically marginalized character. As Hulbert has observed in a perceptive article by the eloquent title of 'Adolescence, Thy Name is Ophelia',

> Her character is defined in terms that include the men around her: she is Polonius's daughter, Laertes's sister, and Hamlet's lover. Her decisions, motivations, actions, and downfall stem from the men of the play, without whose influence she does not make a decision. (Hulbert 2006, p. 202)

In these studies, the character of Ophelia, who becomes the epitome of the modern teenage girl who wants 'to fit in' without fully knowing herself, is inevitably impregnated with contemporary constructions of girlhood, not unlike Klein's and Fiedler's novels. However, while the novels construct a character that moves in the Shakespearean milieu with new awareness and tries to change its ending by evading the prison of a predestined role, these social inquiries tend to give a stereotypical interpretation of the character – implicitly asking contemporary girls to reject the Shakespearean Ophelia. This is a remarkably different approach to the character from the more empowered representations of Ophelia that can be found in these fictions based on *Hamlet*. One of the roles that these characters flatly refuse to play is that of the sexual victim (which tends to characterize Victorian and Edwardian Ophelias): these 'narratives of survival' stage empowered characters that challenge Elizabethan gender politics and theatrical scripts (one only needs to think of Nerissa in *The Turquoise Ring*), constructing forms of Shakespearean Young Adulthood that transgress both the Elizabethan code of gender behaviour and the Great Code of canonical literature. These novels address a new sisterhood of readers whom they require to engage with the canon in creative ways, entertaining notions of femininity that are simultaneously canonical and oppositional. In the absence of family education, these characters educate themselves, thus refashioning gender identities that are resilient and rebellious rather than passive and obedient. While Clarke's appropriations are 'pioneering' in giving space to marginal female characters but are still constructed as cautionary tales, Klein's and Fiedler's Ophelias, as well as Tiffany's Xanthe and Pressler's Dalilah (Jessica's empowered alter ego), embrace an identity of a storyteller and narrator, a woman's voice which opens up new narrative possibilities and pastes them onto the patriarchal script: 'I cannot rest while this story remains untold', declares Klein's Ophelia, 'I will dispel the darkness about me and cast a light upon the truth. So I take up my pen and write: here is my story' (2006, p. 3).

## Notes

1   See Gary Blackwood's trilogy starting with *The Shakespeare Stealer*, 1998.
2   Lisa Fiedler's *Dating Hamlet*, 2002, Lisa Klein's *Ophelia*, 2006, and Matt Haig's *The Dead Fathers Club*, 2006.
3   Grace Tiffany's *My Father had a Daughter*, 2003 and Peter Hassinger's *Shakespeare's Daughter*, 2004.
4   For a detailed discussion of Pressler's representation of the Jewish community in *Shylock's Daughter*, see Jana Mikota's essay in this collection.
5   Klein's Ophelia, in particular, is quite an intellectual: 'Sometimes I wished I had been born a man, so I could have been a scholar' (2006, p. 49).

## List of works cited

Bamber, Linda (1982), *Comic Women, Tragic Men. A Study of Gender and Genre in Shakespeare*. Stanford, CA: Stanford University Press.

Black, William (1983, 1884), *Judith Shakespeare. A Romance*. London: Sampson Low, Marston & Company.

Blackwood, Gary (1998), *The Shakespeare Stealer*. New York: Dutton.

Britton, Fay Adams (1907), *Shakespearean Fairy Tales*. Chicago, IL: The Reilly and Britton.

Brown, Sarah Annes (2005), 'The prequel as palinode: Mary Cowden Clarke's girlhood of Shakespeare's heroines'. *Shakespeare Survey*, 58: 95–106.

Carter, Thomas (1910), *Stories from Shakespeare*. London: Harrap & Company.

Clarke, Mary Cowden (1887), 'Shakespeare as the girl's friend'. *Shakespeariana*, 4: 355–69.

— (2009, 1850–52), *The Girlhood of Shakespeare's Heroines*. 3 vols. Cambridge: Cambridge University Press.

Fiedler, Lisa (2003), *Dating Hamlet*. London: Collins Flamingo.

Genette, Gerard (1997), *Palimpsests: Literature in the Second Degree*. Lincoln, NE: University of Nebranska Press.

Haig, Matt (2006), *The Dead Fathers Club*. London: Jonathan Cape.

Hankey, Julie (1994), 'Victorian Portias: Shakespeare's borderline heroine'. *Shakespeare Quarterly*, 45(4): 426–48.

Hassinger, Peter (2004), *Shakespeare's Daughter*. New York: Harpercollins.

Hateley, Erika (2009), *Shakespeare in Children's Literature. Gender and Cultural Capital*. New York and London: Routledge.

Hoffman, Alice Spencer (1911), *The Children's Shakespeare*. London: Dent; New York: Dutton.

Holmer, Joan Ozark (2002), 'Jewish daughters. The question of philo-Semitism in Elizabethan drama', in J. Mahon and E. Macleod Mahon (eds), *The Merchant of Venice. New Critical Essays*. New York and London: Routledge, pp. 107–43.

Hulbert, Jennifer (2006), '"Adolescence, thy name is Ophelia!": The Ophelia-ization of the contemporary teenage girl', in J. Hulbert, K. Wetmore, Jr. and R. L. York (eds), *Shakespeare and Youth Culture*. New York: Palgrave Macmillan, pp. 199–220.

James, Felicity (2006), '"Wild tales" from Shakespeare: readings of Charles and Mary Lamb'. *Shakespeare,* 2(2): 152–67.

Jameson, Anna (1858, 1832), *Characteristics of Women. Moral, Poetical and Historical*. 2 vols. London: Saunders and Otley.

Klein, Lisa (2006), *Ophelia*. London: Bloomsbury.

Kott, Ian (1996, 1965), *Shakespeare Our Contemporary*. London: Routledge.

Lamb, Charles (1809), *Tales from Shakespeare, Designed for the Use of Young Persons*. 2 vols. London: M. J. Godwin at the Juvenile Library.

Lamb, Charles and Lamb, Mary (2007, 1807), *Tales from Shakespeare*. London: Penguin Classics.

Macleod, Mary (1944, 1902), *The Shakespeare Story-Book*. London: Wells Gardner, Darton and Co.

Marsden, Jean I. (1989), 'Shakespeare for girls: Mary Lamb and tales from Shakespeare'. *Children's Literature*, 1: 47–63.

Marshall, Gail (2009), *Shakespeare and Victorian Women*. Cambridge: Cambridge University Press.

Palmer, Henrietta Lee (1859), *The Stratford Gallery, or the Shakspeare Sisterhood: Comprising Forty-five Ideal Portraits*. New York: D. Appleton and Company.

Pressler, Mirjam (2000, 1999), *Shylock's Daughter*. Trans. Brian Murdoch. London: Macmillan.

Richardson, Abbey Sage (1871), *Stories from Old English Poetry*. Boston, MA: Houghton, Mifflin and Company.

Rozmovitz, Linda (1998), *Shakespeare and the Politics of Culture in Late Victorian England*. Baltimore and London: The Johns Hopkins University Press.

Ruskin, John (1905), 'Of Queen's gardens', in E. T. Cook and A. Wedderburn (eds), *Sesame and Lilies. The Works of John Ruskin*, vol. 18. London: George Allen, pp. 109–44.

Sanders, Julie (2006), *Adaptation and Appropriation*. London and New York: Routledge.

Sterling, Sara Hawks (1905), *Shakespeare's Sweetheart*. Jacobs (no place).

Stidolph, Ada Baynes (1902), *The Children's Shakespeare*. London: Allman and Son.

Taylor, Gary (1989), *Reinventing Shakespeare. A Cultural History from the Restoration to the Present*. London: The Hogarth Press.

Thompson, Ann and Roberts, Sasha (1993), 'Mary Cowden Clarke: marriage, gender and the Victorian woman critic of Shakespeare', in G. Marshall and A. Poole (eds), *Victorian Shakespeare, Volume 2. Literature and Culture*. New York and Basingstoke: Palgrave Macmillan, pp. 170–89.

—(eds) (1997), *Women Reading Shakespeare 1660–1900. An Anthology of Criticism*. Manchester and New York: Manchester University Press.

Tiffany, Grace (2005), *The Turquoise Ring*. New York: Berkley.

Wolfson, Susan (1990), 'Explaining to her sisters: Mary Lamb's Tales from Shakespeare', in M. Novy (ed.), *Women's Re-Visions of Shakespeare. On the Responses of Dickinson, Woolf, Rich, H. D., George Eliot, and Others*. Urbana and Chicago: University of Illinois Press, pp. 16–40.

Ziegler, Giorgianna, Dolan, Frances and Addison Roberts, Jeanne (1997), *Shakespeare's Unruly Women*. Washington: The Folger Shakespeare Library.

2

# Shylock's Daughter (*Shylocks Tochter*) – *Nathan and his Children* (*Nathan und seine Kinder*): Mirjam Pressler's Adaptations of European Classics for Young Adult Readers

Jana Mikota

## Introduction

Mirjam Pressler (neé 1940) is one of the most important contemporary German authors of fiction for children and young adults. Her novels display a high diversity of topics and genres. They have received numerous awards and they have initiated paradigm shifts within German children's and young-adult literature. The student revolt and the feminist movement of the 1960s and early 1970s also had a modernizing impact on both the contents and the narrative strategies of German literature for children and young adults. Not only did new topics, such as divorce or unemployment, enter the genre, the relationship between adults and children was represented differently, too. The child characters began to engage with adult norms and values. The much favoured first-person or personal narrators tell the respective stories from a child's perspective. Mirjam Pressler's novels have made an important contribution to these changes. In 1981, Pressler made her debut with the novel *Bitterschokolade* (*Dark Chocolate*), which addressed a central topic of her future creative work: broken childhood. At the beginning of her career, Pressler concentrated on problem novels for children and young adult readers, defining herself as a children's advocate within the understanding of 1970s' children's and young adult fiction. Drawing attention to various worries and fears, she considerably expanded the field of children's and young adult fiction with new topics. One of her central concerns is the Shoa. Pressler translated *The Diary of Anne Frank* into German and she has described how children experienced National Socialism, the Shoa and the post-war period. Again and again, she addresses Jewish subjects in her novels. Besides, Pressler is one of the most important translators of Hebraic (children's and young-adult) literature in Germany.

The following chapter discusses two novels by Mirjam Pressler that share the above-mentioned concerns: *Shylock's Daughter* (*Shylock's Tochter* 2008) and *Nathan and his Children* (*Nathan und seine Kinder* 2009). Both novels take up characters of world literature – *Nathan the Wise* (1779) by Gotthold Ephraim Lessing [1729–1781] and *The Merchant of Venice* (1600) by William Shakespeare [1564–1616] – and adapt them for young adult readers. For instance, each of the two novels places children at the centre of action, widens the arsenal of characters and highlights the relation between Christians and Jews (in the case of *Nathan*, the relation between Christians, Jews and Muslims) more explicitly than in the originals. In the following chapter, I will scrutinize individual characters, the use of language and the depiction of space in order to demonstrate their function in an adaptation of canonical texts for a young adult readership. A major part of my interpretation will take cognizance of the fact that Pressler's adaptations of these European classics are highly influenced by the experience of the Shoa and the urge to convey this fundamental collective experience to the following generations.

## *Shylock's Daughter*

*Shylock's Daughter* was first published in 1999; a revised edition appeared in 2008. Pressler uses Shakespeare's *The Merchant of Venice* as a prototype from which she develops her own story. Focusing on the moneylender Shylock and his daughter Jessica, Mirjam Pressler's adaptation for young adults highlights Jessica's separation from her parents' generation and her break with traditions and conventions. As the readers learn why Shylock fights so bitterly, the Shakespearean comedy, which has often been regarded as highly problematic for its anti-Semitic subtext by post-war critics (cf. Ludewig 2008), is transformed into an appeal for more tolerance and understanding.

Together with her father, her foster sister Dalilah and the housekeeper Amelia, 16-year-old Jessica lives in the Jewish ghetto of Venice in 1568. Jessica suffers from the restrictions that are imposed on her, such as the prohibition of feasts or splendid clothing for Jews. She longs for freedom. When she makes the acquaintance of the Christian aristocrat Lorenzo, she immediately falls in love with him. Knowing that her father would never agree to this relationship, she raids his savings, secretly leaves her family home, marries Lorenzo and converts to Christianity. Shylock is deeply affected by the loss of his daughter and seeks revenge. When he does not get back the money he lent to the Christian Antonio, Shylock insists on his claim to cut one pound of flesh out of Antonio's chest. However, he loses his claims before the Christian court and is left a broken man.

The title of Pressler's novel already hints at its dramatic source, but the focus of the story has clearly moved to Shylock's daughter. Moreover, Pressler's novel is set in Venice, and Belmont plays a less important role than in the dramatic original. The choice of setting also creates a new aspect in Pressler's novel, because the action mostly takes place in the Jewish ghetto, especially in Shylock's house in the ghetto area. Shakespeare, on the contrary, did not represent the ghetto. Both Pressler and Shakespeare, however, share an interest in the differences between Jewish and Christian lives. Pressler expands on this topic by referring to the lives of the Sephardi and Ashkenazi, thus portraying a considerably more differentiated view of Jewish life than Shakespeare's play. This is already obvious in the openings of both works: Whereas *The Merchant of Venice* begins in the streets of Venice, with the characters Antonio, Solarino and Salanio, Mirjam Pressler gives the first appearance to Shylock's daughter Jessica and thus endows her with a far more important voice.

As far as the depiction of the Jewish world is concerned, Shakespeare's portrayal of this world is mainly through its dark embodiment by the merchant Shylock. Shylock's cheerlessness is supported in his use of a language that appears to be equally deprived of joy. The aristocratic world, on the other hand, is characterized by pleasure, luxury and colours. It is the world of trade and the world of senses, which is primarily located in Belmont. This spatial contrast also informs the structure of Shakespeare's work: the scenes alternate between locations, and Belmont almost appears like a fairy tale. The riddle that is to be solved by Portia's suitors contributes to this fairy tale character.

Pressler also displays the contrast between the Christian and the Jewish world, but she demonstrates that the Jewish world is far more differentiated than Shakespeare's work makes believe. Pressler's setting, the ghetto, on the one hand offers protection to the Jewish population; on the other hand, it causes confinement. 'You don't know what the Ghetto is? Oh, it's a prison or a place of safety – it all depends what you want it to be and you want to do' (Pressler 2000,

p. 276) says one of the characters. In her novel, Pressler manages to capture the atmosphere of the ghetto through the perspective of her personal narrator:

> Jessica went through the gateway to the palazzo. She felt, as she always did, that she was going into another world, a wonderful beautiful happy world – one that suited her far more than the Ghetto – a world where she really belonged. And as usual, this line of thought gave rise to a dull sense of shame, as if she shouldn't really think that way, because it went against her father, against Amalia and Dalilah, and against the place in the world ordained for her by the Everlasting One, blessed be He. (Pressler 2000, p. 4)

Jessica, too, experiences the world inside the ghetto as bleak, dark and grey. These feelings are enhanced by the numerous laws that were imposed on the Jewish population by the *condottiere*, that is, the law of settlement on Venetian national territory. Outside the ghetto, Jessica encounters a different, colourful world and, finally, her love to Lorenzo. The conflict between the Christian and the Jewish world is, thus, displayed less on a materialistic level rather than on a personal one. In addition to that, Pressler also addresses the question of Jewish identity. The contrast between the two cultures is particularly expressed through Jessica's unfulfilled desires:

> Why aren't we allowed to buy flowers like the Christians do? she thought angrily. Why are we only allowed to buy a little bunch of flowers and no sweets and can't even have preserves? Extravagance, – yes, she longed for extravagance, for bright colours, for pretty clothes, for flowers, for excess, for all the cakes and pastries that they served in Levi Meshullam's house. (Pressler 2000, p. 13f.)

This quotation illustrates Jessica's dissatisfaction as well as the different ways of life within the Jewish Community. Levi Meschullam is a Sephardic Jew, Shylock an Ashkenazim, and both follow different laws. Pressler, thus, portrays the heterogeneity within Jewish communities as well as the possible resulting conflicts which Shakespeare completely left aside. This passage also illustrates Pressler's use of an intradiegetic narrator who will be superseded, in a few chapters, by Dalilah, Jessica's foster sister, who appears as a homodiegetic, first-person narrator. Pressler's narrative uses a diversity of focalizers, so that the readers can follow Jessica's, Shylock's, Amalia's and Dalilah's thoughts. In other words, Pressler's narrative mode employs a Jewish perspective, whereas the thoughts of Christian characters are not rendered. With the help of this narrative choice, Pressler manages to eschew the biased perspective that informs Shakespeare's play. In what follows, I am going to show how this choice of narrative perspective additionally helps to create round, multidimensional Jewish characters.

To begin with, let me take a closer look at Jessica, whom Pressler has transformed from a marginal character in Shakespeare's play into the protagonist of her novel. In addition to the Jewish merchant, Shakespeare's play uses, with Jessica, another topos of literary history, namely the beautiful Jewess. Reiterating this topos, Jessica appears lovely, and her beauty serves as a foil against which Shylock's hideousness becomes even more apparent. It is important to keep in mind, however, that Jessica in *The Merchant of Venice* is no well-behaved, loving daughter: she not only decides against home, leaves Shylock and takes his riches with her, but also marries Lorenzo and converts to Christianity:

> Alack, what heinous sin is it in me
> To be ashamed to be my father's child!
> But thought I am a daughter to his blood
> I am not to his manners: O Lorenzo,
> If thou keep promise, I shall end this strife,
> Become a Christian and thy loving wife. (*MV*: II 3: 16–21)

Apparently, Jessica cannot resign herself to life in the Jewish community; she rejects her father's way of life and is ready to give up everything, including her faith. Lorenzo is supposed to help and marry her. Her wish for an interesting, colourful life induces her to take this step.

> Es war kein liebloser Vater, den sie verließ, den sie beraubte, den sie verrieth … Schändlicher Verrath! Sie macht gemeinsame Sache mit den Feinden Shylocks, und wenn diese zu Belmont allerlei Missreden über ihn führen, schlägt Jessika nicht die Augen nieder, erbleichen nicht die Lippen Jessikas, sondern Jessika spricht von ihrem Vater das Schlimmste … Entsetzlicher Frevel! Sie hat kein Gemüth, sondern abendtheuerlichen Sinn. Sie langweilte sich in dem strengen, 'ehrbaren' Hause des bittermüthigen Juden, das ihr endlich eine Hölle dünkte. Das leichtfertige Herz wurde allzu sehr angezogen von den heiteren Tönen der Trommel und der quer gehalsten Pfeife. Hat Shakespeare hier eine Jüdin schildern wollen? Wahrlich, er schildert nur eine Tochter Evas, eine jener schönen Vögel, die, wenn sie flügge geworden, aus dem väterlichen Nest fortflattern zu den geliebten Männchen. (Heine 1993, p. 124)[1]

With such words Heinrich Heine criticized Shakespeare's Jessica, who betrayed both her father and her Jewish identity. Although Jessica was largely designed a marginal character, her actions leave a deep impact on Shylock. Shylock himself loves his daughter, but she emotionally distances herself from him to pursue her own plans. Nevertheless, Heine clearly perceived the reason for Jessica's misbehaviour not in her Jewishness but in her being a woman.

The characters' attitude towards money is another difference between the Christian and the Jewish community that is established in Shakespeare's play. Shylock is a merchant, he lends money to others in order to make profit. If Shylock does not get his money back, his debtor is at his disposal. In contrast, the merchant Antonio and his friends use their money to celebrate and enjoy life. Their money is allowed to circulate freely, without any worry about interest rates. The Jewish merchant, therefore, appears to block free economic flow, because he is only interested in his own profit, hence a unidirectional flow of money (into his own purse). His opponents, on the contrary, are given almost altruistic features, economically speaking, as they help money to circulate.

This difference between a dynamic Christian world and a petrified Jewish one is also mediated through language: Antonio, Portia and other Christian characters in Shakespeare's *Merchant* play with language; they enhance it through poetic imagery, adapt it to the current situation and revel in ambiguities and *double entendre*. Shylock's language, in contrast, is marked by cliché and set phrases, for example from the Old Testament, it is brusque and devoid of any playfulness.[2]

By focusing on Jessica's unease with her Jewish identity, Pressler takes up a question that frequently surfaces in texts by Jewish writers[3]:

> Jessica shook Dalilah's arms away and jumped up. "But I don't want to stop!" she shouted. "I want to get out of here! Just look out of that window. A row of houses round a big square, that's all, and that's supposed to be all there is to life? I want to have gardenparties too. I want flowers. . . . You've told me often enough yourself that I look like one of them. And you're quite right. It's only an accident that I was born a Jew's daughter – a mistake of nature, yes, just like you sometimes get a white mouse in a litter of grey ones. Yes, I was born into a Jewish family, but what if a husband makes me a Christian?" (Pressler 2000, p. 19f.)

For Jessica, flowers and garden parties symbolize a freedom she cannot enjoy in the ghetto. There, she feels lonely, misunderstood and imprisoned. Whereas Jessica characterizes herself as lonely and resigned, she simultaneously appears to others as a conceited, narcissistic and egotistical girl, who may easily hurt others' feelings.

Despite these features, Jessica is certainly lovely, and, above all, her beauty and wealth eventually captivate Lorenzo. After her wedding, Jessica has to change: as she converts to Christianity, she completely breaks with her origins and traditions – and feels displaced in the aristocratic world. Pressler shows Jessica in Belmont, where she does not only enjoy the ease of aristocratic life but is also continuously reminded of her father and her affiliation to the Jewish community. Among her new peers, Shylock is mocked and Antonio's triumph is celebrated. At first, Jessica does not defend her father but later, she feels pangs of guilt, and it becomes clear that Jessica does not feel at home among Christians either:

> She would have liked to smash the glass out of her hand and shout: Is that what you wanted? Did you want to destroy your father's life? Go on eat the preserves, eat until you're sick. Buy flowers, buy them, but they'll never please you. And what is life of riches and elegance worth if you always have your father before your eyes? What use are concerts when you can hear your father weeping behind that music? . . . I wanted to be free, I wanted feasts, a life in comfort. I wanted to get away from the Ghetto . . . (Pressler 2000, p. 261)

Ridden by her bad conscience, Jessica finds it hard to break with her traditions and origins. What is more, she is confronted with the aristocracy's anti-Semitism. Pressler takes up Heine's critique of Shakespeare as she portrays the Jewish girl in a more differentiated manner, showing the problems she encounters, her scruples, inner struggles and fears. Pressler's Jessica may be designed as a loving daughter; nevertheless, her love for Lorenzo is even stronger and clashes with that of her father.

Apart from the alterations in Jessica, Pressler also adapts the character of the merchant Shylock. Pressler's Shylock appears more human than in Shakespeare's play; more importantly, he is now given a past. In Shakespeare's play, Shylock's outsider position is most obviously displayed in the third act, when he tries to justify his revenge on Antonio. In this scene, he is a humiliated person who may evoke sympathy and tolerance for his actions. Pressler gives depth to Shylock's character by endowing him with thoughts and feelings. He explains himself to his friends and is given more room to operate than in *The Merchant of Venice*. At the same time, Shylock is also characterized by Jessica:

> He was a hard, miserly man, he would never give way. . . . And now there was this bond with Antonio. With a pound of his flesh as security. He was a wicked old pawnbroker, her father, the kind of man a daughter could only be ashamed of. (Pressler 2000, p. 51)

Pressler takes up the motive of the pound of flesh, but Shylock's friends object to the contract and warn him. After Jessica's escape, Shylock rejects every warning and insists on his rights. He plots revenge:

> Shylock's back was bent, his shoulders stooped forward. He had lost everything that he loved, first Leah and now Jessica as well, and his life had become

meaningless. But then he straightened himself up and a little of his earlier strength came back to him. His life did have some meaning. Revenge. He would get his revenge. Suddenly his head felt clearer, his confused feelings had disappeared. At last he was able to think of something other than what he had lost. Of revenge. And it was a sweet feeling. (Pressler 2000, p. 183)

In the reversed perspective of Pressler's novel, the Christian characters are, in contrast, presented with less differentiation. Antonio, in particular, is introduced as a hater of Jews and an anti-Semite. Although the world of the Christian community is portrayed as gay and full of fun and games, Jessica gradually realizes that it is not necessarily worth living in. Over and over, Pressler describes how Christians and Jews live together and elucidates the persecutions and humiliations Jews have had to endure over the centuries. Although her representation of the two worlds is much more differentiated than Shakespeare's in *The Merchant of Venice*, Pressler borrows verbatim from Shakespeare's play. Consider, for instance, the following exclamation of Shakespeare's Jessica:

Alack, what heinous sin is it me
To be ashamed to be my father's child! (*MV*: II 3: 16–17)

The same passage surfaces in Pressler's novel: 'He was a wicked old pawnbroker, her father, the kind of man a daughter could only be ashamed of' (Pressler 2000, p. 51). Both texts express Jessica's affliction, yet Pressler's novel continuously offers additional insights into Shylock's home, including further female characters with Dalilah and Amalia. By representing Jessica's thoughts after her conversion, Pressler demonstrates that Jessica's shift to Christianity is not a seamless one, but induces considerable ruptures.

The novel's concluding sentence neatly hints at the differences between Shakespeare's and Pressler's work: 'Children, children, that is a long story, a very long and very Jewish story' (Pressler 2000, p. 277). Mirjam Pressler wrote a novel in which Shylock is moved from the periphery into the centre and therefore becomes more comprehensible. Her Shylock is also a result of the twentieth century and her novel focuses more on Jewish life. Despite her alterations, Pressler does not simplify Shakespeare's play for a younger readership. In her adaptation, she rather expands on the conflicts, rendering the original constellation more complex and differentiated. Her particular concern lies with representing the fears of the Jewish population and addressing the persecutions and harassments by Christians. Pressler has accurate knowledge about the composition of Venice's Jewish population; she includes explanations in her text and the glossary can be read as evidence for young adult fiction. In the text itself, the Thora is repeatedly quoted and, as these quotations are written in italics, they stand out from the overall text. With such an agenda of intercultural understanding in mind, I argue that it is important for Pressler to illuminate Jewish ways of life for her readers and to create a more qualified image of Shylock, the Jewish merchant. With this reversal of sympathizing strategies, Pressler urges her juvenile readers to reflect on alterity and to empathize, where Shakespeare resorted to stereotype and othering.

## *Nathan und seine Kinder*

Published in 2009, Pressler's novel *Nathan und seine Kinder* adapts Lessing's drama *Nathan the Wise* for young readers. The plot of *Nathan the Wise* is set in 1192 Jerusalem. It is the time of the Crusades and a war of religions. Sultan Saladin has conquered the city and had all Templers killed except Curd von Stauffen. Curd von Stauffen's reprieve causes a chain reaction of events when the young Templar rescues Recha, the adoptive daughter of the wealthy and respected Jew Nathan, nicknamed the Wise, from a burning house. The young woman falls in love with her hero, but a relationship between Christians and Jews is impossible. However, Curd von Stauffen finds out that Recha is adopted and had a Christian mother. With this knowledge he goes to the patriarch of Jerusalem to find out whether Recha is a Christian or a Jew. While doing so, he unintentionally delivers Nathan to the Christians.

Nathan himself has already experienced extreme sorrow: Christians set fire to his house, causing the death of his wife and his nine children. Nevertheless, he does not retaliate, does not lust for revenge but forgives. Soon, Nathan is confronted with new danger when the Sultan desires his possessions, orders Nathan to his court and asks the wise Jew which religion is the only true one. Nathan falls into this trap with his famous parable of the three rings, which earns him the respect and friendship of the Sultan. Nathan presents himself as an intelligent and tolerant teacher who accepts the distinctive features of different religions and looks for a common denominator. He does not suspect that, in the meantime, the patriarch of Jerusalem and the Muslim captain Abu Hassan are plotting against his life. When Nathan falls prey to robbers, it remains unclear who are the culprits: the Patriarch as representative of the Christians? Or the fanatic Muslim Abu Hassan, whom Pressler added to the story?

In contrast to *Shylock's Daughter*, Mirjam Pressler already reveals the connection between her novel and Lessing's drama in the paratext, quoting directly from Lessing's *Nathan* in one of the mottoes:

> Lasst lächelnd wenigstens ihr einen Wahn,
> In dem sich Jud' und Christ und Muselmann
> Vereinigen; – so einen süßen Wahn (qtd in Pressler 2009)[4]

Originally, these lines are spoken by Daja and refer to the topic of both drama and novel, namely the utopia of a peaceful coexistence of Christians, Jews and Muslims. Moreover, Pressler writes an epilogue explaining her intentions of adapting Lessing's drama:

> Lessings *Nathan der Weise* ist eine weltanschauliche Erörterung in Form eines Dramas, und das ist unter anderem ein Grund dafür, dass das Stück heute schwer lesbar ist, ganz abgesehen davon, dass die meisten Menschen ungern Theaterstücke lesen. Zudem erscheinen Lessings Figuren doch sehr im Dienst der Gedanken zu stehen, die er verbreiten wollte; die Menschen als Charaktere kommen mir dabei zu kurz. Mein Bedürfnis war es, sie etwas plastischer darzustellen, lebendiger. Das lässt sich in einem Roman natürlich viel einfacher machen als in einem Drama. (Pressler 2009, p. 250)[5]

As a consequence, Pressler enlarges the range of *dramatis personae*, including Christians, Jews and Muslims. To the original characters, Nathan, Al-Hafi, Saladin, Recha, Templar, Daja, Sitah and the Patriarch, Pressler adds to her novel Abu Hassan, a captain of Saladin, Geschem, a boy in Nathan's house, Elijahu, an administrator of Nathan and Zipora, Nathan's cook. As each chapter is dedicated to another character, different thoughts and points of view are communicated to the reader. Pressler uses multiple first-person narrators, shifting points of view among the individual chapters: Sittah, Saladin's sister, Abu Hassan, Recha, Nathan's daughter, Daja, Recha's companion, Geschem, Elijahu, Templar Leu von Filnek, and Al Hafi, a dervish who serves Saladin – they all assume the narrator's role respectively. Nathan and the situation in Jerusalem around 1191/92 are accordingly presented from Christian, Jewish and Muslim perspectives. Nathan is characterized indirectly by different characters or by his own speech. The characters that appear in both works are characterized similarly in Lessing's and Pressler's versions, but they appear more vivid and multidimensional in Pressler's novel.

Both texts share a similar opening – the fire in Nathan's house and the rescue of Recha by the Templar – but the descriptions of the events are different. Having different characters tell about the fire, Pressler delivers a variety of impressions – even in Nathan's household. In Lessing, Nathan enters the stage, and it is Daja, who relates the fire among other things.

Pressler claimed she did not intend to rewrite Lessing's play but tried to 'stay as close to Lessing's guidelines ... if only to make a reference to the original'.[6] She does not see her novel as a counterpart to Lessing's drama but as a 'variation' (Pressler 2009, p. 251). The basic concept and the idea of tolerance, which eventually climaxes in the Ring Parable, are preserved, and the characterizations of the individual figures are reminiscent of Lessing's *Nathan the Wise*.

Nathan emerges as a generous, wise and wealthy merchant. Unlike Shylock in Shakespeare's play, Nathan helps his fellow men regardless of their religion. At the beginning of the novel, the reader learns about Nathan's past and how he lost his wife and seven children in a fire caused by Christians:

> Viele Stunden lang tobte Nathan, und die Nachbarn und ich hatten alle Hände voll zu tun, ihn festzuhalten und daran zu hindern, sich auf die nächstbesten Christen zu stürzen und sich für den Tod seiner Lieben zu rächen. Alle waren sie verbrannt, seine Frau, seine sieben Söhne, sein Bruder, die Knechte und Mägde. (Pressler 2009, p. 46)[7]

Friends help Nathan to calm down, Recha comes to him as a baby and he summons new courage to face life: 'Gott ist fern, aber die Menschen sind nah. Glaube mir, Elijahu, das höchste Ziel der Menschen muss die Vernunft sein. Vernunft und die Liebe zu anderen Menschen' (Pressler 2009, p. 48).[8] With this idea in mind, Nathan and Recha move to Jerusalem and their next years are ruled by reason. Lessing's drama includes such a passage, too, in what may be called a "key scene" of the play. In Act IV, Scene 7, a secret of Nathan's past is presented when Nathan relates how, after Christian soldiers had murdered his family, his days were determined by despair and a thirst for vengeance. For some time, he quarrelled with God, but then he acknowledges reason as his guiding principle:

> Doch nun kam die Vernunft allmählich wieder.
> Sie sprach mit sanfter Stimm': "und doch ist Gott!
> Doch war auch Gottes Ratschluß das! Wohlan!
> Komm! übe, was du längst begriffen hast,
> Was sicherlich zu üben schwerer nicht,
> Als zu begreifen ist, wenn du nur willst.
> Steh auf!" – Ich stand! Und rief zu Gott: Ich will!
> Willst du nur, daß ich will! (Lessing 1984, IV, 7; p. 708)[9]

Notwithstanding the importance of Nathan, Pressler's novel places Recha, Nathan's (adoptive) daughter, at the centre of attention. Unlike Lessing, Pressler gives a voice to women, particularly Jewish women, and describes their everyday lives. Minor characters are employed to depict the lot of married and unmarried women; Recha, for instance, experiences that her friends marry and change.

A central conflict of the novel consists in Recha's love for the Templar. As in the original, their love cannot be realized in Pressler's adaptation, either. Even when the Templar finds out that Recha is, in fact, a Christian who was raised in Nathan's house in Jewish tradition and faith, he cannot marry her. The ending of the novel implies that Recha finally decides to keep her Jewish identity in order to honour the memory of her father:

> Ich hob den Kopf und blickte Leu von Filnek ins Gesicht. "Nein, ich war nicht verlassen", sagte ich [Recha] noch einmal. "Ich hatte einen Vater. Kein Kind könnte sich einem liebevolleren und zärtlicheren Vater wünschen. Und glaube mir, die Liebe ist ein starkes Band, manchmal noch stärker als Blut." (Pressler 2009, p. 246)[10]

In the play, the revelation of the sibling relationship between Recha and the Templar ultimately forbids sexual fulfilment. Pressler remains opaque about Recha's background; it is Recha herself who decides against the Templar and stays in Nathan's house. This action expresses an intimate and loving relationship between foster father and daughter. After Nathan's death, Recha follows his earlier example. Recha perseveres in her faith; she stays on in Nathan's house and, so the novel insinuates, will most probably continue his work. She does not plot revenge but hopes for peace between the religions: 'Die hohen Feiertage rückten näher und bald danach würde der ersehnte Regen fallen und die Zisternen würden sich wieder füllen' (Pressler 2009, p. 248).[11] With this ending, Pressler alters Lessing's drama where Nathan survives. Nevertheless, Lessing's is not a hopeful ending since the war of religions continues and Nathan is left behind alone.

Mirjam Pressler's Jewish world is opposed to the Muslim and the Christian worlds, yet it is above all the Christian world that has reservations about the Jews and rejects them. The Templar Leu von Filnek, for instance, calls the country 'ein Land der Barbarei und des Todes' (Pressler 2009, p. 67)[12] and completely ignores its beauty; a beauty that is repeatedly emphasized by Recha who especially hints at its fragrance. Leu von Filnek falls in love with Recha but cannot marry her because he refuses a relationship with a Jew; he cannot even imagine it. The Patriarch reacts as follows: 'Dafür gibt es eine eindeutige

Aussage unserer heiligen Kirche. Der Jude, der so etwas getan hat, verdient den Tod. Er muss sterben. Er muss auf dem Scheiterhaufen verbrannt werden' (Pressler 2009, p. 186).[13] The passage makes clear that Jews were prohibited from raising Christian children and providing them with a home. Too late, Leu von Filnek realizes what he has done, but in order to ease his conscience, he reassures himself that, after all, he is 'only' betraying a Jew (compare Pressler 2009, p. 189). In Pressler's novel, as well as in Lessing's drama, the Patriarch is portrayed as a fanatic who is the antagonist of Nathan. He embodies the unenlightened human being. In the novel, only a few persons manage to live according to the principles of Nathan because they allow themselves to be determined by envy, resentment or homesickness. Although the contrast between the worlds of the different religions is not contrasted as sharply as in her adaptation of *The Merchant of Venice*, Pressler's agenda is again clearly didactic, appealing to her young readers to develop tolerance and intercultural understanding. With this goal, Pressler follows Lessing's equally moralizing stance.

# Conclusion

The two novels discussed in this chapter are based on literary models which they interpret freshly and originally, expanding and placing a Jewish perspective at the centre of attention. Pressler shows how these works by eminent canonical writers can be adapted for a young adult readership. Her books exemplify that these are novels written after the Shoa and therefore need reconsideration and rewriting of their pre-Shoa material. My analysis of the texts has revealed that Pressler focused on the drama *The Merchant of Venice* in order to tone down the anti-Semitic subtext of Shakespeare's play. Apart from the Jewish perspective and the idea of Jewish origins and traditions, it is above all the female perspective which distinguishes *Nathan and his Children* and *Shylock's Daughter* from their original versions. Female characters remain marginal in both Lessing's and Shakespeare's works. In both *Nathan and his Children* and *Shylock's Daughter*, female characters are used to illustrate the conflict between Christianity, Islam and Judaism. But unlike Shakespeare, Pressler uses the trope of the beautiful Jewess not for mere embellishment but in order to render Shylock more humane. The female protagonists are used as projection screens for the male figures. In *Nathan and his Children*, Pressler alters the ending of her source. Contrary to the play, Nathan is murdered in the novel; his murderer is not revealed. One could interpret this ending so that Nathan's idea of tolerance, common sense and responsibility eventually fail. As I have demonstrated in my analysis, however, Pressler's novel still concludes full of hope as the new protagonist, Recha, becomes the voice of a new generation.

In sum, Pressler adapts canonical texts from two different national literatures for a young adult readership in various ways:

1. Pressler elaborates more thoroughly on Jewish traditions, drawing, among other things, on the Thora;
2. Women, especially Jewish women, are given a voice; women's daily life is presented in different centuries;
3. By deploying children or young adults as protagonists, narrators or focalizers, Pressler clearly takes cognizance of the wishes of her target audience for identification.

*The Merchant of Venice*, as well as *Nathan the Wise*, forms part of the canon of world literature. Pressler's adaptations of these works for a young readership make a significant contribution to the European cultural memory. Her work gives ample evidence for the little recognized fact that literature for children and young adults is part of our cultural memory and, hence, continues certain traditions, subjects and motives. She enhances the works by giving those persons a voice that until then have remained in the background. Pressler uses the genre of young adult fiction to adapt canonical works for the tastes of young readers and thus to preserve those works in the cultural memory. Her novels aim to break down prejudices between Jews, Christians and Muslims. Thus, Pressler's books are significant, not only because of their literary merits, but also because of their purpose to create empathy and understanding for other cultures. Pressler's youthful characters are carriers of hope for a better world. With this goal, literature for young adults fulfils an educational function in a double sense: it makes young readers familiar with canonical texts and presents them with ethical role models.

## Notes

1 'He was no loveless father, whom she deserted, robbed, betrayed . . . Abominable treachery! She conspires with Shylock's enemies, and if they talk slander about him at Belmont, Jessica's eyes are not cast down, Jessica's lips do not quiver, but Jessica says the worst about her father . . . Terrible iniquity! She has no feeling but an adventurous spirit. The strict, "honourable" house of the embittered Jew

was tedious to her, seemed hell to her. Light-hearted, she was too easily lured by the serene beating of the drum and the melodious pipe. Did Shakespeare thus want to depict a Jewess? Indeed, he did not but depicts one of Eva's daughters, one of those young birds who, once fledged, take to the air and flutter, away from the father's nest to a mate.' (my translation, J. M.)

2  Cf.: [Shylock]: 'Ho, no, no, no, no: my meaning in saying he is a good man, is to have you understand me that he is sufficient, – yet his means are in supposition; he hath an argosy bound to Tripolis, another to the Indies, I understand moreover upon the Rialto, he hath a third at Mexico, a fourth for England, and other verntures he hath squand'red abroad, – but ships are but boards, sailors but men, there be land-rats, and water-rats, water-thieves, and land-thieves, I mean pirates, and then there is the peril of waters, winds, and rocks: the man is notwithstanding sufficient, – three thousands ducats, – I think I may take his bond' (*MV*: I 3: 13–24).

[Portia]: 'How all the other passions fleet to air:
As doubtful thoughts, and rash-embrac'd despair,
And shudd'ring fear, and green-eyed jealousy.
O love, be moderate, allay thy extasy,
In measure rain the joy, scant this excess!
I feel too much thy blessing, make it less
For fear I surfeit.' (*MV*: III 2: 108–14)

3  Cf., for instance Leon de Winter, Robert Menasse, Fanny Lewald, Philip Roth.

4  'Let smiling her at least this one illusion,
In which Jew and Christ and Mahometan
Unite; – oh such a sweet illusion' (my translation, J. M.)

5  'Lessing's Nathan the Wise is a philosophical exposition in form of a drama, and this is, among other things, one reason for the piece being a difficult read, notwithstanding the fact that most people do not like reading plays. What is more, Lessing's figures very much appear to serve the thoughts he wanted to unfold; they rather fall short as characters. I desired to render them more pliant, more lively. Of course, this is much more easily done in a novel than in a drama' (my translation, J. M.).

6  Translated from German: 'so weit wie möglich an Lessings Vorgaben . . . , schon um ihm eine Referenz zu erweisen' (Pressler 2009, p. 251).

7  'Nathan raved for hours, and the neighbours and I had a handful to hold him back and keep him from attacking the next Christian in sight to revenge the deaths of his beloved ones. They had all burnt: his wife, his seven sons, his brother, his servants and maids' (my translation, J. M.).

8 'God is far, but people are close. Believe me Elijahu, man's highest goal must be
reason. Reason and love for other human beings' (my translation, J. M.).

9 'But now, reason returned by degree.

She talked with tongues sweet: "and still there's God!

Yet even this his council! Well!

Come! Do what you have long conceived,

What certainly is harder not to do

Than to conceive, if thou but wish'st.

Get up!" – I stood! And cried to God: I will!

If only thou will that I will!' (my translation, J. M.)

10 'I lifted my head and looked Leu von Filnek straight into the face. "No, I wasn't
abandoned", I [Recha] repeated. "I had a father. No child could wish for a more
loving and tender father. And believe me, love is a strong bond, sometimes even
stronger than blood."' (my translation, J. M.)

11 'The holidays were approaching and soon after the long awaited rain would fall
and fill the cisterns again' (my translation, J. M.).

12 'A land of barbarity and death'. (my translation, J. M.)

13 'Our holy church has a clear regulation for such cases: A jew who committed
such a thing, deserves death. He must die. He must be burnt at the stake'
(my translation, J. M.).

# List of works cited

Heine, Heinrich (1993), 'Shakespeares Mädchen und Frauen und kleinere
literaturwissenschaftliche Schriften', in Manfred Windfuhr (ed.), *Historisch-kritische
Gesamtausgabe der Werke*, vol. 10. Hamburg: Hoffmann und Campe, p. 124.

Lessing, Gotthold Ephraim (1984), 'Nathan der Weise', in Kurt Wölfel (ed.), Gotthold
Ephraim Lessing, *Dramen*. Frankfurt a. M.: Insel, pp. 593–740.

Ludewig, Anna Dorothea (2008), '"Schönste Heidin, süßeste Jüdin!" Die "Schöne
Jüdin" in der europäischen Literatur zwischen dem 17. und 19. Jahrhundert – ein
Querschnitt', in *Medaon*, 3, <http://medaon.de/archiv-3-2008-artikel.html>.

Pressler, Mirjam (2000, 1999), *Shylock's Daughter*. London: Macmillan Children's Books.

— (2009), *Nathan und seine Kinder*. Weinheim: Beltz & Gelberg.

Shakespeare, William (2006), *The Merchant of Venice/Der Kaufmann von Venedig*.
Barbara Puschmann-Nalenz (trans) (ed.). Stuttgart: Reclam.

# 3

# Shakespeare in Children's Literature; Two Approaches: Susan Cooper's *King of Shadows* and Tad Williams' *Caliban's Hour*

Eva Oppermann

After the publication of Charles and Mary Lamb's *Tales from Shakespeare* (1807), the works of the English playwright have entered the nursery and the classroom in different ways. Among the contemporary publications are Tad Williams' *Caliban's Hour* (1993) and, more recently, Susan Cooper's *King of Shadows* (1999). Both novels are based on Shakespeare's two Magic Plays: Williams' on *The Tempest* (1611) and Cooper's on *A Midsummer Night's Dream* (1598/99). The two novels, however, differ significantly in the way they deal with the respective plays. Whereas Williams retells the story from a remembering Caliban's point of view in order to give him the chance of having some revenge, Cooper uses *A Midsummer Night's Dream* for two purposes. First, acting helps her main protagonist come to terms with his past, especially his father's death. Nat Field is a Shakespeare fan if ever there was one at his age, even before he meets the great playwright in person when he travels back in time. Second, Cooper seems willing to teach her readers as much as possible about Shakespeare's time and his theatre, taking *A Midsummer Night's Dream* as an exemplary drama. Within this chapter, I am going to compare the two different approaches of the novels to the plays. My main focus on Williams' text will be its interpretation as an underdog's 'writing back' to both *The Tempest*'s main character and the concept of civilization and education he embodies. In the case of *King of Shadows*, I am interested especially in the way Cooper uses her hero's confrontation with Puck from *A Midsummer Night's Dream* to guide him from escapism to acceptance of loss and death and in the way how she selects parts from the play in order to achieve her aim.

As may be inferred from the above, *King of Shadows* is not an adaptation in a narrow sense; it is neither narrated by a character from *A Midsummer Night's Dream* nor does it share the play's setting. Still, I argue that it corresponds to the concept of adaptation developed by Linda Hutcheon. Hutcheon writes:

> In short, adaptations can be described as the following:
>
> - An acknowledged transposition of a recognizable other work or works,
> - A creative and an interpretative act of appropriation/salvaging
> - An extended intertextual engagement with the adapted text.
>
> Therefore, an adaptation is a derivation that is not derivative–a work that is second without being secondary. It is its own palimpsestic thing. (Hutcheon 2006, pp. 8–9)

Since all three characteristics can be applied to both Cooper's and Williams' work, regarding them as adaptations of the respective plays is justified. As far as the intertextual character of adaptations is concerned, I am indebted to Gerd Rohmann's concept of creative intertextuality, which 'means ... to create new, experimental texts from the *déjà lu* of literary pretexts,' (Rohmann/Oppermann 2005, p. 9, original emphasis) and which is based on the same theoretical foundation by Bakhtin and Kristeva as Hutcheon's concept of adaptation (see Hutcheon 2006, p. 21, Rohmann/Oppermann 2005, p. 1). Accordingly, adaptations can be regarded as experiments because they not only have to remain true to their pretexts but also have to treat them critically.

The term 'Magic Plays' is my own; it is confirmed by Sarkar: '[n]owhere is the power of magic so apparent as in *A Midsummer Night's Dream* and *The Tempest*: both are plays which, for many, end with uneasy questions about the effects of magic' (Sarkar 1999, p. 252). It is not surprising that these two of all Shakespeare's plays are used for children's adaptations; their magic plots relate them to the fairy tale genre (Bausinger 1997, p. 178). This may also be the reason why they were transformed into the first two tales of the Lambs' collection (v). With *The Tempest*, this may have been the case because it was the first play in the First Folio, but *A Midsummer Night's Dream* was not the second, as a look into the catalogue of the First Folio reveals. In the Romantic Period, the age of the Grimm Brothers and their collection of fairy tales, the Lambs' two adaptations may have been regarded as particularly appealing to children, girls in particular (Chedgzoy 2007, p. 186) and may still be so today, especially if one considers the importance of fantasy. Even if the fairy tale collections were not intended for children alone (Bausinger 1997, pp. 174–5), it is evident that children belonged to their audience. Thus, it does not come as a surprise that these two plays have been adapted into children's books.

## Susan Cooper, *King of Shadows*

Cooper seems to have read thoroughly about Shakespeare's plays. The ease with which she describes work at the Globe Theatre and Elizabethan everyday life reveals this. However, she tries not to force her knowledge onto her readers in any way that interferes with the pleasures of consuming the story, hence her learnedness remains covert. Rather, she uses the techniques of the historical novel to transport her knowledge and thus avoids obtrusiveness.[1] Part of her knowledge is transferred by Nat himself when he talks to the readers about his hobby, play-acting, so that there is no authoritative figure speaking. Cooper's didacticism is rather of the kind Crouch describes as valid for Science Fiction,[2] not the obvious moralist teaching style present in the exempla of former centuries (cf. Oppermann 2005, pp. 308–9). On the contrary, when Gil Warnum mentions critic Andrew Gurr, whom 'Arby thinks he's God' (Cooper 2001, p. 168), there is even some irony involved, as if Cooper wanted to give her readers the chance to take one of the world's best Shakespeare theatre specialists not too seriously.

Nat travels back to the year 1599 and lives at Shakespeare's side and in his house long enough to give the readers a thorough, yet lively, image of both Elizabethan London and the Elizabethan Stage:

> For three days the time went by with much the same pattern to each day: Classes or rehearsal in the morning, work during the performance, an hour or two with the other apprentices before supper and bed. . . .
>
> There was hardly a moment when I wasn't aware that I didn't belong. I suppose a lot of it was what they call culture shock: the business of suddenly finding yourself without all the little everyday goodies that a kid living in the twentieth century takes for granted. Not only all the people and places of my life were missing but all the support systems too: electricity, gas, plumbing, running water, refrigeration, central heating, regular plates and knives and forks, packaged food, canned food, paper tissues, toilet paper... Without any of those, living in 1599 was like being on a permanent camping trip in a third world country. I began to feel grubby all the time, and itchy, and hungry, and vaguely sick. (Cooper 2001, p. 68)

The readers are introduced to the locations and the persons through Nat's being there and meeting them. In this 'identity of the realms of existence on the narrator and the other characters', as Stanzel calls it (Stanzel 1995, p. 76/'Typenkreis', n. p.), places and characters are immediately introduced. This manner of introducing characters and places is typical of literary fantasies such as *King of Shadows*. Therefore, I cannot agree with Teel's statement that '[y]oung readers who aren't familiar with names such as Burbage, Marlowe, Essex and Cecil might find themselves as lost in history as Nat initially was' (Teel 2007, n. p.), especially if we assume that the implied readers of the text are young people in their teens. Young readers can recognize that the scenes in question are about politics and that something very secret and interesting is going on. Neither Nat nor the readers need to know more about any person mentioned than what Nat finds out from his mentor and the other apprentices. The only name dropped by Cooper without explanation is that of Christopher Marlowe (Cooper 2001, p. 85), and even in this case, one can imagine that he was Shakespeare's colleague and got into trouble.

Cooper does not rewrite *A Midsummer Night's Dream* either; she is even reluctant with the use she makes of the play. The story of the lovers is only related indirectly and so is the so-called tragedy performed by the craftsmen. Cooper's main focus lies on Puck and his relationship with Oberon, which is not the most important feature in the play, although, of course, Puck is responsible for much of the chaos which happens onstage. In fact, the lovers' story is only of interest for Cooper as the background of Puck's actions. Most of the speeches quoted from *A Midsummer Night's Dream* in the first third of the book are from the scenes in which the fairy folk are present. The lovers' story is only summarized by Nat as far as it is necessary to give the readers sufficient information about the context of Puck's actions.

> So Gil went on with the scene, until the point where Demetrius comes on, pursued by the unlucky Helena (who loves him) ungratefully trying to get rid of her as he hunts the eloping Hermia (whom he loves) and Lysander. . . .
>
> Oberon has seen Demetrius being mean to Helena, and felt sorry for her, so he tells Puck to squeeze the magic juice on *his* eyes too, so that he'll switch from Hermia to Helena. Unfortunately Puck mistakes Lysander for Demetrius, and instead of sorting out the lovers he makes things worse. Pretty soon neither girl has the right guy in love with her, each of them is mad at the other, and the men are threatening to kill one another. (Cooper 2001, pp. 26–7, original emphasis)

Thus, the reader receives a good impression of the contents of the play without receiving genuine summaries which would have appeared artificial in the novel.

Cooper has chosen well both the role Nat plays and the play in which he is to act. *A Midsummer Night's Dream*, 'a happy comedy if there ever was one' (Wilson 1962, p. 13), may well be suited to distract Nat from his father's death and the resulting guilt complex. It does not come as a surprise that Nat does not have any difficulties with the characters being 'more important than [he is]' (Cooper 2001, p. 7). In the first rehearsal which is described in the novel '[he is jarred] out of [his] happy time, [his] acting time' (Cooper 2001, p. 28) for a moment. This serves to introduce the reader to Nat's personal situation. Nat is 'okay', but only 'as long as the play would last' (Cooper 2001, p. 28). Puck also is a suitable role for Nat since he is described as being free from emotions:

> "*What hast thou done?*" Master Shakespeare thundered at me, and for a moment it was terrifying to be attacked by the magnificent unearthly presence. But I remembered something he had said to me in rehearsal: "Puck is all mischief," he had said. "He loves jokes, and causing trouble – he has no heart. Don't let him *feel*, like you or me." (Cooper 2001, pp. 126–7, original emphasis)

By making Puck 'all mischief', Cooper interprets him as a figure who is characterized especially as not capable of displaying emotions such as fright or grief. Puck constantly enjoys what he does. He can even laugh off the attack he receives from Oberon. As such, he is a perfect figure for Nat's escapism since while he is Puck Nat can leave his too troublesome emotions behind. However, his escape can only be temporary since questions are always certain to be asked, and then, he has to cope with his memories again.

Only when he is transported into Shakespeare's London, to which he so much wishes to belong, and is confronted with his worst memories by seeing a dog bleed to death much like his father did, he realizes that it does not make sense to run away from the past and his troubles but to face them. Luckily, Nat finds an understanding friend in his new mentor, Shakespeare. Because of his son's death, Shakespeare is experienced both in grief and in the experience of losing a child deeply loved. He is the first and only person who is able to explain to Nat that he is not guilty of his father's suicide, that he was not 'not enough' (Cooper 2001, p. 74). Their resulting deep relationship, which I would even describe as a form of love (Oppermann 2006, pp. 82–3,[3] see also Chedgzoy 2007, p. 192), helps him overcome both his trauma and loss.

Nat Field is a suitable character for identification, not only because he is the narrator of the story but also because of his character, age and experiences. Young readers do not need dead parents or siblings to wish for escape from everyday life and to feel excluded from the peers at school or in the neighbourhood. Bullying is a common activity among teenagers, especially at school, and in such a situation, an adult friend can indeed be the best thing which could happen to be. Teel states:

> The lessons learned are about finding one's place, making the most of what one is given, and learning to grieve without judgment or resentment. Nat has some very realistic trouble adjusting to all the things that happen to him, both in the course of the unfolding story and in the backstory. (Teel 2007, n. p.)

That Nat manages to turn Roper into a friend because he – luckily again – is able to save him from choking by the use of the Heimlich manoeuvre,[4] is a side effect which adds interest to the plot but is not necessarily important (Derochea, n. d.). In fact, it may even be a piece of wish-fulfilment which may not necessarily be regarded as realistic. I do not share Derochea's statement that Nat's use of the Heimlich-manoeuvre was a mistake which caused him further trouble.

It is interesting that Cooper includes *The Tempest* in this context, interpreting Nat both as an inspiration for and as a future actor of Ariel. Without going too deeply into Shakespeare's and Nat's psychology of giving a beloved one free (Oppermann 2006, p. 82), one can argue that not only has Nat lost Shakespeare, but also Shakespeare lost Nat. This hints at another stage of development, both in grief and in friendships. Arby's idea that Shakespeare 'wrote [Nat] into [*The Tempest*]' (Cooper 2001, p. 185) may be justified by the thought that friends sometimes have to give up on a friendship when they are either separated by a long distance or when they have developed in a way that has rendered them estranged from each other. Ariel constantly reminds Prospero of his promise to set him free, and Arby wishes for a time to come, in which Nat can also 'go free of grieving' (Cooper 2001, p. 186).

In fact, in *The Tempest*, Ariel emphasizes the wish for freedom from his first appearance onstage onwards. Dialogues such as the following may have inspired Cooper to ascribe this role to Nat in the future:

> Ariel: Is there more toil? Since thou dost give me pains,
> Let me remember thee what thou hast promised
> Which is not yet performed me.
> Prospero: How now? Moody?

What is't thou canst demand?
Ariel: My liberty.
Prospero: Before the time be out? No more!
Ariel: I prithee,
Remember I have done thee worthy service,
Told thee no lies, made no mistakings, served
Without or grudge, or grumblings. Thou did promise
To bate me a full year.
Prospero: Dost thou forget
From what a torment I did free thee?
Ariel: No. (*Tmp.*: I 2: 244–52).

Scenes like this are repeated several times. Prospero promises Ariel to fulfil his longing for freedom whenever a new task is required. In contrast to Puck, who serves his master out of his own intention and enjoys it, Ariel wants to be free from Prospero in spite of being in the latter's debt. Puck enjoys the tasks he is given:

Puck: Thou speak's aright;
I am the merry wanderer of the night.
I jest to Oberon, and make him smile
When I a fat and bean–fed horse beguile,
Neighing in likeness of a filly foal;
. . . (*MND*: II 1: 42–6).

In fact, according to Greenblatt's definition of a Puck (Shakespeare 1997a, p. 821), Puck is indeed a spirit capable of working for others, whereas Ariel is only depicted as a 'magical spirit in various occult texts' (Shakespeare 1997b, p. 3062). In contrast to these descriptions, Ariel has more to do than make Prospero laugh; he has to make sure that his master's plans lead to success. Nevertheless, both characters are rather equal, especially when emotions are concerned (Frosch 2007, p. 501). Like Puck, Ariel is devoid of humane emotions:

Ariel has nothing of humanity – he has only an imaginative apprehension of the pity he would feel "were he human" – being pure intelligence, "free from all gross and putrifying mass of a body, immortall, unsensible, assisting all, having Influence [sic] over all". (Shakespeare 1954, p. 143)

This is indeed strongly reminiscent of what Cooper has Shakespeare say about Puck; the only major difference being that Puck is described as 'all mischief' (see above) and Ariel as 'all intelligence'.

When Prospero finally releases Ariel, one can indeed say that both Prospero and Ariel are in a situation in which they have to come to terms with their separation. For Nat, too, playing time is over. He will have to come to terms with the loss of his father and his best friend, but he has their literary heritage, and he will always be able to find them again in their texts (see also Chedgzoy 2007, pp. 195–6). For Nat, remembering both Shakespeare and his father without grieving is something to yearn for. It may well be that Cooper had this in mind when she added *The Tempest* to *A Midsummer Night's Dream* at the ending of her novel. Kermode (Shakespeare 1954, p. 144) says that Puck reappears as Ariel; it may well be that Cooper has read his Arden edition of the play.

Cooper's approach to Shakespeare's play reveals a way out of trauma and loneliness which is suitable reading for teenage outsiders. In addition, she introduces her readers to one of Shakespeare's most famous comedies with the help of a time travel plot (which is popular among children). Thus, she creates a good foundation from which child readers may embark to find out more about England's most famous playwright.

## Tad Williams, *Caliban's Hour*

Tad Williams has chosen a different approach towards his adaptation of Shakespeare. His is a classical case of 'writing back' (Bute 2000, p. 165), in which Caliban's experience on Prospero's island is retold from the anti-hero's point of view. It makes sense to regard *Caliban's Hour* as a teenage novel to be read at the same age as *King of Shadows*. The topics which are dealt with (growing up, the discovery of sexuality and the escapade into the adult world) are of particular interest for this age group (Clausen 1981, pp. 142–3). In addition, Williams makes use of a genre well established in children's literature. Owing to the fact that Sycorax and Caliban were stranded on the island, the text fits into the genre of Robinsonades, among which there are many children's classics. Caliban, however, is a savage Robinson who has neither a jointed house nor a field to cultivate. However, he lives in perfect harmony with his surroundings, perhaps with the exception of the sow which attacks him and which he later kills. Only with Prospero, civilization is introduced to the island. Sycorax, supposedly due to despair and the injuries she suffered when she was cast out of Algiers, was unable to teach her son. With civilization, there arrive on the island, albeit not yet obviously, alienation from nature and class consciousness. Like *Lord of the Flies*,

*Caliban's Hour* presents an island society gone wrong. The chance to develop on the island what Duncan calls a 'natural Society' (1980, p. 45) is missed:

> In the dialectic of comedy, especially romantic comedy like Shakespeare's, a young couple typically overcome an artificial society to restore a paradisal "natural society" in which characters identify with the miraculous reviving power of nature and discover their true selves. This "Natural Society" may be established in Shakespeare's regenerative "green world" (the Forest of Arden, Perdita's Bohemia, or in Portia's Belmont or on Prospero's isle. (Duncan 1980, p. 44)

Prospero tries to establish his original Milanese society on the island straightaway and destroys not only Caliban's way of life but also the chance to socialize with him. The magician abuses both his power and his education on an innocent fellow human.

Like Cooper, Williams seems to have read his share of *Tempest* criticism, as the following examples show. They can be regarded as direct responses to pieces of criticism such as: 'Caliban ... represents the natural man. This figure is not, as in pastoral generally, a virtuous shepherd, but a savage and deformed slave' (Shakespeare 1954, p. xxxviii).

> *Look, Miranda,* [Prospero] said. His voice was as coldly interested as if he had found me lying dead and decayed upon the sand. *This apparently deserted island seems to have at least a few larger inhabitants. An ape, I think – no, perhaps something a shade more interesting. A so-called "natural man", a savage, a cannibal.* (Williams 1994, p. 73, original emphasis)

Not only does the phrase 'natural man', which both Williams and Kermode use for Prospero, reveal how close Williams' description of his hero is connected to criticism. The same can be seen in a comparison between Johnson's and Williams' manners of commenting on Caliban's discovery of the names the 'things' around him have:

> *Caliban* has learned to speak of *Prospero* and his daughter, he had no names for the sun and moon before their arrival, and could not have invented a language of his own without more understanding than *Shakespeare* has thought it proper to bestow on him. (Johnson 1991, p. 41, original emphasis)
>
> On my island I existed in a world of unquestionable *things.* The great rock above the beach had no name, but I knew it, and knew what it was: something I could climb to see far out across the ocean's face. A family of lizards nested there, small, brown, striped with yellow, and though they fled before my approach,

skitting into crevices to lie in silent panic until I passed them by, I did not think of them as being more alive than the great stone, or of some higher order of being – no more than I thought of myself. . . .

In my mind, that great rock was a thing, just as the lizards were things, each one, and I did not compare them with anything else. It simply was. *I* simply was. (Williams 1994, pp. 26–7, original emphasis)

Even without the Lockean concept of the *tabula rasa* and the Rousseauean noble savage in mind, one can recognize the cultural clash within Williams' novel. However, this does not seem to go astray from the play's tone. The way how Prospero takes away the island from Caliban and opens a new world for him with his newly gathered words corresponds to Shakespeare's presentation in the play. The only change in the example given is that Williams shows how Caliban has become what he is at the time of the play.

But Williams does not only confront his readers with novelties in the literary field. Nor does he openly make Shakespeare a matter of teaching in his book. Like Cooper's, his novel is governed by strong emotions, but this time, they are destructive. While Nat is 'froze[n] into a little ice block' (Cooper 2001, p. 183), Caliban burns with rage (cf. Williams 1994, p. 93), and from his point of view he has a right to do so. Not only is he punished unjustly, he has also been robbed of his island and his peace of mind. Even after Prospero and Miranda had left, he was unable to retain the latter because he now possessed language, and with it the means to contemplate his situation in a way unknown to him before. However, in retrospect, he understands only too well what had happened to him, and during his encounter with the wild sow,[5] he had learnt about hatred in the hard way.

Caliban never regards the island as his own; however, it is obvious that Prospero does so once he has arrived. Even if he adopts Caliban into his small family, the boy never has the same role in it as Miranda. In addition, Prospero lures Caliban into working for him, even if the latter does not understand this at first. Caliban sacrifices his freedom for the society of other humans, but he finds out that he is kept in an inferior position. The name 'Prospero' becomes 'Master' (Williams 1994, p. 97). Caliban has no chance to break free from the relationships he has developed. Neither can he manage to become – far less remain – part of the small family on the island he longs for so much, nor does he really gain from the work he does: 'How can you [Prospero] *give* me a single room in a house which I built?' (Williams 1994, p. 129, original emphasis). The older Caliban gets, the more of an outsider he becomes.

The same can be said about Caliban's attempted rape of Miranda. D'haen remarks that the sexual approach Caliban made towards Miranda was, if not appreciated, though still accepted, and likely favourably accepted by her and that she turned against Caliban only later when she saw her honour and position threatened (D'haen 1997, p. 316). Although I agree with this point of view, I could imagine another reason why Miranda may have turned away from, and even against, Caliban. According to Williams, Miranda must have been about 11 to 12 years old at the time of this incident; even for the Renaissance rather a young girl for a first sexual experience. In addition, it is questionable how much she knew about sexuality; even if Prospero has talked to her, this does not automatically imply practical knowledge. Whereas the narrator Caliban obviously intends sexual contact, Miranda seems to be at least uncertain about Caliban's approach:

> *Your breathing is so loud, Caliban...!*
> My other hand coiled about your waist and held you snug while my fingers dipped down from your neck and smeared the drops of water beading above your faintly freckled breasts. Your bodice was still untied and I loosened it further.
> *What are you doing?* You sounded a little surprised, but I heard no fear.
> *I ... want ...*
> My hand found the hardening tips of your breasts and you shuddered. I pressed my face into your neck and felt your blood, warm and swift–flowing beneath the skin, beat against my mouth. I wanted, not to devour you, but to absorb you, to become with you a single thing, naked and indivisible. You pulled away, but when I did not loose my grip on your waist, you leaned back toward me and your leg lifted beneath your heavy skirt that you could press yourself against me. (Williams 1994, pp. 152–3, original emphasis)

Miranda is excited at this moment, and only seconds later she is frightened by the voice of Ariel, who, as she believes, has seen what was going on. Her first sexual experience and the experience of fright are thus connected. It comes as no surprise that she talks to her father, especially as she believes she was observed. In addition, we must not forget that Prospero always saw Caliban as the 'savage' who could never be part of the family no matter how much Caliban longed for this, and he certainly had warned Miranda against getting too close with him. It appears obvious throughout the story – as it is in the play – that Prospero intends Miranda to marry, one day, according to her rank.

His plans, however, seem to have failed at least partially. After her time on the island Miranda, a much more civilized version of Robinson than Caliban and possibly much happier by the comforts of civilized life, may have been happy to return to a civilized country and even be on top of court the wife of a model-husband, Ferdinand. However, her daughter Giulietta, also in her teens, is by far too adventurous to marry the heir she is intended to. In a way, Giulietta, too, is caught in the courtly etiquette and the everyday life of representing and childbearing (at most), and 'writes back' when she agrees to return with Caliban in her mother's stead. Thus, she not only saves her mother's life but also escapes from the narrow confinements of Naples Society.

Nevertheless, one should not forget that, even if she is willing to join Caliban in the life on his island, Giulietta is not, and will never be, Miranda. The age conflict between the two will not ease the relationship; the only exception may be that Caliban treats Giulietta as he wanted to be treated by Prospero, by whom he always wanted to be accepted as a son, and whom he regarded as a father for a long while; that is, as a beloved and respected, albeit adopted, child. This may not be entirely illusionary; after all, Prospero was the victim Caliban originally intended to murder after he had managed to leave the island. Caliban's relationship with Miranda, important as it may be, is always overshadowed by his relationship with her father. It is Prospero who, in a way, 'tames' Caliban, Prospero who first teaches Caliban his language, Prospero, whose respect Caliban wants to earn by working for him. Caliban seems to have suffered even more under the loss of Prospero's well-meaning than under Miranda's broken friendship. Possibly, Giulietta's company is Caliban's only chance to receive a happy, harmonious family on his island. Even if Miranda cannot offer to her daughter what she needs to be happy, Caliban may. Thus, perhaps at the conclusion not only of *The Tempest*, but also of *Caliban's Hour*, 'all have found their true selves, "Where no man was his own" (*Tmp.*: V 1: 211–12)' (Duncan 1980, p. 45).

Williams' novel deals with paternal conflicts. For both Caliban and Giulietta, the circumstances under which they grow up are intolerable. Even though the characters' situations are extreme, teenagers will certainly be able to identify with them if they feel misunderstood or unloved by their parents (especially when lovers or friends are not appreciated!) and caught in a way of life society expects of them. Therefore, the elopement of the couple at the end of the novel can be read as a symbolic escape. In addition, the art of 'writing back' may enable teenagers to develop a sense of changes in perspective.

Cooper's and Williams' novels are a vital part of what adaptions from Shakespeare's plays have been produced for teenage readers. In both texts, strong emotions are the main themes which carry the story. The characters, especially the main protagonists, offer ample possibilities of identification for the readers and, in the case of *King of Shadows*, sufficient background information about Shakespeare to make the novel a good introductory reading. The difference between the two novels also reveals an, albeit limited, impression of what forms of adapting for children and young adults Shakespeare's plays are capable. It is more than likely that the reading of one of these books will kindle a lively interest for the original plays in the readers, so that Shakespeare's popularity will continue to exist, despite very early modern English expressions and a blank verse which teenagers nowadays are not used to.

Cooper has achieved a book which is both psychologically and historically attractive to read. It is easy to imagine that many readers will turn to Shakespeare's plays, if they have not yet read them before, soon after having finished *King of Shadows*. Williams' adaption may be less interesting historically, its psychological meaning, however, can be regarded as even stronger, so that also *Caliban's Hour* can be expected to draw its readers towards *The Tempest*.

# Notes

1   For an exact description of the genre, see Fisher (1996), pp. 368–76, concerning Shakespeare, his time and his plays especially, see Ibid., p. 374.

2   'Sophisticated science fiction often regards itself with a seriousness which is literally deadly . . . no crisis is so breath-stopping that it will prevent one astronaut from quizzing or instructing another about the technical reasons for their dilemma. . . . Science fiction is inevitably didactic. The author cannot tell his story without putting it into its proper theoretical setting. With many writers, indeed most, this comes between the reader and his enjoyment of the story.' (Crouch 1972, pp. 53–5; see also Oppermann 2005, p. 141)

3   In this chapter, I argue that I consider Nat's relationship with Shakespeare as close to a homosexual relationship as a boy at his age and a much older man can get. I am certain that Nat has a crush on Will. I do not agree, however, with Chedgzoy's interpretation of the trust training scene (2007, p. 192). Chedgzoy states that this is meant to reveal Nat's trauma because his fellow actor's betrayal re-evokes the loss of trust in his father from which Nat suffers and which results from his father's suicide. In my opinion, this scene is meant rather to reveal Arby's character than Nat's trauma. Nat does not think about his father in that situation. Arby's reaction, which appears to be overly severe to all but Gill, is hotly discussed by the boys.

4 The Heimlich manoeuvre is used to prevent a person from suffocating because of an obstructed windpipe. The victim is clasped around the waist from the back, and with a clenched fist, its strength supported by the other hand, a hard upward thrust is applied, so that the air pressed from the lungs throws out the obstruction from the windpipe. Nat uses this first aid device to free Roper from a piece of apple he has just bitten off while fooling around after a success onstage.

5 Normally, a sow does not have tusks or teeth which are able to cause wounds as the ones described in the text. It seems to me as if Williams has created this special brand of wild pig in order to demonstrate how strong female power can be when it comes to protecting its breed. In this respect, the sow also stands in contrast to the human mothers in the novel because neither Sycorax nor Miranda is able to care for their children as well as the sow.

## List of works cited

Bausinger, Hermann (1997), 'Märchen', in H. Brackert and J. Stückrath (eds), *Literaturwissenschaft*. Reinbek: Rowohlt, pp. 173–85.

Bute, Jonathan (2000), 'Caliban and Ariel write back', in Catherine M. S. Alexander and Stanley Wells (eds), *Shakespeare and Race*. Cambridge: Cambridge University Press, pp. 165–76.

Chedgzoy, Kate (2007), 'Shakespeare in the company of boys', in K. Chedgzoy, S. Greenhalgh and R. Shaughnessy (eds), *Shakespeare and Childhood*. Cambridge: Cambridge University Press, pp. 184–99.

Clausen, Christopher (1981), 'Home and away in children's fiction'. *Children's Literature*, 10: 141–52.

Cooper, Susan (2001), *King of Shadows*. New York: Aladdin Paperbacks.

Crouch, Marcus (1972), *The Nesbit Tradition*. London: Ernest Benn.

Derochea, Beth (n.d.), 'Review of *King of Shadows*', *Rambles*, viewed 1 March 2010, <http://www.rambles.net/cooper_shadows.html>.

D'haen, Theo (1997), '*The Tempest* now and twenty years after', in N. Lie and T. D'haen (eds), *Constellation Caliban*. Amsterdam: Rodopi, pp. 313–31.

Duncan, Joseph E. (1980), 'Archetypes in Milton's earthly paradise'. *Milton Studies*, 14: 25–58.

Fisher, Janet (1996), 'Historical fiction', in P. Hunt and S. Ray (eds), *The International Companion Encyclopedia of Children's Literature*. London: Routledge, pp. 368–76.

Frosch, Thomas R. (2007), 'The missing child in *A Midsummer Night's Dream*'. *American Imago*, 64: 485–513.

Hutcheon, Linda (2006), *A Theory of Adaptation*. New York: Routledge.

Johnson, Samuel (1991), 'Caliban's language', in D. J. Paulsen (ed.), *Shakespeare: The Tempest*. Basingstoke: Palgrave Macmillan, p. 41.

Lamb, Charles and Lamb, Mary (1994), *Tales from Shakespeare*. London: Puffin.

Oppermann, Eva (2005), *Englischsprachige Kinderbücher: 'Kinderkram' oder anspruchsvolle Literatur auch für Erwachsene?* Kassel: Kassel University Press.

— (2006), '"On love, and loving": Shakespeare's sonnet 116 and its role in Susan Cooper's *King of Shadows*', in E. Oppermann (ed.), *Literatur und Lebenskunst/ Literature and the Art of Living: Festschrift für Gerd Rohmann*. Kassel: Kassel University Press, pp. 69–85.

Rohmann, Gerd and Oppermann, Eva (2005), 'Literature and intertextuality'. *The Atlantic Critical Review*, 4(4): 1–15.

Sarkar, Malabika (1999), 'The magic of Shakespeare's sonnets'. *Renaissance Studies*, 12(2): 251–60.

Shakespeare, William (1623), 'The First Folio', *Internet Shakespeare Editions*. Brandeis University, viewed 23 October 2010, <http://internetshakespeare.uvic.ca/Library/facsimile/book/Bran_F1/17/?size=small&view_mode=normal&content_type=>.

— (1954, 1611), *The Tempest*, F. Kermode (ed.). London: Methuen.

— (1997a, 1598/99), 'A Midsummer Night's Dream', in S. Greenblatt et al. (eds), *The Norton Shakespeare*. London and New York: Norton, pp. 805–63.

— (1997b, 1611), 'The Tempest', in S. Greenblatt et al. (eds), *The Norton Shakespeare*. London and New York: Norton, pp. 3047–107.

Stanzel, Franz K. (1995), *Theorie des Erzählens*. Göttingen: Vandenhoeck & Ruprecht.

Teel, Katherine (2007), 'Book Reviews: *King of Shadows*, by Susan Cooper', *Helium*, viewed 1 March 2010, <http://www.helium.com/items/656242-book-reviews-king-of-shadows-by-susan-cooper>.

Williams, Tad (1994), *Caliban's Hour*. New York: Harper Paperbacks.

Wilson, John D. (1962), *Shakespeare's Happy Comedies*. London: Faber & Faber.

# 4

# Shakespeare for Beginners: The *Animated Tales from Shakespeare* and the Case Study of *Julius Caesar*

## Maddalena Pennacchia

The *Animated Tales from Shakespeare* originated as a television project started in 1991 by S4C, the Welsh-language TV channel, in association with Soyuzmultfilms, the prestigious state-run cartoon and animation studio established in Moscow in 1935 and since credited for making fairy tales in the Soviet Union 'a main staple of films produced for children and adults' (Zipes 2011, p. 323). This audio-visual joint venture, which claimed in its very title an authoritative connection to Charles and Mary Lamb's narrative adaptations for children, *Tales from Shakespeare Designed for the Use of Young Persons* (1807), produced 12 30-minute animated films of a selection of plays, which were released in two series and broadcasted in 1992 and 1994, respectively.[1] The animations display a vast range of techniques from stop-motion puppets, to cel animation, to painting on glass and watercolour.

When the S4C producers decided to launch the project, only two years had passed since the fall of the Berlin Wall and people were still optimistic about the future of a united Europe. Not surprisingly, the *Animated Tales* are defined in their 'making of' documentary – now available on the DVD set that collects them – as 'a remarkable example of collaboration between East and West'. As a matter of fact, the whole process implied a continuous exchange of ideas and materials between Cardiff and Moscow, as the series' producer-director, Dave Edwards, had the chance to experience when commuting back and forth between the two cities in order to permit the 'works of England's greatest playwright' to be 'reinterpreted by an unlikely alliance of Welsh and Russian filmmakers' (quot. from the DVD documentary, Edwards 2005). After having been considerably abridged by the British writer Leon Garfield, the Shakespearean texts had to be recorded in the Welsh studios by classical actors (many of them trained in the RSC) and subsequently sent to the Russian visual artists who worked to create images that could match the 30-minute audio tracks. Chris Grace, Head of animation at S4C and executive producer of the series, described his motivation for such a laborious enterprise in terms that clearly reveal its cultural politics: 'I envisage the great European cultural heritage being animated – opera Shakespeare, Dickens – and being seen at peak viewing time as a counterpoint to Disney' (quot. in Bottoms 2001, p. 4). It is no surprise that The *Animated Tales* are defined by their difference from Disney, for, as Deborah Cartmell reminds us, 'the Disney corporation has been the most prolific and lucrative twentieth-century adaptor of classic children's fiction', but its approach has been, to say the least, distinctively invasive: 'as is frequently observed, the ambition of a Disney adaptation is to usurp its source . . . so that the film-adaptation triumphs over its literary original' (Cartmell 2007, p. 169).

As I will try to point out in the following pages, however, despite their repeated professions of 'fidelity', the *Animated Tales* both build on and undermine the notion of reverence for the Shakespearean text, whose manipulation is theoretically justified from the beginning by the intrinsic necessity of making Shakespeare more accessible to young and inexpert viewers so that they may better appreciate the Bard's work in the future. After briefly considering how the *Animated Tales* came to form, almost accidentally, a Shakespearean canon for children, I will focus on a single animation out of the 12 in the series, that is *Julius Caesar* (dir. Yuri Kulakov 1994). I believe that the intercultural and intermedial quality of this specific adaptation may be a fair example of the complexity of the Welsh-Russian series of animations as a whole. Indeed, these animated adaptations seem to me more subversive than might be thought from their being one of the most widely used didactic tools in British primary and secondary schools.

## Shakespeare, education and the cultural market

In an article entitled 'Abbreviated Shakespeare', Peter Holland highlights that while in most instances of popular curtailments of Shakespeare the main stylistic elements are parody and irony, in the *Animated Tales* a feeling of deep respect almost amounting to veneration prevails, since their aim is

> to educate their audience into an appreciation and love of Shakespeare, out of a
> conviction of Shakespeare as a cultural artifact available to all, not restricted to

a narrowly defined form of performance. Screened in dozens of countries (and easily dubbed since animation creates no need for subtitling), The *Animated Tales* is Shakespeare as cultural educational television available to all, Shakespeare in the classroom, or, more often, ... in the modern home. (Holland 2007, p. 44)

Of course, Holland is not mistaken when he suggests that the project was a massive educational undertaking. The *Animated Tales* were explicitly conceived with a didactic aim and addressed to a broad global audience, mainly of children, but also including all those adults who, not having received an introduction to the Bard's work for a variety of reasons, may appreciate a safe, so to speak, and authorized short cut in order to approach him. However, Laurie Osborne, in stressing the 'not-so-veiled cultural imperialism' (1997, p. 105) of the enterprise, reports Prince Charles' words of praise about it: 'I welcome this pioneering project which will bring Shakespeare's great wisdom, insight and all-encompassing view of mankind to many millions from all parts of the globe, who have never been in his company before' (quot. in Osborne 1997, p. 105). For such a lofty goal, a scholar of no less calibre than Stanley Wells was sought after as literary advisor of the series – someone whose very name would guarantee Shakespearean correctness.

Holland also suggests, in passing, that the sentiment of reverence in the *Animated Tales* can already be detected in Leon Garfield's abridged scripts (2007, p. 44). The writer, who meaningfully described his work as a sort of Titanic miniaturization process, only comparable to 'paint[ing] the Sistine Chapel onto a postage stamp' (quoted in Williams 2003, p. 32), has repeatedly insisted on the painful task of having to choose what to include and what to leave out of Shakespeare's original words. The S4C production decided to entrust him with the task of writing the series' screenplays because he was a renowned author of children's literature and he had already published a famous collection of narrative adaptations of the plays, *Shakespeare Stories* (1985). This volume, which had become a children's literary classic almost overnight, presented itself as an updated version of Charles and Mary Lamb's experiment of transposing Shakespearean texts from the dramatic into a narrative mode. In his retelling of the stories, Garfield introduced an omniscient narrator – a legacy which, as Laura Tosi highlights, is directly drawn from the Lambs:

one of the innovations of *The Tales from Shakespeare*, which the Lambs bequeathed to adaptations to come, was the voice of the narrator, who, as in fairy tales, describes the characters and the meaning of action so that there are no ambiguities for the reader. (Tosi 2009, p. 129)

Garfield is no exception to this, for in his narrative adaptations he considerably tones down ambiguities for the young and/or inexpert readers through a narrator who remains invisible and is, therefore, able to describe the scene both from his point of view and as if it were objective. The narrator device once mastered in the written narratives must have proven particularly useful when Garfield had to abridge the original Shakespearean texts for the *Animated Tales*. The change from print to an audio-visual medium must have led almost naturally to the transformation of the narrator into a voice-over device. Since the plays had to be reduced to a length of a short half hour, a voice-over narrator summarizing events and linking them in meaningful sequences must have seemed almost indispensable.

If reverence, scholarly dedication and a strong educational purpose are common to such works as Charles and Mary Lamb's *Tales*, Garfield's *Stories* and the *Animated Tales*, another less immediately obvious aspect links them additionally: an awareness of the economic value of Shakespeare and, at the same time, a controversial attitude towards it. This aspect already comes to the surface in the 'Introduction' to the Lambs' *Tales*, where the original plays are unexpectedly described as 'rich treasures from which these small and valueless coins are extracted' (Lamb 1995, p. 6): however 'small and valueless', the adaptations are still explicitly compared to coins, revealing the otherwise hidden discourse of 'Shakespeare' as a source of money making. In one of her acute articles devoted to the series, Laurie Osborne points out to the same controversial feeling in the production of the *Animated Tales*, when she underlines that the 'financial potential' of the project was constantly denied by producers, who in open opposition to Disney's commercial politics, rhetorically substituted such potential with the more appropriate artistic potential of the series:

> The Welsh-Soviet partnership and the relative poverty and difficulty of Soviet animators' working conditions justify the financial gains while analyzes of the varied strategies of animation in the series stress the importance of combined European skills (i.e. Soviet artistic animation rather than commercial American version). (Osborne 1997, p. 105)

The point is, in any case, that each of the *Animated Tales* is a cultural product to be put on the market and advertised if it is to achieve the high purpose of educating people to appreciate Shakespeare's art all over the world: 'Even though founded in contrast to Disney's heavily commercialized popular appeal, the *Tales'* own extensive marketing collapses this opposition between commercial and artistic, popular and elite' (Osborne 1997, p. 105).

Moreover, the use of such products 'in the classroom' and 'in the modern home', as stressed by Holland, has been possible only thanks to the fast development of recording technologies. The *Animated Tales* almost immediately became a VHS series of separate cassettes, thus turning from a transient televised message into products to be used and watched at will. An even more radical change affected them when they were copied from analogous to digital recording. Since 2005, the whole series has been available on a DVD box set entitled *Shakespeare: the Animated Tales*, which offers interactive menus with subtitles, a *Shakespeare Timeline* file and two documentaries on *The Making of the Animated Tales* and the *Shakespeare Schools Festival*.

As Richard Burt underlines in his introduction to *Shakespeare the Movie II*, the digitalization of film on DVD has transformed our way of viewing and understanding the audio-visual product:

> We are now invited to attend not only to a given Shakespeare film as shown in theatrical release and on the DVD but to a series of DVD extras such as menu trailers, deleted scenes, audio commentaries, interviews, "making of" documentaries, music videos, video games, and so on. Taking Shakespeare on DVD into account also involves taking into consideration the circulation of film and television adaptation not only in cinematographic and televisual contexts but, more broadly, in other mass media such as comics, novelizations, advertising, video games and live performances in theatres of various kinds. (Burt 2003, pp. 1–2)

The phenomenon pointed out by Burt is typical of what a number of critics now call 'media convergence' (Jenkins 2006; Murray 2003), and it is a major change brought about by the coming of age of digitalization. Thanks to digitalization, all media have been rendered capable of interfacing with each other, thus engendering a complex and closely interconnected system in which messages of all kinds, shaped in different expressive codes but all 'speaking' the same bit-language, are continuously remediated and circulated. This technological change has had a tremendous impact on the cultural industry, now mainly dominated by transnational media corporation companies, so that a (cultural) message is now conceived of, since its first inception, as a product that must travel the whole media circuit in order to approach the greatest number of customers/ users possible. Therefore, the cultural message in question, in adapting itself to any media environment it crosses, assumes different objective shapes, thus turning into a series of products (or media tie-ins) all slightly different from one another and still all referencing one another (Pennacchia 2007).

The *Animated Tales* have been an early example of the case in point. When the videos became commercially available, Garfield's abridged scripts were also published as a series of books, more often than not used by teachers in the classroom, with illustrations similar but not identical to the Russian ones, thus bringing back Shakespeare's curtailed words to the printed page. It is interesting to read the 'Product description' of the latest collection of abridged scripts on Amazon's website:

> Leon Garfield skilfully abridged twelve of Shakespeare's most famous plays – *Macbeth, The Tempest, A Midsummer Night's Dream, Twelfth Night, The Winter's Tale, Romeo and Juliet, Hamlet, The Taming of the Shrew, As You Like It, Richard III, Othello* and *Julius Caesar* – to create individual thirty minute scripts. These plays are a workable length for classrooms while still maintaining Shakespeare's language, and have become favourites with teachers bringing the drama of Shakespeare to children for the first time. Their widely spaced, readable format makes them an ideal way to introduce what can be difficult language for the unfamiliar. This is the first time the twelve plays have been available in one volume. The competitive price point also makes them affordable, both for teachers and for families. (Web. 31 January 2012)

Cultural customers, therefore, have at their disposal many kinds of abridged texts, all claiming to use as many of Shakespeare's original words as possible; it has been noticed, for example, that Garfield's printed scripts have suffered fewer cuts and alterations than the scripts performed on the videos (Osborne 1997, p. 104).

The astonishing consequence of this coexistence, in the contemporary hyper-mediated environment, of all these slightly different abridged versions of the plays, is that the popular perception of the Bard's 'original text' is deeply affected. In other words, younger generations of readers/viewers, to whom these products are mainly addressed in order to inspire a sort of veneration for Shakespeare's original words, may actually lose a sense of origin or of a given hierarchical order among original texts and (different kinds of) adaptations. There may be nothing shocking in this, because as every Shakespearean scholar well knows, Shakespeare's texts are 'naturally' unstable (Honigmann 1965), a fact that should always be kept in mind when approaching the 'Bard' at any stage of learning. Still, if the didactic purpose of The *Animated Tales* is to work properly, it would be advisable that children were made aware of the complexity of such dynamics.

# A new Shakespearean canon for children?

Although 'the first task . . . of a writer adapting Shakespeare is to choose the plays' (Tosi 2009, p. 129), I must confess I have not been able to find any evidence of the selecting criteria that guided the producers in the choice of the plays. In the above-mentioned documentary about the making of the series, for instance, this important piece of information has been omitted.

I would suggest, however, that the production relied heavily on the selection already operated by Leon Garfield in *Shakespeare Stories*, in which 12 of the 36 canonical plays, those printed in the Folio, had been adapted: *Twelfth Night*, *King Lear*, *The Tempest*, *The Merchant of Venice*, *The Taming of the Shrew*, *King Richard II*, *King Henry IV Part One*, *Hamlet*, *Romeo and Juliet*, *Othello*, *A Midsummer Night's Dream*, and *Macbeth*.

The *Animated Tales* cut Garfield's selection in half, producing and broadcasting only six episodes in the first season on Channel 4: *A Midsummer Night's Dream* (9 November 1992), *The Tempest* (16 November 1992), *Macbeth* (23 November 1992), *Romeo and Juliet* (30 November 1992), *Hamlet* (7 December 1992) and *Twelfth Night* (14 December 1992).

In 1994, a second volume by Garfield was published, *Shakespeare Stories II*, which added nine more plays to the previous ones: *Much Ado About Nothing*, *Julius Caesar*, *Antony and Cleopatra*, *Measure for Measure*, *As You Like It*, *Cymbeline*, *King Richard III*, *The Comedy of Errors*, and *The Winter's Tale*. In the same year, the second season of the *Animated Tales* was released and six new episodes aired. It is not rash, therefore, to infer that Garfield might have chosen the new plays with an eye to the already planned new animated series. At any rate, the new episodes were *King Richard III* (2 November 1994), *The Taming of the Shrew* (9 November 1994), *As You Like It* (16 November 1994), *Julius Caesar* (30 November 1994), *The Winter's Tale* (7 December 1994), and *Othello* (14 December 1994). To sum up for the sake of clarity: out of the original 36 plays in the Folio, 21 were turned into narrative adaptations for children by Leon Garfield, and of these 12 were also adapted by him for the screen and animated by Russian artists.

When the animated tales were rearranged in the DVD box set that now collects them, what may have been quite a haphazard or idiosyncratic process of selection was transformed, supposedly for marketing reasons, into a new Shakespearean canon. In the DVD box set (2005), the plays were grouped together in three separate discs apparently not with respect to their chronological order of production or to their different artistic techniques, but according to a principle of imitation of the Folio's well-known division in Comedies, Histories and Tragedies. But let us inspect this audio-visual product more closely: disk one contains four Tragedies (*Macbeth*, *Hamlet*, *Romeo and Juliet*, and *Othello*); disk two contains five Comedies (*Twelfth Night*, *As You Like It*, *A Midsummer Night's Dream*, *Taming of the Shrew*, and *The Winter's Tale*), and disk three contains three Histories (*The Tempest*, *Julius Caesar*, and *Richard III*). If we may rather safely say that the Tragedies' section proposes, almost unaltered, A. C. Bradley's famous idea of the tragic canon (with the sensational exclusion of *King Lear*) and that the Comedies' section offers meaningful examples both from the early comedies and the romantic ones (plus one Romance), it appears clear that the editors had to solve the problem of filling in the Histories' section (what is, in fact, *The Tempest* doing there?). Generally speaking, the Histories were a new genre somewhat invented by Shakespeare and made visible by John Heminges and Henry Condell when they introduced it to divide the two classic genres of Comedy and Tragedy, thus grouping together Shakespeare's numerous plays dealing with English history (Danson 2000, p. 8). What happens to the Histories in the narrative adaptations for children we have thus far considered? If Charles and Mary Lamb completely excluded them (together with all the Roman plays, with the exception of *Cymbeline*), Garfield only included three Histories in his first volume of *Shakespeare Stories* (*King Richard II*, *King Henry IV Part One*, and *King Richard III*) and added three Roman plays in the second volume (*Julius Caesar*, *Antony and Cleopatra*, and *Cymbeline*). Finally, only two out of the six adapted historical narratives by Garfield were selected for the *Animated Tales*, namely *Richard III* and *Julius Caesar*. It is interesting to note, in passing, that at the time of the production, the discussion about the teaching of history in schools, as Robert Phillips underlines, was raging:

> [l]ittle wonder, then, that at the high point of the controversy over the National Curriculum in the 1990s, Margaret Thatcher should have become directly involved in the debate.... Political interest in school history was not merely confined to one political party, as politicians from a range of political persuasions expressed a view, including John Major and Tony Blair during the 1996 election campaign. (Phillips 2000, p. 11)

Now, if *Richard III* is one of the more 'universal' Histories in terms of dramatic cogency, the choice of *Julius Caesar* and its positioning in the Histories' section (while in the *Folio* it is classified as a tragedy) might have been determined by the need to present viewers with a historical character less involved in the making of Britain and of broader interest to a global audience than English royalty members. And who better than Julius Caesar, whose name, as Miriam Griffin reminds us, is almost synonymous with ancient history and 'has been used in various local forms – Kaiser, Czar, Tsar – as the highest title for rulers far from Rome in place and time' (Griffin 2009, p. 1).

If there is always an 'impulse both to collect Shakespeare's plays and to divide them', as Laurie Osborne rightly remarks (Osborne 2003, p. 140), what seems to me undeniable in this decision to imitate the Folio's division is the ambitious claim that *Shakespeare: the Animated Tales* makes in presenting itself as the new authoritative canon of Shakespeare for children. An ambition which has been supported through the years by a huge cultural project, the Shakespeare Schools Festival, which was set up by the same producers, as we read in the 'about us' section of the official website:

> In 2000, Chris Grace, Director of Animation at S4C and Executive Producer of *Shakespeare: The Animated Tales*, and Penelope Middelboe, Series Editor of *Shakespeare: The Animated Tales*, launched the Shakespeare Schools Festival (SSF). Pupils from 8 schools in Pembrokeshire performed over two nights to sell-out audiences at the Torch Theatre, Milford Haven.... . Ninety per cent of the UK's secondary schools now use the *Tales* as their introduction to the language and plays of Shakespeare for years 7–10 (11–15 year olds), making it BBC Education's most popular series. In 2009 the films were made available by the DCSF to all English primary schools. (Web. 31 January 2012 <http://www.ssf.uk.com/about-us/history>)

It may well be, therefore, that for British children, the *Animated Tales* are the new Shakespearean canon.


## 'Slave language and subversive images': The animated *Julius Caesar*

In Michael Hoffman's *The Emperor's Club* (2002), one witnesses a questionable use of Shakespeare in the classroom, when Professor Hundert, a history teacher in an American prep school, assigns his pupils the task of reading *Julius Caesar* that they may understand the Roman events of 44 BC, not an unusual practice, as Samuel Crowl would remind us, for 'Shakespeare's play has served from Jefferson and Washington to the present, as a key source for linking the American democracy with the Roman republic in the popular imagination'

(Crowl 2009, p. 106). When discussing the play, Professor Hundert is quite sure the boys will take Brutus' side, but unexpectedly Sedgewick, the cunning and troubled adolescent son of an unscrupulous Senator, who seems to understand *realpolitik* more than his history teacher does, refuses to put himself in line with the mainstream interpretation. Sedgewick openly accuses the Roman hero of being a coward for not having killed Antony at the right time, thus both spoiling the success of the conspiracy and dooming his fellow conspirators to their death. Sedgewick's rejection of professor Hundert's interpretation, highlights the inherent ambiguities of Shakespeare's play and those of any political order represented in it.

The fact is, of course, that *Julius Caesar* is not a straightforward book of history, a truism that can be forgotten in the classroom with disastrous results: it is an adaptation for the stage of different historical sources, some of them at odds with one another, which Shakespeare wrote in order to entertain Elizabethan playgoers of different ages, classes and of both sexes. *Julius Caesar* was the first play to be performed at the Globe when it was inaugurated in 1599 (Wilson 2002, p. 8): the story of a man whose name immediately recalled ancient Rome, the city/world, was an appropriate choice for the opening production of such an ambitious theatre. And since Renaissance England saw itself as the true heir to that ancient Empire, its authoritative example became an all-important model for both its imitators and detractors (Del Sapio Garbero 2009)[2]; Shakespeare – who held a share in the Globe as a member of the Lord Chamberlain's Men – was also keeping an eye on the box office when he offered his countrymen such an instance of popular adaptation from ancient and authoritative historical sources, (mainly but not only Plutarch's lives of Julius Caesar, Brutus and Mark Antony).

Professor Hundert's understanding of Shakespeare's political ethos in clear-cut terms may well parallel Joseph Mankiewicz's black-and-white approach to the play in his Hollywood adaptation of 1953. Where Shakespeare's text never shows signs of rooting for one side or the other in the contention between republicans and caesarians – only a worried concern for the consequences of civil wars emerges – in Mankiewicz's version Brutus unequivocally appears as the true and only hero of the story, a spotless defender of liberty and democratic values, so much so that he gets almost 'locked into his rectitude' – as Gilles Deleuze once wrote in a comment on the film (Deleuze 1989, p. 53). However, the film is still considered by many critics 'the finest Shakespeare film ever done by a major Hollywood studio' (Sinyard 1986, p. 13) and has undoubtedly influenced the understanding of this specific play for at least half a century, especially when we consider that, because of its acknowledged artistic value and its availability on video tapes and DVDs, it is still very much used in classrooms all over the world.[3]

The reason why I am lingering on Mankiewicz's adaptation for MGM is that one of the most self-evident aspects of the animated *Julius Caesar*, directed by Yuri Kulakov, is a striking visual similarity to precisely that film, as others also have noticed (Coursen 2002, p. 119). Kulakov's modeling of his cel animation[4] on Mankiewicz's film can be detected, for instance, in the stately Roman setting, in the cinematic solution of some crucial dramatic situations (Brutus in his orchard, or Antony's and Brutus' famous speeches delivered in the market place), and in the astonishing likeness of some of the animated characters to the actors in the film (if Cassius looks like John Gielgud, Antony *is* Marlon Brando).

Of 'visual echoes which [the *Animated Tales*] offer of earlier [Shakespearean] films' Laurie Osborne also speaks (Osborne 1997, p. 106), when she acutely highlights that just as the Lambs' abridgements introduced young nineteenth-century readers to the literary mode that was to dominate the British panorama for a long time – that is, narrative – so these animations train children's sensibility to an understanding of film as one of the most influential contemporary media: 'they prepare their audience to understand the play cinematically rather than theatrically or literarily' (Osborne 1997, p. 103). In the case of *Julius Caesar*, however, the Russian animation almost seems a subversive repetition of Hollywood's most famous film adaptation of the play, thus turning into what Linda Hutcheon might call a postmodernist parody, or 'a form of imitation ... characterized by ironic inversion' (Hutcheon 2000, p. 6), one capable of generating a creative tension not only between the two different media at stake (film and cartoon), but also between the two cultural contexts of production, the American context and that of the former Soviet Union that had long been major opponents in the Cold War.

Not only can the animated *Julius Caesar* be investigated as a postmodern parody, but it might also be better understood in terms of what Jack Zipes, in his latest book on film adaptation of fairy tales, sees as a specific characteristic of Russian animation, that is the interplay between 'slave language' (*Sklavensprache*), and its disruption through 'subversive images':

> the Russians had to learn how to employ slave language and soon became linguistic and artistic masters of dissent through complicity. Dissent took many forms of subterfuge, and a genre that served writers, artists and filmmakers well was the fairy tale because of its metaphorical ambivalent language. (Zipes 2011, pp. 322–3)

I think this strategy can be detected in many of Soyuzmultfilm's *Animated Tales*, but in particular in the animated *Julius Caesar*, where the parodic approach to Hollywood's hegemonic interpretation of the play is further articulated through the use of an editing technique typical of Soviet cinema, one theorized by Eisenstein since his earliest essays. The great Russian film director and theorist wrote in 1923 about what he called 'montage of attractions', meaning the use of sudden 'aggressive effects' which are capable of shocking the spectators to the point of making them more emotionally aware of the overall ideological message (Eisenstein 1923, p. 230). What is extremely interesting in the animated *Julius Caesar* is how the continuity editing characteristic of Hollywood (and of Mankiewicz's filming) seems to be interspersed with 'attractions', that is intercuts of 'aggressive' images, which can create an interpretative tension especially between Hollywood's downplaying of Caesar and Kulakov's fascination with him. In the original play, Rome, on the verge of revolution, is described as a site of fire eruptions, earth tremors and landslides, whirling winds and rainstorms, in which baroque convolution appears to be the dominant form; MGM's adaptation, on the contrary, turned this tumultuous movement into a geometrical fixedness. The 'American' Rome was designed by the art directors, Edward Carfagno and Cedric Gibbons, with dominant right angles and straight lines which reflected and enhanced Manckiewicz's extremely formal shots, which have been described as 'rigidly frontal and composed in geometrical patterns: circles, triangles and squares' (Jorgens 1977, p. 101). As a consequence, the City seemed almost frozen into an unchanging classical form, eventually even turning into a marmoreal cenotaph. On the contrary, Kulakov brings colours back to Shakespeare's Rome, making the colour red the dominant tint of the City and thus re-emphasizing the numerous images of fire present in the original text and expunged from the film. Moreover, these images are directly linked by Kulakov to the figure of Caesar, which in the animation acquires a strong capacity to engage the eye of the viewers and win their attention.

It is true that Julius Caesar is a controversial figure in Shakespeare's tragedy; his heroic status is deeply questioned in the play, perhaps as a consequence of the contradictory and conflicting relationship of Elizabethan culture to ancient Rome. Far from being the great young leader who had expanded Rome's borders beyond imagination, Caesar is represented by Shakespeare as an old, deaf, conceited man, whose Roman virtue is now but a faint echo of past greatness. Faithful to this aspect, Mankiewicz even more markedly diminishes the greatness of Caesar, who, in the film, is played by an aged, bald and overweight Louis Calhern, a supporting actor in an all-star cast.

Conversely in the Russian animated version, Caesar is drawn as a still vigorous man, with the handsome features of the Cesare Chiaramonti (a famous sculpted head in the Musei Vaticani). He is the first figure to appear on screen after the title frame, in which his name is surrounded by red flames, and he appears as a noble knight, laurel-crowned, riding his white horse clad in a floating red mantle, a *toga purpurea*, an all-purple toga worn by the early kings and possibly adopted by some emperors. This scene is, thus, commented upon by the voice-over narrator: 'All Rome was wild with joy. Julius Caesar, having conquered his great rival, Pompey, has returned in triumph, the ruler of the world'. Caesar will appear three more times as a riding knight, galloping suspended in the air: when he comes back as a ghost to disturb Brutus' night before the battle, when he 'flies' on the battlefield and just before Cassius' suicide. This figure very much reminds one of the warriors described in the biblical *Book of Revelation* (19: 11–16) as a knight on a white horse, who according to the prophecy will descend from heaven to punish the wicked in the latter days.

If images of fire cluster around the figure of Caesar from the very beginning of the animation, there is a striking intercut shot of a few seconds (another 'attraction') both in the sequence of the conspiracy night and in that of the assassination. There we see a firebird hatching from an ancient stone vase and flying away. In the original play, Caesar is indeed compared to a majestic bird, perhaps an eagle, by Flavius, the tribune who takes it upon himself to disrobe the great man's statues, removing the 'ceremonies' with which the rabble had adorned them. As we read in the Shakespearean text:

> These growing feathers plucked from Caesar's wing
> Will make him fly an ordinary pitch,
> Who else would soar above the view of men,
> and keep us all in servile fearfulness. (*JC*: I 1: 72–5)

In Mankiewicz's adaptation of *Julius Caesar*, the landing of the Roman eagle on American soil was explicitly (and ironically) represented, as Samuel Crowl noticed, at the very beginning of the film:

> we move from the roar of the MGM lion to a close-up of a military standard bearing the Roman eagle: the symbol of a cultural empire in the making laying claim to the still powerful legacy of a political empire long dead. (Crowl 1994, p. 150)

Mankiewicz seemed to be almost consciously reproducing the very act of repositioning and re-mediating Rome that had been performed before him by Shakespeare himself (Pennacchia 2009). But the Russian artists' decision to focus on the 'aggressive' image of the firebird, instead of the eagle, appears shocking when we consider not only that the phoenix is a powerful animal in Russian folklore, but that it has always been a symbol of eternity both in the Eastern and Western culture. And this might lead us to further reflect on the difference between the American and the Russian approach to *Julius Caesar*. Mankiewicz's adaptation – shot in black and white to recall the war newsreel – was explicitly engaged in making a parallel between Caesar's as well as Mussolini's Rome, not to speak of Hitler's Berlin and, I would add, Stalin's Moscow. However, if in that adaptation Caesar appears as the *ur*-model of the tyrant deserving to be rightfully overthrown, in its Russian parody the phoenix-like leader radiates an uncanny enchantment.[5]

As may be inferred even by a limited analysis of just one out of the 12 *Animated Tales*, these audio-visual adaptations for children and young adults present themselves as extremely sophisticated intermedial and intercultural texts, which might be tremendously helpful to teachers who care to train their students in the complex but rewarding task of interpreting Shakespeare's plays.

# Notes

1   All the original air dates quoted in this chapter are taken from the IMDB website (Web 31 Jan 2012. http://www.imdb.com/title/tt0147788/episodes).

2   I am indebted to Maria Del Sapio Garbero who has conceived and coordinated the Research Programme based in Roma Tre 'La Roma antica in Shakespeare e nel Rinascimento europeo: modelli culturali e appropriazioni' in which I have participated for the last few years with much profit and satisfaction. See Del Sapio Garbero 2009.

3   In the United Kingdom, the practice of watching Shakespeare on film in the classroom was very much encouraged in official documents issued on occasion of the introduction of the National Curriculum approximately in the same years of the *Animated Tales* project. As Janet Bottoms remarks: '[i]n 1989, the Cox Report, *English for Ages 5–16*, which was to form the basis of the statutory National Curriculum in English, recommended that all secondary school pupils should "gain some experience of the works of Shakespeare," though not all should be expected to study them in textual detail. Instead the "once-traditional . . . desk bound" methods might be replaced by a variety of practical and active approaches, including the "use of film and video recording"' (Bottoms 2001,

p. 4). In fact, the use of Shakespeare plays and of their film adaptations was meant for History classes as well, as may be inferred for example by the *History Non-Statutory Guidance* (1991), a short guide to the teaching of history in the National Curriculum, where teachers were exhorted 'to consider a great variety of interpretations: historical novels, museum displays, film and television, and oral history' (McAleavy 2000, p. 74).

4   As Laurie Osborne concisely explains, cel animation is a technique that 'uses images created on layers of transparent acetate so that parts of the background can remain unchanged as images move in front of them. To create the illusion of depth of field, cel animators sometimes use a device called a 'multiplane camera', which places the layers of acetate at varying distances from the lens' (Osborne 1997, p. 108).

5   In his articulated response to a paper I gave at the seminar 'Negotiating Conflict in Cinematic and New Media' (Convenors: Thomas Cartelli and Mariacristina Cavecchi, ESRA, Pisa 2009), Evghenii Muzica (Middlesex County College, NJ, USA) reminded me that Stalin died in 1953, the year Mankiewicz's *Julius Caesar* was released, and during his rule, Soviet directors made a lot of films dedicated to the so-called 'role of the personality in history' – that is, films about tyrants. The most acclaimed one was Sergei Eisenstein's 1944 *Ivan the Terrible* – a biopic-trilogy about Russia's sixteenth-century tsar Ivan IV, a (to say the least) controversial figure who, very much like Caesar, fought tirelessly and ruthlessly to unify the country and turn it into an absolute monarchy. Stalin might have liked to be compared to Caesar and, ironically enough, when he died rumors spread about a presumed conspiracy that modelled his end after the myth of Caesar's death. For the meaning of Caesar in the Soviet Union and the Marxist and post-Marxist thought, see Canfora 2009.

# List of works cited

Bottoms, Janet (2001), 'Speech, image, action: animating tales from Shakespeare'. *Children's Literature in Education*, 32(1): 3–15.

Burt, Richard (2003), 'Introduction: editor's cut', in R. Burt and L. E. Boose (eds), *Shakespeare the Movie II: Popularizing the Plays on Film, TV Video, and DVD*. London and New York: Routledge, pp. 1–13.

Canfora, Luciano (2009), 'Caesar for communists and fascists', in M. Griffin (ed.), *A Companion to Julius Caesar*. Oxford: Blackwell, pp. 431–40.

Cartmell, Deborah (2007), 'Adapting children's literature', in D. Cartmell and I.
  Whelehan (eds), *The Cambridge Companion to Literature On Screen*. Cambridge and
  New York: Cambridge University Press, pp. 167–80.
Coursen, H. R. (2002), 'Animated Shakespeare: second season', *Shakespeare in Space:
  Recent Shakespeare Productions on Screen*. New York: Peter Lang, pp. 113–28.
Crowl, Samuel (1994), 'A world elsewhere: the Roman plays on film and television', in A.
  Davies and S. Wells (eds), *Shakespeare and the Moving Image. The Plays on Film and
  Television*. Cambridge and New York: Cambridge University Press, pp. 146–62.
— (2009), 'Mirrors, shadows, and lofty scenes: modern film versions of *Julius Caesar*', in
  S. Hatchuel and N. Vienne-Guerrin (eds), *Shakespeare on Screen. The Roman Plays*.
  Mayenne: Publications des Universités de Rouen et du Havre, pp. 105–22.
Danson, Lawrence (2000), *Shakespeare's Dramatic Genres*. Oxford and New York:
  Oxford University Press.
Deleuze, Gilles (1989), *Cinema 2. The Time-Image*. Minneapolis, MN: University of
  Minnesota Press.
Del Sapio Garbero, Maria (2009), 'Fostering the question "who plays the host?"', in
  M. Del Sapio Garbero (ed.), *Identity, Otherness and Empire in Shakespeare's Rome*.
  Farnham and Burlington: Ashgate, pp. 91–104.
Edwards, Dave (2005), *Shakespeare: The Animated Tales*, DVD, BBC-Metrodome.
Eisenstein, Sergei (1975, 1923), 'Montage of attraction', in J. Ley (ed.), *The Film Sense*.
  San Diego: Harvest Book, pp. 230–33.
Garfield, Leon (1997, 1985), *Shakespeare Stories*. London: Puffin.
— (1998, 1994), *Shakespeare Stories II*. London: Puffin.
— (2002), *Shakespeare: The Animated Tales*. London: Egmont Books.
Griffin, Miriam (2009), *A Companion to Julius Caesar*. Oxford: Blackwell.
Holland, Peter (2007), 'Shakespeare abbreviated', in R. Shaughnessy (ed.),
  *The Cambridge Companion to Shakespeare and Popular Culture*. Cambridge and New
  York: Cambridge University Press, pp. 26–45.
Honigmann, E. A. J. (1965), *The Stability of Shakespeare's Text*. London: Edward Arnold.
Hutcheon, Linda (2000), *A Theory of Parody. The Teachings of Twentieth-Century Art
  Forms*. Urbana and Chicago: University of Illinois Press.
Jenkins, Henry (2006), *Convergence Culture: Where Old and New Media Collide*. New
  York and London: New York University Press.
Jorgens, J. J. (1977), 'Joseph Mankiewicz's *Julius Caesar*', *Shakespeare on Film*.
  Bloomington and London: Indiana University Press, pp. 92–105.
Lamb, Charles and Lamb, Mary (1995, 1807), *Tales from Shakespeare*. Harmondsworth:
  Penguin Popular Classics.
McAleavy, Tony (2000), 'Teaching about interpretation', in J. Arthur and R. Phillips
  (eds), *Issues in History Teaching*. London and New York: Routledge, pp. 72–82.
Murray, Simone (2003), 'Media convergence's third wave: content streaming'.
  *Convergence the Journal of Research into New Media Technologies*, 9(1): 8–22.

Osborne, Laurie (1997), 'Poetry in motion: animating Shakespeare', in L. E. Boose and
    R. Burt (eds), *Shakespeare, the Movie: Popularizing the Plays on Film, TV, and Video*.
    London and New York: Routledge, pp. 103–20.
— (2003), 'Mixing media and animating Shakespeare tales', in R. Burt and L. E. Boose
    (eds), *Shakespeare, the Movie II: Popularizing the Plays on Film, TV, Video, and DVD*.
    London and New York: Routledge, pp. 140–53.
Pennacchia, Maddalena (2007), 'Literary intermediality: an introduction', in M.
    Pennacchia (ed.), *Literary Intermediality. The Transit of Literature Through the Media
    Circuit*. Bern: Peter Lang, pp. 9–23.
— (2009), 'Antony's ring: remediating ancient rhetoric on the Elizabethan stage', in
    M. Del Sapio Garbero (ed.), *Identity, Otherness and Empire in Shakespeare's Rome*.
    Farnham and Burlington: Ashgate, pp. 49–59.
Phillips, Robert (2000), 'Government policies, the state and the teaching of history',
    in J. Arthur and R. Phillips (eds), *Issues in History Teaching*. London and New York:
    Routledge, pp. 11–23.
Shakespeare, William (2006), *Julius Caesar*, D. Daniell (ed.). London: Arden
    Shakespeare.
Sinyard, Neil (1986), *Filming Literature. The Art of Screen Adaptation*. London and
    Sydney: Croom Helm.
Tosi, Laura (2009), '"I could a tale unfold. . .": adaptations of Shakespeare's supernatural
    for children, from the Lambs to Marcia Williams'. *New Review of Children's Literature
    and Librarianship*, 15(2): 128–47.
Williams, Marcia (2003), 'Bravo, Mr William Shakespeare', in N. J. Miller (ed.),
    *Reimagining Shakespeare for Children and Young Adults*. London and New York:
    Routledge, pp. 29–39.
Wilson, Richard (2002), 'Introduction', in R. Wilson (ed.), *Julius Caesar. New Casebooks*.
    Basingstoke: Palgrave, pp. 1–28.
Zipes, Jack (2011), *The Enchanted Screen: The Unknown History of Fairy-Tale Films*.
    New York and London: Routledge.

5

# Adapting and Parodying Shakespeare for Young Adults: John Marsden's *Hamlet* and Andy Griffiths' *Just Macbeth!*

Mark MacLeod

## Shakespeare and critical literacy

The question of whether Shakespeare should continue to occupy a privileged position on the list of texts set for the study of English in Australian schools was a logical response to the influence of critical literacy and to the increasingly multicultural nature of Australian society from the 1970s onwards. And under Prime Minister John Howard (1996–2007), it was among the most passionately contested issues of the conservative government's campaign to assert greater control over school education with the introduction of a national curriculum.

Howard and his government had been voted out by the time Australia's two most popular children's writers published adaptations of Shakespearean tragedies: John Marsden in his novel *Hamlet* (2008) and Andy Griffiths in his *Just Macbeth!* (2009). At first glance, these texts appear to represent polarities in the national conversation about Shakespeare during the Howard years.

The publications could hardly be more different. With a dust jacket – itself now rare in Australian publishing – its embossed matt lamination, elegant design and cream paper stock, the production values of Marsden's *Hamlet* announce its function unambiguously: to do homage to Shakespeare's greatest tragedy, edit it for a generation who might be challenged by three hours in the theatre, let alone five, and through the more linear medium of prose perhaps make the density of its poetic language more accessible.

Griffiths' *Just Macbeth!*, in stark contrast, is published in paperback, with inexpensive paper stock, a crowned head on the cover with a dagger through it, illustrated by Terry Denton with his trade mark bug eyes and fun-park mouth, and the kind of starburst taglines you might find on a box of laundry detergent: 'DOUBLE, DOUBLE, TOIL AND TROUBLE!' and 'MURDER, MADNESS AND WIZZ FIZZ!' Inside are hundreds of tiny illustrations around the margins of the word text, some of them in long sequences that create moving cartoon images like the pages of an old-fashioned flick-book. This is the format that has made six previous collaborations by Griffiths and Denton in the *Just* series – beginning with *Just Tricking!* in 1997 – a best-selling, if not award-winning, success. The function of the apparently anarchic layout is clearly to carnivalize a classic text in parody for a generation who appear to take little but their social networking seriously.

Both Marsden and Griffiths have been teachers, however, and this chapter argues that, although more obviously the product of a generation of critical literacy, Griffiths' *Just Macbeth!* confirms Shakespeare's canonical position just as clearly as Marsden's more overtly respectful adaptation does.

## Why Shakespeare and why now? Australia's 'culture wars'

To understand why these writers would suddenly turn to Shakespeare at this time, it is useful to consider briefly the so-called culture wars that were waged by Howard and his supporters, after 13 years of government by the Australian Labor Party. During this period, populist scare campaigns constructed the ongoing conversation about the need to revise the English syllabus in Australian schools as a simplistic choice between critical literacy on the one hand and 'back-to-basics' on the other. Although education has traditionally been the responsibility of the individual state governments in Australia, the federal government began to attach to its funding of state programmes specific conditions that appeared explicitly political in their emphasis on back-to-basics, a policy to allow parents to compare schools' results in national literacy and numeracy testing, and on such 'core values' as the flying of the Australian flag. The federal Minister for Education expressed the view that: 'Significant damage will be done to this nation's future if most young people do not leave school having been acquainted with Shakespeare, Hardy, Austen, White, Steinbeck and many others' (Nelson 2005). Although extending the list beyond Shakespeare was clearly designed to placate any groups lobbying for the inclusion of writing by women, Australians and Americans, or for working-class subject matter, it carefully avoided addressing the indigenous and multicultural emphasis in Australian education since the 1970s.

To influential conservative spokespeople, policies associated with multicul-turalism had compromised traditional consensus standards. Educator Kevin Donnelly constructed any broadening of the curriculum as a left-inspired political attack:

> Great literature was once valued for its aesthetic and moral value. The impact of "neo-Marxism", "feminism", "postmodernism" and "theories of transgression" (in particular "queer theory") now means that such an approach is considered "Eurocentric", "homophobic" and "patriarchal". So students at the University of Melbourne spend their time "reading diverse cultural forms (the family home, the amusement park) and practices (shopping, fandom)" and learning how "pop-feminist and post-feminist discourses conceptualised the relation between gender, sexuality and embodiment".
>
> Not only has the definition of what are considered worthwhile texts for study (such as Shakespeare, Patrick White, Joseph Conrad and Jane Austen) been exploded to include "the fashion industry, daytime television, cyber-feminism, plastic surgery", but concepts like truth and beauty are replaced by "concepts such as authenticity, identity, historical revisionism, mimicry and hybridity". (Donnelly 2005, pp. 56–7)

In his statements on the teaching of literature and history, Prime Minister John Howard targeted repeatedly the concept of critical literacy: 'When television's Big Brother or a text message jostles with Shakespeare and classical literature for a place in the English curriculum, we are robbing children of their cultural inheritance' (Howard 2007). At first it seems odd that a prime minister would bother to comment on the inclusion of canonical texts in the school syllabus. But the need to provide good-quality reading material for children is a motherhood issue attracting easy votes and, while it appears to support parents' emotional investment in the future of their children, more significantly it exploits nostalgia to validate their own past.

An earlier speech by the Roman Catholic Archbishop of Sydney, Cardinal Pell, with a title borrowed from the new Pope, 'The Dictatorship of Relativism', had made it clear that the cultural inheritance at risk was primarily that of moral values.

> While parents wonder why their children have never heard of the Romantic poets, Yeats or the Great War poets and never ploughed through a Brontë, Orwell or Dickens novel, their children are engaged in analysing a variety of "texts" including films, magazines, advertisements and even road signs as part of critical literacy . . . (Pell 2005)

In a speech that was intended to promote the reading of canonical texts by young people, 'ploughed through' was an ironic choice, but more significant was the curious omission of Shakespeare from the Archbishop's list – a decision more likely due to the bawdiness and violence of the plays, than to Shakespeare's being too easily identified with advocacy for the classics.

Whereas media commentators and members of the general public apparently do not feel qualified to pass judgment on, say, the curriculum in science, in Australia as in the United Kingdom, 'literature has long been one of the subjects most hamstrung by government directives, with politicians on occasion ready to intercede over matters of content, and to legislate about what in the curriculum may or may "not be touched"' (Ward and Connolly 2008, p. 294). Both church and state, then, were advising adult carers that students had to be rescued from the relativist reading of (mostly hypothetical) cereal boxes and made to study the canonical works of English literature. In that context, the term 'Shakespeare' is, as Hately (2003) argues, intensely politicized, and the plan to dump Shakespeare in an English Studies course for non-academic students, reported in Sydney's *Daily Telegraph* on 28 February 2010, makes this one name metonymic for the abandonment of all-consensus metropolitan values.

Although educators such as Sawyer (2007) have challenged the compulsory study of Shakespeare in an increasingly multicultural Australia, political campaigns have ensured that his work stays on the syllabus. Publication of Marsden's *Hamlet* and Griffiths' *Just Macbeth!* is, therefore, not in response to the question of *whether* Shakespeare should be taught. That has been decided. It is a question of *how*, and the assumption is that presenting the original, or even earlier adaptations such as Olivier's Oscar-winning *Hamlet* (1948), will no longer work.

## *Hamlet* and the preoccupations of Marsden's fiction

Like Zeffirelli's (1968) and Luhrmann's (1996) films of *Romeo and Juliet*, Marsden's *Hamlet* is an ambitious attempt to reclaim the youthfulness of the protagonists, which Olivier and his co-stars never made believable, but it assumes that prose fiction is a mode more likely than the original poetry to make the play's themes accessible. At first the choice of Shakespeare's longest play, in which there is far more talk than action, seems an odd one for teens used to extreme sports and high-energy films and games in the digital space. Indeed, much of the play is about *in*action. Its suitability for adaptation as a novel, however, can be inferred from the explanation Hapgood (1999) gives for the play's enduring appeal:

> a major factor in Hamlet's longevity has been the Prince's extraordinary rapport with the audience, an intimacy that Shakespeare enhances by giving him an unmatched number of opportunities to confide his thoughts and feelings, whether to other characters or to the audience in his soliloquies. (Hapgood 1999, p. 3)

With its emphasis on soliloquies, *Hamlet* is perhaps the most novelistic of Shakespeare's plays, and the implied author in Marsden's text focuses – as most literary novelists would – on motivation.

Given the playful meta-narratives of Marsden's contemporaries – including Griffiths – the somewhat old-fashioned focus on the exploration of character is surprising, but both Osborne (2010, p. 50) and Crewe (2006, p. 35) comment on the rehabilitation of character in literary studies after interest in the postmodernist project declined, and they argue that in Shakespeare scholarship this is due to the influence of film adaptations. Crewe avers that, from the general public's point of view, Shakespeare *is* his characters and always has been, particularly in the tragedies, due to 'people's ordinary human interest in other persons' (p. 37), although he points out the plays' availability to postmodernist readings, since 'Shakespeare questions character as much as he produces it' (p. 35).

The indecisiveness of Marsden's Hamlet mirrors that of the novel's implied young adult readers. As the earlier Marsden novels do, the text here proposes sexual tension as the main motivation – not only for Hamlet's interaction with his mother and stepfather and with Ophelia, but also for minor relationships between, for example, Hamlet and Horatio, or Ophelia and Polonius. Polonius' anger is due to his being an older parent and to his jealousy of Hamlet's youthful sexuality. Polonius blames his own young wife for having produced two 'oversexed' (Marsden 2008, p. 49) children in Ophelia and Laertes. In the sexually charged atmosphere of this novel, both Hamlet and Ophelia wonder whether there might be an erotic aspect to the close friendship between Hamlet and Horatio, and worry momentarily about it. The novel, therefore, reads between the lines of Shakespeare's text and infers motives that reflect some of the insecurities of young readers today.

Marsden makes a long-standing interest in Freud explicit in his 1998 book of advice for boys, *Secret Men's Business*, subtitled 'Manhood: the Big Gig'. Controversial at the time it was published, not as much for its frankness about the physical expression of sexuality as for its construction of the relationship between adults and children as a war – a metaphor that becomes literal in Marsden's most famous work *Tomorrow, When the War Began* – *Secret Men's Business* tells its young adult readers:

> Schools, and some parents, want to keep you as a child. They feel you will be easier to control if you are still a child . . . . They might not want to acknowledge the fact that you are now sexually potent. Your father may have been the only sexually potent male in the house up until now and he could feel threatened. . . Your mother could be nervous that there is now another sexually potent male in the house, and she may try to keep you as her "little boy". (Marsden 1998, p. 3)

At the same time as it encourages young male readers to compete with and even supplant their fathers, the chapter in *Secret Men's Business* titled 'Bad Fathers and No Fathers' begins with the blunt statement, 'You need a father' (Marsden 1998, p. 92), and advises those who have no father that there are ways of getting one.

A further context for the themes in both *Secret Men's Business* and Marsden's *Hamlet* is the prevalence in Australia of single-parent families headed by women, which, along with the feminization of Australian schools, was a factor often cited during the 1990s in the national conversation about the need for more books aimed at boys – a conversation that Marsden and such writers as James Moloney (2000), Gary Crew (see Van Putten 1996) and Glyn Parry (1996, pp. 57–9) were frequently invited to take part in. Lacan constructs the battle within Shakespeare's *Hamlet* as a desire for the masculine – not in physical terms, although Marsden's *Hamlet* takes advantage of the contemporary willingness to discuss such a possibility openly, in its questioning of the relationship between Hamlet and Horatio. Hamlet comments, for example, that Horatio is 'getting some muscle' (Marsden 2008, p. 8), and when Bernardo and Horatio enter Hamlet's bedroom to tell him they have seen the ghost, they are uncertain how they should wake him.

> Bernardo was just inside the door. Horatio was closer to the bed. But still Horatio hesitated. He didn't know how to do it. He wanted to stroke Hamlet into gentle awareness but thought it would look too much like love. Instead he shook Hamlet's shoulder roughly, as if he were angry. (Marsden 2008, p. 13)

The equal roughness of Hamlet's response when he is touched – 'What the fuck do you want?' – reflects the reality that, despite the explicit acknowledgement of homoeroticism in contemporary texts for teens, there has been no reduction in the defensive bullying of GLBTQ students in Australian schools.

When Ophelia thinks of Hamlet as the 'prettier' of the two boys (Marsden 2008, p. 41), the text echoes the Elizabethan use of the word, which is not gendered as female, although its feminine connotations are at play here, and Hamlet's fear that his masculinity is inadequate emerges when he sees the well-endowed cook masturbating and fears that he himself would never be able to satisfy Ophelia sexually with 'his little thing' (Marsden 2008, p. 59). Marsden's *Hamlet* should be read, then, in the context of Connell's influential construction of the male as confronting a range of possible masculinities. But at the same time it reflects the dysfunctionality that Walsh identifies as 'the defining feature of masculinity' (2010, p. 4) at the end of the twentieth century. For Lacan, the tragedy of Shakespeare's Hamlet is that he is trapped between two symbolic objects of his desire, and 'confronted on one hand with an eminent, idealized, exalted object – his father – and on the other with the degraded, despicable object, Claudius, the criminal and adulterous brother, Hamlet does not choose' (Lacan 1977, p. 12). If Marsden's Hamlet fails to choose, he will remain the 'boy' that the text labels him throughout.

## Marsden's *Hamlet* and Shakespeare's language

The back cover blurb on the hardback edition of Marsden's novel says simply: 'To be or not to be. That is still the question' (2008). While on the one hand the novel explores some of the spaces between Shakespeare's lines and makes new insights explicit, elsewhere it pares the original right back to an often laconic contemporary text with multi-layered ambiguities to be inferred by the reader. Whereas in the original soliloquy, Hamlet expands on his dilemma, here the layers of meaning revolve around the unspecified subject of the verb 'to be'. Who or what is 'to be'? If the subject is decision and action, then the line refers to constituting the potential as actual. If the subject is Claudius, Gertrude, or Hamlet himself, then the reference is to death. For a writer who, in an earlier young adult novel, *Dear Miffy* (1997), explores the harrowing incidence of teen suicide, this is a powerful reading.

Marsden's *Hamlet*, then, is an adaptation overtly respectful of the original in its exposition of both plot and character and in its tone. There remains, however, the question of Shakespeare's language. In dispensing with some minor characters and simplifying the plot, the novel highlights the structural symmetry between the two sets of parent-child relationships, and underlines important connections, such as that between the Lacanian objects, Gertrude and Ophelia. After Hamlet kills Polonius, for example, he sees Gertrude 'thrashing around on the chair, like a drowning woman' (Marsden 2008, p. 127) – the analogy deftly prefiguring Ophelia's drowning in the river and, in connecting the two women, emphasizes the abjection of the female. But why does this adaptation include so little of the original language – particularly when Marsden was for many years an English teacher?

The question becomes more insistent when the text is compared with Nicki Greenberg's graphic novel *Hamlet* (2010). In this full-colour illustrated adaptation, the characters are black inkblots with limbs, tails and masks, reminiscent of various animated predecessors from Felix the Cat to the comic hybrid beings of Dr Seuss, although Woodhead (2010) likens this adaptation to Tezuma's manga epic, *Buddha*. At 421 large-format pages on heavy art paper stock, the novel might prompt doubts about its portability or reading it in bed, but the page extent is due to Greenberg's use of Shakespeare's original text, somewhat edited, in a hand-lettered font. The whole concept of pairing animated fantasy characters with this text has a strange infantilizing effect that compromises the tragedy, and given the predominance of talk over action in the original, referred to earlier, the decision to adapt *Hamlet* to the graphic novel form at all seems almost perverse. By differentiating the appearance of the characters speaking, however, Greenberg's *Hamlet* does make Shakespeare's dialogue easier for contemporary readers to follow.

Although Cartelli (2010, p. 29) expresses impatience with 'students' growing inability, or reluctance even to try, to grapple with Shakespeare's language', Hogan (2010) accepts that the main impediment to young people enjoying Shakespeare now is the otherness of the language, and she makes no allowance for the fact that the original *Hamlet* was not intended to be read, when – in terms reminiscent of Kanter's justification for his creation of the *Classics Illustrated* series in 1941 (Klatt 2010; Lanier 2010) – she praises the graphic novel form for making the text more accessible.

> The comic form has the enormous advantage that the text – in which Greenberg has stayed true to the original play – is broken up into small balloons, making it easy to quickly apprehend the meaning and to appreciate the humour and vividness of the imagery. For people unfamiliar with Shakespeare's work, the language can be intimidating when they encounter it in great blocks of text, or even when they hear it spoken quickly on stage or screen. (Hogan 2010)

Tony Thompson, an English teacher interviewed during the 'culture wars', points out that those who object to the teaching of Shakespeare in schools because the language is too difficult have not, however, identified the challenge accurately.

> There is a brilliant activity that was shown to me years ago where the teacher gives each student a word from a famous speech. One student will start with "Is", the next with "this", the next with "a dagger", etc. After they have finished the speech, the teacher asks how many students had a word they didn't understand. Nobody puts up their hand except maybe the poor kid with "dudgeon" and it suddenly becomes clear. It isn't the words; it's the funny way they are arranged. This is a big confidence booster at this stage. The next step is to get them to use the punctuation. Reading the sentences without a flourish of rising inflection at the end of each line makes a big difference as well. Usually after the first act, the language ceases to be a problem and then it is just a matter of keeping the damn characters straight. (Thompson 2005)

If that is the main challenge for students, then Greenberg's *Hamlet*, with the original text 'staged on the page', as the book's cover says, could prove to be an unexpected solution, although the potential mismatch between the tone of the visual imagery and the word text may limit its appeal.

Lanier's argument that film adaptation was the catalyst for the 'teening of Shakespeare' (2010, p. 107), however, helps to explain the language of Marsden's *Hamlet*, which quotes the original text sparingly, and subtly modifies contemporary usage to convey a degree of otherness that is still accessible.

> Shakespeare film pushed hard against the textual conceptualization of Shakespeare that was the dominant keynote of much of the twentieth century, the notion that Shakespeare's essence is to be found in the particularities of his language. One of the main achievements of the nineties was to bring Shakespeare in line with late twentieth-century visual culture and in the process loosen the equivalence between Shakespeare and text. (Lanier 2010, p. 105)

Once a space was opened up between 'Shakespeare' and the original language, Lanier argues that far more varied adaptations were possible, in different cultures and on new platforms. Writing at an early stage in the exploration of the digital environment, Maynard, McKnight and Keady (1999) say that children see the classics in hard copy as long and difficult to read. Since Shakespeare was not originally intended to be read anyway, let alone studied, their view supports Groves' warning (Mitchell and Parry 2005) that damage can be done in the classroom by adults eager to force the classics on children before they are ready for them. For Maynard et al., however, new technology satisfies the young reader's need to 'play inside the story' (1999, p. 193). But is that what young readers inevitably want to do?

Lanier sees the producers of graphic novels and digital games pursuing cultural capital in the number of their products that are adapted from Shakespeare, although conversely, he argues, Shakespeare's cultural capital is also renewed by his association with a young audience who are unlikely to encounter his work in the theatre (2010, p. 111). Despite the growing legitimacy of unconventional art forms, however, does an adaptation such as Griffiths' and Denton's *Just Macbeth!* offer the audience anything beyond what Jameson calls 'the self-indulgence of. . . infinite regress' (1991, p. 64) into textuality?

## *Just Macbeth!* and the infinite regress into textuality

Profusely illustrated with cartoons and gags in the margins, the text of *Just Macbeth!* appears immediately as a parody of the original – thoroughly disrespectful and iconoclastic as might be expected from the author of *The Day My Bum Went Psycho* (2001), *The Bad Book* (2004) and the series of short story collections beginning with *Just Tricking!* (1997). Griffiths' fictional narrator Andy and his classmates – familiar from the *Just* series – mount a production of *Macbeth*, because their teacher Ms Livingstone says that performance is the best way to study a play script. Given the daily reporting of increasingly violent incidents perpetrated by children in both the physical and digital environments, Verducci (2000) argues that renewed education in empathy as part of the values curriculum might best be achieved through the use of drama, and Stanislavski's method, in which acting cannot begin until the character's internal feelings are made real. However, just as both Shakespeare's *Hamlet* and *Macbeth* employ the play-within-the-play device, the scenario in *Just Macbeth!* makes empathy almost irrelevant. Notably familiar from British film and television, it sets up a carry-on cast of bumbling amateurs, who find themselves playing in the annual production of some classic, with predictably farcical results.

The title itself challenges anyone inclined to approach an adaptation of Shakespeare with respect. The 'Just' functions as a colloquial shrug. There is nothing special about this dramatic experience; it is merely *Macbeth*. Conversely, the 'Just' also asserts that this is the unadulterated original *Macbeth*: just *Macbeth*, the whole truth and nothing but. So which is it? Or can it be both? *Just Macbeth!* is a live theatre collaboration between Australia's national Bell Shakespeare

Company and Andy Griffiths. It is also published as a book not with literal 'illustrations', rather with a chaotic visual narrative by Terry Denton. The two overlap, but each includes narrative elements that are unique. So the concept of *Just Macbeth!* is slippery from the beginning.

The page layout constructs a print version of the dual narrative, with the initial implication that one is central and the other peripheral. At the centre of Griffiths' plot is Shakespeare's *Macbeth*, and the framing story features the students who are taking part in the class production. This framing story constructs a reflection of the student audience watching *Just Macbeth!* – or reading it – and places them on the stage. The naivety of the character Andy and his fellow students is then used repeatedly to challenge fear of the metaphysical and the occult, the reification of the archaic, of royalty and tradition generally, and the cultural capital of Shakespeare's language. So as members of the audience or readers witness the student actors stumbling through a parody of Shakespeare's text, they observe the inadequacy of their own responses to it.

*Just Macbeth!* opens with a monologue from Griffiths' character Andy. Despite the name, he is not the autobiographical Andy Griffiths, but the deliberate confusion constructs the space between fiction and the actual as a contested site.

> "You know I love Shakespeare.
> And when I say I love Shakespeare, I don't just mean I love Shakespeare, I mean I REALLY love Shakespeare.
> And when I say I REALLY love Shakespeare, I don't just mean I REALLY love Shakespeare: I mean I REALLY REALLY love Shakespeare.
> Not only is he the greatest playwright of all time, but if it wasn't for him, Lisa wouldn't be standing next to me. In my house.
> Yes, you heard right.
> Lisa Mackney.
> The most beautiful girl in the world.
> Is standing next to me!" (Griffiths 2009, p. 1)

What begins as an endorsement, apparently designed to gratify the adult gatekeepers, quickly becomes suspect as Andy protests too much and the endorsement grows more strident. Then the reference to Lisa Mackney explains his enthusiasm. Andy has wanted the attention of this idealized girl through several short story collections, and here she is, playing his wife in the class production of *Macbeth* – doubly ironic since, as Hately argues, Lady Macbeth has long been 'a kind of cultural shorthand for dangerous femininity' (2006, p. 31).

Throughout the narrative, Andy as Macbeth clowns around with his best friend from the *Just* series, Danny – here as Banquo – and the main role of Lisa as Lady Macbeth is to deplore their immaturity. Where Marsden's Hamlet agonizes over his desire to become a man, the characters in *Just Macbeth!* revel in their boyishness. Neither Griffiths as the writer nor Denton as the illustrator misses an opportunity to milk the comic potential of this scenario. There are frequent intertextual references to earlier Griffiths/Denton texts, such as the story 'Bandaid' from *Just Crazy!* (2000), in which Andy anticipates the pain of ripping off a band-aid and his mother's predictable response when blood gushes out and he has to ask her for a new one: 'Do you think we're made of bandaids? Do you think bandaids grow on trees?' (p. 2). Here, for example, Danny as Banquo's ghost turns up after the murder:

DANNY: My head hurts.
ANDY: Go away! You're dead!
DANNY: I need a bandaid.
[Andy takes a box of bandaids from his sporran and throws a bandaid at the ghost]
ANDY: There! Now go!
DANNY: I need another bandaid.
[Andy throws another one.]
    And another. . .
[He throws another one.]
    And another. . .
[He throws another one.]
    I need *lots* of bandaids.
ANDY: Aaaagh! Take the whole box! (Griffiths and Denton 2000, pp. 125–6)

Such a scene does nothing to illuminate a young reader's understanding of Shakespeare's *Macbeth*, and yet the recognition that it evokes does empower young readers with confidence in their knowledge of literature – albeit of a contemporary Australian 'classic', rather than the canonical text. And that confidence may make them more enthusiastic readers and theatregoers. Behind both Marsden's adaptation of *Hamlet* and this parody of *Macbeth*, then, is the contemporary concern with the literacy of young people, particularly boys.

## Shakespeare and literacy

Partly motivated by adult fears of their children's enthusiasm for new technology, the concern with literacy expressed in the 'back-to-basics' political campaign emerges unmistakably in Terry Denton's illustrations, which acknowledge the growing number of boys who are visually literate, but struggle with extended word texts and are, therefore, increasingly drawn to the digital space, rather than books or traditional live theatre, for entertainment. When Danny as Banquo is killed, his horse wanders around the margins for several pages, eating stray ellipses, looking for a job and finally taking off on page 128 when he is told, 'You're needed on page 144' (Griffiths and Denton 2009, p. 128). No doubt some adult readers will regard this as a 'dumbing down' of Shakespeare, but the intelligence of such metafictional games should not be dismissed. Nor should Linda Hutcheon's contention (1989, p. 101) that while parody subverts the original, it also 'legitimises' it.

Ironically, for all its apparent irreverence, *Just Macbeth!* includes far more of the original text than Marsden's *Hamlet* does. Although Hecate is edited out as an unnecessary complication, almost the whole of the witches' chant is included, for example, apart from 'Liver of blaspheming Jew' becoming 'Liver of blaspheming boy' (although 'Nose of Turk' is retained), and that in turn results in 'slips of yew' becoming 'raw bok choy' (Marsden 2008, p. 135). Those changes aside, the scene is straight Shakespeare, subverted perhaps only by the fear that the tone is becoming too serious, as the witches subside into playground quarrelling after they have finished mixing their potion.

The frequent inclusion of passages from Shakespeare should not, of course, be surprising, given the involvement of the Bell Shakespeare Company in the project. Their agenda is obviously to attract young people to their serious Shakespeare repertory, not turn them away. Nevertheless, the inclusion becomes more frequent in the second half of *Just Macbeth!* – significantly after Andy as Macbeth has to murder Duncan, in the scene titled 'Horror! Horror! Horror!' (Griffiths and Denton 2009, pp. 84–8). In the book, this is the longest of just five scenes that are rendered almost entirely by illustration, and it is the darkest. The tiny bust of Shakespeare that announces the page numbers – or in printing jargon, 'folios' – at the foot of each page attempts a couple of lame jokes while the murder is being enacted wordlessly overhead across five pages, but on the final page it simply utters the words 'Murder most foul' (Griffiths and Denton 2009, p. 88). This hiatus in the madcap banter that dominates the narrative up to this point changes the balance in the tone of *Just Macbeth!*

The narrative begins and ends with the colloquial use of the verb 'kill', all too common among both children and parents in Australia. When, for example, Andy's older sister Jen sees the mess he and his friends have made in the kitchen, using their mother's food processor to blend up a witches' potion, she sneers:

> JEN: And by the way. . .Mum is *definitely* going to kill you!
> ANDY: [picking up a large knife] Not when she finds out that I killed you first. She'll *thank* me! (Griffiths and Denton 2009, p. 195)

The silent murder scene at the centre of the narrative has given this final exchange a slightly more serious edge. But can it be argued that a change of tone in the second half of *Just Macbeth!* constitutes a learning experience in moral values that the young audience or reader is conscious of?

Challenged to defend the anarchic morality of the cautionary tales in his controversial collection *The Bad Book* (2004), Griffiths argues that his only obligations as a writer are to keep his young readers turning the pages and to entertain them.

> Our prime purpose in writing *The Bad Book* is not to "encourage young people to be better". This is more appropriately a project for moral instruction, not fiction. Both (illustrator) Terry (Denton) and I believe that children's book writers have one overwhelming duty: to fire the reader's imagination and encourage a love of reading. (Griffiths and Denton 2004)

Even at its silliest, *Just Macbeth!* cannot be read simply as just a series of textual games, so Griffiths' assurance of his and Denton's intentions is suspect. The multi-layering of narratives in the *Just* series, epitomized by *Just Macbeth!*, appeals, as this chapter has suggested, to readers and audiences from a wide age range, but the inclusion of adults in that range has not always been acknowledged. The fact that in the year it was published *The Bad Book* was the most frequently challenged and banned book in Australian schools (Knox 2004), and also one of the top sellers, suggests that adults often tolerate Griffiths' work in the name of literacy. Read in that context, there is a significant subtext to the apparently farcical scene in *Just Macbeth!* when the courtiers observe that Macbeth does not look well. Lisa as Lady Macbeth is unconcerned and says that it is only because he has just watched too many horror movies on DVD. But who is she referring to: Andy or Macbeth? When the stage direction has her snap at Andy to get a grip and stop talking about visions of daggers (Griffiths and Denton 2009, p. 127), he answers as Macbeth, and continues to do so. Andy's guilt at having to murder Duncan, even in play, has affected him and Shakespeare's text takes an increasingly firm hold of the narrative.

## Parody and the restatement of the original

There are two points to note about the reference to DVDs. In order to set up the joke, the text light-heartedly includes historical information for its young readers, when Lennox is puzzled by Lisa's use of the term.

> LENNOX: [utterly confounded, given that it's the eleventh century and DVD technology won't be invented for another nine hundred years] Digital what? (Griffiths and Denton 2009, p. 127)

The stage direction here supports Hately's argument that for this audience it is difficult to create a parody without restating the original:

> the offering of Shakespeare to young readers is in general a vexed enterprise: there can be no guarantee that a child reader will have a preexisting knowledge of Shakespeare, and so authors must often provide the very cultural competency they wish to critique. (Hately 2009, p. 60)

The running gag about the effect of DVDs on young people and adults alike (since Andy is a young boy playing the adult Macbeth) is a playful reference to the controversy over the violence in *The Bad Book*, a shrug at the notion that fiction can constitute the actual and affect behaviour and at the same time a mischievous suggestion that the rules may be different where Shakespeare is concerned. The banter among the student characters leading up to the murder of Duncan is alternately silly and cartoon-violent, but the change in tone, the silence and Andy's eventual involuntary uttering of Shakespeare's original words suggest that, in having to perform and witness the act of murder, these naïve young characters 'get' the classic play. While *Just Macbeth!* sets out to subvert the iconic status of the original and seems to epitomize Jameson's view that postmodern parody forfeits all moral reference in its infinite regress, it finally demonstrates Hutcheon's thesis that, in contesting the original, parody also confirms it and, despite Griffiths' disavowal of any intention other than entertainment, aligns this text more closely with the evidently serious ambitions of Marsden's *Hamlet* than it might at first appear.

## List of works cited

Cartelli, Thomas (2010), 'Doing it slant: reconceiving Shakespeare in the Shakespeare aftermath'. *Shakespeare Studies*, 38: 26–36.

Connell, Robert W. (1995), *Masculinities*. St Leonards: Allen & Unwin.

Crewe, Jonathan (2006), 'Reclaiming character'. *Shakespeare Studies*, 34: 35–40.

*Daily Telegraph* (2010), 'Shakespeare too hard for HSC English', 28 February, viewed 13 March 2011, <http://www.news.com.au/national/shakespeare-too-hard-for-hsc-english/story-e6frfkvr-1225835374675>.

Donnelly, Kevin (2005), 'The Culture Wars in the schools'. *Quadrant*, 49(4): 56–61.

Greenberg, Nicki (2010), *Shakespeare's Hamlet: Staged on the Page*. Sydney: Allen & Unwin.

Griffiths, Andy (2001), *The Day My Bum Went Psycho*. Sydney: Pan Macmillan.

Griffiths, Andy and Terry Denton (1997), *Just Tricking!* Sydney: Pan Macmillan.

— (2000), *Just Crazy!* Sydney: Pan Macmillan.

— (2004), 'Bad book "not good enough"'. *Age*, 25 September, viewed 13 November 2009, <http://www.theage.com.au/articles/2004/09/24/1095961856737.html?oneclick=true>.

— (2009), *Just Macbeth!* Sydney: Pan Macmillan.

Hapgood, Robert (ed.) (1999), *Hamlet Prince of Denmark*. Cambridge: Cambridge University Press.

Hately, Erica (2003), 'Shakespeare as national discourse in contemporary children's literature'. *Papers: Explorations into Children's Literature*, 13(1): 11–24.

— (2006), 'Lady Macbeth in detective fiction: criminalising the female Reader'. *Clues: A Journal of Detection*, 24(4): 31–46.

— (2009), 'De-colonising Shakespeare? Agency and (masculine) authority in Gregory Rogers's *The Boy, The Bear, The Baron, The Bard*'. *Papers: Explorations Into Children's Literature*, 19(1): 59–68.

Hogan, Sandra (2010), 'Review of Nicki Greenberg's *Hamlet*', *Perilous Adventures* (blog), viewed 14 April 2011, <http://www.perilousadventures.net/1101/hamlethogan.html>.

Howard, John (2007), 'I want the best for our kids', *Herald Sun*, 9 February, viewed 11 January 2009, <http://www.pandf.org.au/data/portal/00000005/content/49294001171865502257.pdf>.

Hutcheon, Linda (1989), *The Politics of Postmodernism*. New York: Routledge.

Jameson, Fredric (1991), *Postmodernism, or the Cultural Logic of Late Capitalism*. Durham, NC: Duke University Press.

Klatt, Wayne (2010), 'Classics illustrated'. *Antiques & Collecting Magazine*, 1 April, 20–25.

Knox, Malcolm (2004), 'Booksellers go psycho as poo hits the fans'. *Sydney Morning Herald*, 25 September, 1.

Lacan, Jacques (1977), 'Desire and the interpretation of desire in *Hamlet*', James Hulbert (trans) and Jacques-Alain Miller (ed.). *Yale French Studies*, 55/56: 11–52.

Lanier, Douglas (2010), 'Recent Shakespeare adaptation and the mutation of cultural capital'. *Shakespeare Studies*, 38: 104–13.

Marsden, John (1997), *Dear Miffy*. Sydney: Pan Macmillan.

— (1998), *Secret Men's Business*. Sydney: Pan Macmillan.

— (2008), *Hamlet*. Melbourne: Text Publishing.

Maynard, Sally, McKnight, Cliff and Keady, Melanie (1999), 'Children's classics in the electronic medium'. *The Lion and the Unicorn* 23(2): 184–201.

Mitchell, Lisa and Parry, Leigh (2005), 'Pop goes the Bard', *Age*, 3 October, viewed 12 April 2011, <http://www.theage.com.au/news/education-news/pop-goes-the bard/2005/09/30/1127804655965.html>.

Moloney, James (2000), *Boys and Books: Building a Culture of Reading Around Our Boys*. Sydney: ABC Books.

Nelson, Brendan (2005), *Transcript of the Address Recorded for the Schooling for the 21st Century Conference*. Canberra: Australian Government Media Centre, viewed 10 April 2011, <http://www.dest.gov.au/Ministers/Media/Nelson/2005/09/ tran1280905.asp>.

Osborne, Laurie (2010), 'iShakespeare: digital art/games, intermediality and the future of Shakespearean film'. *Shakespeare Studies*, 38: 48–57.

Parry, Glyn (1996), 'Boys are beautiful'. *Australian Book Review*, 181: 57–9.

Pell, George (2005), 'The dictatorship of relativism: address to the National Press Club', 21 September, viewed 13 March 2011, <http://newlearningonline.com/new-learning/chapter-7-knowledge-and-learning/george-pell-on-the-dictatorship-of-relativism/>.

Sawyer, Wayne (2007), 'The powerfully literate citizen', *English in Australia*, 42(2): 44–7.

Thompson, Tony (2005), *Transcript of ABC Radio National program 'Lingua Franca'*, 29 October, viewed 30 March 2011, <http://www.abc.net.au/rn/linguafranca/ stories/2005/1493101.htm>.

Van Putten, Val (1996), 'The faults, failings and future of the CBC'. *Reading Time*, 40(3): 13–5.

Verducci, Susan (2000), 'A moral method? Thoughts on cultivating empathy through method acting'. *Journal of Moral Education*, 29(1): 87–99.

Walsh, Fintan (2010), *Male Trouble: Masculinity and the Performance of Crisis*. Basingstoke: Palgrave.

Ward, Sophie and Connolly, Roy (2008), 'Let them eat Shakespeare: prescribed authors and the national curriculum'. *The Curriculum Journal*, 19(4): 293–307.

Woodhead, Cameron (2010), '*Hamlet* by Nicki Greenberg: book review', *Behind the Critical Curtain* (blog), 30 October, viewed 8 April 2011, <http:// cameronwoodhead.com/archives/hamlet-by-nicki-greenberg-book-review/>.

# 6

# Shakespeare Comic Books: Visualizing the Bard for a Young Audience

Anja Müller

## Introduction

It is hardly surprising that William Shakespeare is the most commonly adapted author in English literature and culture, no matter whether the adaptation is targeted at adults or at a young audience. As the chapters in the present volume reflect, Shakespeare adaptations also rank first as far as critical attention is concerned. Whereas the first adaptations of Shakespeare for children tended to be in narrative form (see Laura Tosi's chapter in this volume), visual adaptations have become ever more important in the twentieth and twenty-first centuries. Baz Luhrmann's *Romeo and Juliet* is probably the most prominent effort to adapt the Bard for a decidedly young cinema audience, who may be attracted to watch the movie with Leonardo di Caprio in the lead role rather than by the story of the star-crossed lovers. Apart from film, comic books are particularly suitable to visually adapt canonical texts for a young readership. In the bookshop of the new Globe Theatre, such adaptations take almost as many shelves as critical studies or critical editions of Shakespeare's texts. Although comics have always appealed to a broad audience, covering all age groups, they still tend to be associated with child or teenage readers. The Comics Code, established in the United States in 1954, ostracized "'all scenes of horror, excessive bloodshed, gory or gruesome crimes, depravity, lust, sadism, [and] masochism'" (qtd in Duncan and Smith 2009, p. 41) to prevent what was believed to be unsuitable material for young readers. Such self-regulatory sanitizing, despite its underlying moral agenda, can add fuel to those critics who argue that comic book adaptations are bound to be reductive in complexity. Add to this some prejudices concerning the alleged superiority of the word over the image as well as the inferior status of popular art, especially art for non-adult audiences, and the contested status of comic books becomes inevitable. Fears that comic book adaptations of canonical texts debase the original or, worse, substitute it and lure young readers away from the true text have been frequently expressed.[1] But, as Kevin Wetmore reminds us, comic adaptations only do what comes naturally in adaptation processes, such as the staging of a drama text or intertextual references: they abridge or recycle. Only the status of the comic as a popular, juvenile genre accounts for the disparaging of its adaptational work (cf. Wetmore 2009, p. 174). A contrary position might argue that the status of the comic book genre may be raised by adapting a canonical text and thus profiting from its profound qualities.

The reasons for offering canonical texts to young readers in form of comics are manifold. Among them is the belief that children are visually literate by intuition, especially when growing up in today's age of visual media, therefore, visually coded texts are supposed to be more accessible and attractive to younger readers.[2] As far as comic book adaptations of dramatic texts are concerned, comics seem to be a particularly suitable medium of adaptation because of their inherent theatricality. Wetmore perceives correspondences between comics and theatrical art in the collaborative process of production, the importance of visual setting and the influence that stage poses may have on character representation in comic panels (see Wetmore 2009, p. 172 and p. 177). 'What theatre does in time, comic books do in space: juxtapose text and image to tell a story', says Wetmore (2009, p. 173). I would argue that the affinity between both genres is even closer, as the sequential character of the comic book genre, especially the significance of the gutter (the varying gaps between the individual panels), combines spatial and temporal elements. It is, therefore, no wonder that one can observe instances of mutual influence between theatre and comic art, as Wetmore and Jean-Marie Bouissou do with regard to Japanese manga and Kabuki theatre (see Wetmore 2009, p. 173 and Bouissou 2010, p. 20).

My chapter will take it for granted that adaptations of Shakespeare in comic books should not raise any questions about who is to debase or raise in esteem whom. Instead, I am interested in the motivations, operations and effects of the adaptational process. For that purpose, I assess four comic book adaptations of *Macbeth* (from Marcia Williams, over Classical Comics to two Manga versions) in order to explore the peculiarities which this type of visualizing Shakespeare for young readers might entail. With its action-driven plot, *Macbeth* lends itself to visualization rather easily (see also Hayley 2010, p. 276). Besides, its brevity makes it one of the Shakespeare plays that are most often introduced at school. On the other hand, the violent nature of the Scottish Play might also raise doubts about its suitability for young readers. By focusing on the modes of adaptation which the different comic book series employ, I intend to examine how the individual adaptations handle these challenges and create versions of the play for readers of different ages and how, by doing so, they also reflect on the relationship between their own genre and that of the canonical text they adapt.

## Marcia Williams, *Mr. William Shakespeare's Plays*

Marcia Williams' *Macbeth* forms part of her picture book *Mr. William Shakespeare's Plays* for young readers of up to 10 years. In *Re-Imagining Shakespeare for Children and Young Adults*, edited by Naomi J. Miller, Marcia Williams writes at some length about her ideas and intentions when 'messing with the Bard' (2003, pp. 29–38). Her own introduction to Shakespeare, she says, was through *Tales from Shakespeare*, which she found a terrible read. Her major quibble with the Lambs is their lack of illustration, which did not convey adequately the visual experience of a stage performance, although it is the stage performance that eventually gives life to the drama text.[3] Williams considers this visual experience essential for children, because '[w]e now live in a fast-moving, visual world and work for children and young people should reflect this' (Williams 2003, p. 32). Adapting Shakespeare for children, therefore, exceeds working on language or plot; it should create a sensual experience. The children Williams writes for are neither rational nor sensible (sentimental) children, who make their encounter with a canonical text through reading and readerly imagination. They belong to a generation that has grown up with educational principles based on sensual experience, development of creativity and encouragement to express oneself. It is no wonder that Marcia Williams, who describes herself more as a doodling student from the back row than a scholar (Williams 2003, p. 33), is most intrigued by the conditions of Elizabethan theatre performances, by the mixed audience (including children), the noise and the lack of propriety among the spectators for whom their own social performance in the theatre may have been as important as the performance on stage.

Williams tries to capture this theatrical atmosphere in the panels of her comic book versions of Shakespeare's plays and even calls her own adaptations 'performances' (Williams 2000, preface). Framing the panels with an audience that also illustrates the different seats available in an Elizabethan theatre (including the groundlings' floor), the comic integrates stage and audience into the page. The panels consist of three parts:

> The words that Shakespeare actually wrote are those spoken by the actors; the story, or plot of the play, is told underneath the pictures; and the spectators – who are famously rude and noisy – can be seen and heard around the stage. (Williams 2000, prefatory page)

Williams cuts the dialogue down to a few remarkable lines of the original and adds audience reactions for the reader's identification, focalization and comic relief. Through this device she supplies the drama text with a narrative element mediating between drama text and reader. The frames are yet another visual device of narrativization, because they have a mediating function, as well. They guide the reader's attention to certain details, either comment on or evaluate scenes. For Williams, these parts are the quintessential adaptive transformation that opens up Shakespeare's plays for a contemporary child audience. Whereas, despite the necessary rigorous abridgement, she largely leaves the plot and the language of Shakespeare's play intact, the depicted audience allows her to include a more modern language, even anachronisms. 'While the rest of the book may be considered my retelling of Shakespeare's conversation with his reader, the audiences' speech bubbles are my conversation with my reader, our personal interaction, gossip, and backchat' (Williams 2003, p. 34). Williams, thus, unites two levels of asserting the 'timelessness' of Shakespeare's plays: By presenting plot and language rigorously curtailed, but unchanged in wording, she establishes a continuity to her model, which is underscored by visualizing the historical setting and costumes of Shakespeare's time. On the other hand, the audience frame implies that the 'timelessness' of Shakespeare's plays consists in their adaptability to different tasks and needs.

For Marcia Williams, the comic book format suits the needs of children extremely well, not only because of its visual appeal, but also because she believes this format is best suited to children's literacy. Adults may have problems with the complexity and simultaneity of pictures that are not supposed to be read in a linear sequence. Children at primary school age, however, may respond much more easily to this particular form of representation. The different visual and verbal levels of the strips, like repetitions of gestures or reappearing figures, are said to correspond ideally with 'Shakespeare's own multilayered texts' (Williams 2003, p. 35).

What is at stake for Williams is to adapt Shakespeare for an audience of all ages. She sees her contribution not as a dumbing down of the Bard, but as a door opener. Her attitude to adaptations for children is expressed in the following chewing-gum metaphor: 'You can stretch it [the adaptation] and stretch it, but you must not let it snap' (Williams 2003, p. 36; original quote taken from Gerald Scarfe). This clearly reveals that the overall agenda of Williams' books – despite their emphasis on riotousness – is eventually educational insofar as she wishes to introduce children to the most eminent representative of the English literary canon. If an adaptation for children is to retain this function of enculturation, then the idea of fidelity to an authoritative original – and be it ever so condensed – is hard to eschew.

## Classical Comics *Macbeth*

The Classical Comics series to some extent offers a compromise for the attempt to unite the entertaining and attracting functions of comic book adaptations of canonical texts with an educational agenda. As they make concessions to readers who may have difficulties understanding the language of texts published before 1900, they also develop an interesting marketing strategy. Classical Comics *Macbeth* exists in three different versions: First, an unabridged, 'Original Text' (2008a): 'This is the full, original script – just as The Bard intended. This version is ideal for purists, students and for readers who want to experience the unaltered text; all of the text, all of the excitement' (p. 142 in any Classical Comics edition of *Macbeth*). Second, the 'Plain Text' version (2008b) translates Shakespeare's text line by line into modern English: 'If you've ever wanted to fully appreciate the works of Shakespeare, but find the original language rather cryptic, then this is the version for you!' (Ibid.). Finally, the 'Quick Text' version (2008c) is praised as '[a] revolution in graphic novels! We take the dialogue and reduce it to as few words as possible, but still retain the full essence of the story. This version allows readers to enter into and enjoy the stories quickly' (Ibid.). Although this tripartite publication model is also used for other canonical texts, such as *Frankenstein, Jane Eyre* or *Great Expectations*, its use for Shakespeare adaptations seems particularly suitable. After all, one could say that the three versions of the Classical Comics series reflect the diversity of Shakespearean audiences, which Williams tried to capture in the single panel of her 'performance strips': the connoisseur and scholar, those trying to appreciate art but being put off by the alterity of language, and those just enjoying a good story.

What is at stake here is a reader-oriented treatment of the relationship of dialogue and plot in a dramatic text. The Classical Comics adaptation clearly considers the relevance of dialogue, plot and performance to be audience-specific. The drama text, hence, does not need to be inviolate to retain the identity of, say, *Macbeth*. The invariable constants in the series are the plot, which remains unaltered, and its visualization in the panels, which remains the same in all three versions. The book covers are remarkable in this respect: The Plain Text cover features a character study of the protagonist; both Original and Quick Text depict a group of the chief protagonists. Whereas these figures are clearly identifiable in the coloured cover of the Quick Text, the Original Text cover is held in black, with glossy black outlines of the characters. This handling of the paratext corresponds with the versions' different agendas: Quick Text aims at a clearly identifiable story. Original Text acknowledges the sometimes opaque character of Shakespeare's text. It also signals 'quality' and the readiness to look closely at the work instead of reading quickly and superficially for the plot.

According to its educational agenda, the volumes include an introduction to the historical context of the play and an appendix with chapters on Shakespeare, on the 'real Macbeth', the textual history of *Macbeth*, and some 'making of' pages on how the comic was drafted.[4] Although published in Britain, the series follows the conventions of an American comic style. The characters, who are introduced by a cast list, are modelled on familiar types from sword and dagger movies or comics on medieval topics such as *Prince Valiant*. The villains Macbeth and Lady Macbeth are clearly identifiable by their black hair. Lady Macbeth's red dress indicates (sexual) aggression and prevents her from looking, with her extraordinarily long black plaits, like Pocahontas in a Scottish castle. Most of the panels are held in dark colours – after all, this is a tragedy. Black and red predominate, the latter especially in the panels surrounding King Duncan's murder, which remains unrepresented itself.

If the illustrations are supposed to substitute stage performance, one can say that the Classical Comics *Macbeth*, like Williams', aims at historical accuracy. The setting of the castle is drawn realistically and with many details, people are clad in historical costume complete with the odd kilt. The perspective is mostly that of an external focalizer who observes the scene from a distance. The theatrical aspect is further increased by the dominant use of subject-to-subject transitions between panels, which creates the impression of a fast-paced action and demands a considerable amount of reader involvement to follow the action (see also McCloud 1993, p. 71). Close-ups show faces in strong emotions, gestures are reminiscent of stage poses, all of which contributing to an atmosphere of intense and powerful emotions. Even if the proximity of the facial expressions is more reminiscent of film, the grandeur of the figures' poses clearly helps to create an overall 'theatrical' impression of the Classical Comics *Macbeth*. With its typecast figures and emphasis on a fast-paced plot, the Classical Comic Series is less interested in subtle characterization or complex layers of meaning than in retelling a thrilling story. Nevertheless, entertainment is not the first and foremost goal of the series:

> I'm fascinated by your approach to the play and its language. I find them gripping, dramatic and, although for me the original Shakespeare is always my reason for turning to these plays, I think that what you are doing in illuminating and making perhaps more lucid, especially for young people, is clever and meaningful.

This quotation on the back cover of all three editions comprehensively reflects the double agenda of the series, namely to attract and entertain through sensational representation ('dramatic', 'gripping') while always pointing to that covert original in the background, which should be the ultimate motivation for reading any version of Shakespeare's plays. The adaptation is granted a value of its own, as it may help to render the original more understandable and as it is 'meaningful' in its own way. This double act between high and popular culture is embodied by the person to whom the quote is attributed, namely Patrick Stewart, who is famous as both a high-profile actor in London's West End theatres and as *Star Trek Next Generation's* Captain Jean-Luc Picard. Nevertheless, the Classical Comics series does not escape a hierarchization of high and low culture, because the quote subtly but unmistakenly prioritizes the original Shakespeare over an adaptation aimed at 'young people'. After all, the title of the series, 'Classical Comics', already invokes its debt to the literary canon. This attitude is further expressed by the deliberately historical visual representation and an ostentatious fidelity towards the original plot (and text). The identity of the three editions, despite their differences, finally insinuates a stability of the work that endures over textual variations. These adaptations of Shakespeare plays for a comic book format try to legitimate their existence in a supposedly less respected medium by almost overstating their roots in the canonical original. The comic book format, then, is only legitimate as a means to an end, namely to attract a readership to a canonical author and thus to perpetuate his future appraisal. A new visual language is tentatively offered to lure young readers, to lower the barriers or bridge the gap between high and low cultures. The aim, however, is clearly evaluated: quality lies with the original, and the desirable goal is to educate the young reader to dare a direct encounter with the 'Bard' and learn to understand him properly. The two roads taken here are the text and an interest in historical background and cultural history. Shakespeare's *Macbeth* thus is presented as both a piece of literature and a part of British cultural history.

## Shakespeare's *Macbeth, The Manga Edition*

Contrary to the overtly educational agenda of the Classical Comics series, The Manga Edition of *Macbeth* puts emphasis on its entertaining function. The preface contends: 'The graphic novels known as manga (Japanese for 'whimsical pictures') are a natural medium for Shakespeare's work' (Sexton 2008, p. 2). Like Marcia Williams, Adam Sexton, the editor of the series *Shakespeare – The Manga Edition*, stresses the aspect of visuality. Yet to him, this is a genre-specific quality, not a demand of a young readership: Shakespeare's plays were written to be performed on stage, and any adaptation, therefore, must take cognisance of this visuality. Manga, the originally Japanese comic book genre that is nowadays so popular with young readers, seems to Sexton an ideal genre to transform Shakespearean drama into:

> In fact, a manga is potentially more visual than a stage production of one of the plays of Shakespeare. Unbound by the physical realities of the theatre, the graphic novel can depict any situation, no matter how fantastical or violent, that its creators are able to pencil, ink, and shade. (Sexton 2008, p. 2)[5]

Sexton especially has in mind the ability of comics to visualize what happens offstage in theatre due to technical limits or conventional taboos. In his opinion, he is supported by Douglas King, whose article 'Mediating the Supernatural' (2003) suggests that precisely this quality of illustrations is an advantage when it comes to adapt Shakespeare's plays for children: magic, the supernatural and verbal imagery can, thus, be visualized. These concrete images are meant to clarify situations or textual passages as well as to appeal to a young reader's imagination.

The second supposed advantage of manga over drama, according to Sexton, concerns its accessibility on the printed page:

> [I]n a production of one of the plays onstage or onscreen, we can hear the words but can't see them. Though Shakespeare is never easy, reading helps. And that is precisely what manga adaptations of the plays allow. Perusing a Shakespeare manga, the reader can linger over speeches, rereading them in part or altogether.

Especially in the long and intricate soliloquies typical of Shakespearean tragedy, this allows for an appreciation of the playwright's craft that is difficult if not impossible as those soliloquies move past us during a performance. (Sexton 2008, p. 3)

The unique character of a theatre performance, thus, becomes an impediment for the understanding of young readers. Here, Shakespeare's language is believed to be a burden, an obstacle for modern readers. It is not only an aesthetic treasure, but it can also be a problem or even a deterrent. Unlike my previous examples, the manga editions of Shakespeare do not try to overcome this problem by simplifying the language. They may abridge the text, although not drastically, but they otherwise retain the original drama text and trust completely in the power of printed pages with illustrations. Sexton ties his adaptation to notions of the original insofar as he legitimates his medium of the manga with the purpose to allow its readers to understand the original better.

Like the Classical Comics *Macbeth, The Manga Edition* uses a historical setting and costumes indicating a medieval time frame. Its visual aesthetics, however, follow the conventions of Japanese manga, even if the edition is 'flipped', that is, it follows the usual Western reading sequence from left to right instead of the back-to-front sequence of original Japanese manga. The arrangement of the black-and-white panels also breaks the typical Western reading sequence from time to time. At crucial moments of tension, aspect-to-aspect transitions are used, which suspend time for a moment, simulating simultaneity; this type of transition is typical of manga (see McCloud 1993, p. 72 and pp. 77–9). Another manga feature is the youthful appearance of the characters – including Macbeth (who is blond), Lady Macbeth and even one of the witches.[6] Moreover, the figures are represented by using the so-called masking effect, which deliberately draws stylized lines and bland faces instead of realistic details to represent character. According to Scott McCloud, this style, which is also employed by Hergé's clear-line-style *Tintin* series, is common for traditional manga (McCloud 1993, pp. 42–3). As McCloud explains in *Understanding Comics*, the masking style invites identification, because the blandness of the figures' faces leaves more room for the readers to project themselves into. In *Macbeth, The Manga Edition*, this invitation to identify is additionally supported by the frequent close-ups of eyes or lips in aspect-to-aspect transitions. Whereas the Classical Comics gave its readers a distanced view of the characters, The Manga Edition zooms its readers right into the story and close to the characters. With this appeal to identification, The Manga Edition does not present Shakespeare's play as an eminent artwork to be admired from and with a critical distance. It invites its young readers to come close to the play, to share its intense excitement and to become interested not only in the story but especially in the characters and their psychological conflicts. The approach taken is more affective than critical or appreciative.

Moreover, as Sexton indicates in his preface, *Macbeth, The Manga Edition* revels in visualizing what happens offstage or is verbalized in teichoscopy in Shakespeare's play. Several frames even try to visualize either ideas or what is going on in another place while the character who serves as our focalizer delivers a speech or soliloquy. Macbeth's 'If it were done. . .' monologue, for example, uses the aspect-to-aspect technique to show both Macbeth and what is going on in the hall where King Duncan is still celebrating simultaneously (Sexton 2008, p. 30). Another set of frames illustrates Macbeth's metaphorical language in hyper-realistic fashion: when Macbeth tells his wife 'O, full of scorpions is my mind' and 'Ere the bat hath flown, there shall be done a deed of dreadful note', elaborately drawn scorpions and bats hover over the mask-like faces of Macbeth and Lady Macbeth in the panels (Sexton 2008, p. 94). McCloud explains that this particular use of hyper-realism in manga usually serves to objectify ideas or to highlight the complex significance of the represented object (McCloud 1993, p. 44). To a reader who is familiar with manga aesthetics, this curious way of illustration signals that the bats or scorpions are to be read as abstractions, not as real items. The idiosyncrasies of manga aesthetics are, thus, employed to offer readers who are conversant with this visual language, an easier access to Shakespeare's imagery.

As mentioned above, one common topic of the debate surrounding adaptations of canonical texts for children, especially in comic book format, concerns sanitization. The Manga Edition gives a simple answer to this question: since manga tends to include sex and violence (cf. Bouissou 2010, p. 20 and p. 24), and young readers are familiar with manga aesthetics, representations of violence are not incompatible with this *Macbeth*, either. Following the tradition of fast-paced, action-centred *shonen* manga for boys (see also Hayley 2010, p. 275), the adaptation shows extended violent death scenes, including Duncan's murder and Macbeth's death. The final fight between Macduff and Macbeth is presented with additional details: Macduff is first wounded by Macbeth, but then cunningly surprises Macbeth from a seemingly defeated position; in the following frames, Macbeth's end is shown in close-up, with gory detail, culminating in a full-page panel with Macbeth's severed head (Sexton 2008, pp. 178–83). What may at first sight look like a splatter version, unduly indulging in the violent bits of Shakespeare's play can also be regarded as simply following the aesthetic conventions of the *shonen* manga. The stylized graphics also render representations of extreme violence more bearable than if they appeared in the realistic, colourful 'American' style of the Classical Comics. The particular visual encoding of the manga genre helps to signal to its readers the fictional character of the representation. Young readers today have grown up with television cartoons where characters survive the most lethal fights, accidents and explosions (such as *Tom and Jerry* or *Bugs Bunny*). They may even be already conversant with manga like *Dragonball* or *Pokemon*, featuring futuristic superheroes or mutant creatures, whose sole purpose lies in winning one lethal combat after the other. Such readers can be – and apparently are – trusted not to mix representation with reality when reading manga. The abstraction of the genre here serves as an important distancing device that is also assumed to be understood by younger readers.

## *Manga Shakespeare Macbeth*

Whereas the comic book adaptations discussed so far still retain a historical visualization of Shakespeare's play, *Manga Shakespeare Macbeth*, illustrated by Robert Deas, leaves this beaten track of visual fidelity behind and transports its Shakespearean drama text into an entirely new visual world. 'In this version of Shakespeare's tale of murder and the supernatural, samurai warriors have reclaimed a future post-nuclear world of mutants' (blurb, back cover). *Manga Shakespeare Macbeth* also belongs to the *shonen* genre, but its emphasis on strong female characters may be seen as an attempt to attract readers of both sexes. With a very prominent, strong Lady Macbeth figure, who does not refrain from physically attacking Macbeth, *Manga Shakespeare Macbeth* may even try to establish two protagonists, one male and one female, and thus cross the lines of *shonen* and *shojo* (that is, manga for girls). *Manga Shakespeare Macbeth*, too, is 'flipped', and like in The Manga Edition *Macbeth*, one can find masking style, close-ups and a skilful arrangement of panels and frames, albeit with less frequent use of the aspect-to-aspect technique.

Established in Britain in 2007, *Manga Shakespeare* was the first series to use manga to render Shakespeare more accessible to young readers. The series editor, Emma Hayley, is frank about the financial considerations of her enterprise (the shares of the market of manga had increased 98% between 2004 and 2005; see

Hayley 2010, p. 267); even the later marketing of the books for educational purposes is seen from this perspective (see Hayley 2010, pp. 278–9). The major idea behind the project was, however, to provide a new approach to Shakespeare in a medium that could capture the theatrical aspects of the original and would appeal to a young audience by meeting them in their preferred genres.

Among the features this particular adaptation displays, the careful use of perspective is worth mentioning. In a number of panels, the reader is made to share the protagonist's vision, for example, when Macbeth is looking through a spyglass while observing his wife's conversation with Duncan (*Manga Shakespeare Macbeth* 2008, p. 58). The resulting image hardly conceals its debts to a similar use of perspective in films like *Terminator* or *Robocop*, where views through the visor of a cyborg protagonist have almost become a convention. If such views may also invite identification with Macbeth, further images add psychological depth to the protagonist. This becomes most obvious in Macbeth's lament over his dead wife. In all the other comic book versions, Lady Macbeth's death remains marginal – a mere note on which Macbeth briefly comments; sometimes with one or two frames added that show the suicide. In *Manga Shakespeare Macbeth*, Lady Macbeth's suicide interrupts the action: Macbeth leaves the battlements to go down and embrace the shattered body of his wife a last time, delivering his final monologue in anguish (*Manga Shakespeare Macbeth* 2008, pp. 178–80). This Macbeth fuses the manga hero with the post-1980s super-hero type of Western comic culture – larger than life, aloof, but with some flaws leading to his downfall. This image is further evoked in a number of frames: Again and again, Macbeth is shown on high elevations, observing what is happening below. Before the final battle, we see him climbing an Eiffel Tower-like building (*Manga Shakespeare Macbeth* 2008, p. 184) – a rather pointless act with regard to the action, but a nice visual allusion to King Kong's desperate attempt to escape by climbing up the Empire State building. In other panels, Macbeth is sitting in his royal hall all on his own, surrounded by surveillance screens – and he eventually meets his enemies alone. All these images can be referred to both Japanese manga and Western comic traditions. As the Manga Shakespeare series deliberately employs manga artists from the United Kingdom (Hayley 2010, p. 270), such a hybridization of visual aesthetics can be regarded as a planned result.

Besides, the adaptation process in *Manga Shakespeare Macbeth* does not simply translate Shakespeare's play into manga, with some historical elements or depictions of a stage on page. I would argue that the essence of this adaptation lies in the densely woven web of allusions to popular art and movies. One recognizes the warlords from Japanese anime and manga traditions; Banquo bears the features of a pulp fiction villain, complete with eyepatch and cigar. The setting of Macduff's and Malcolm's meeting resembles similar surroundings in movies or animations about warriors whose superhuman power derives from spiritual, Zen-like practices (compare *Manga Shakespeare Macbeth* 2008, p. 140 to, for instance, the shore scene in *Karate Kid I* or desert combat scenes in *Dragonball Z*). We also have a *déjà vu* with Macbeth's armour: have we not seen that before – in the Bat Cave (*Manga Shakespeare Macbeth* 2008, p. 168)? Does not the visual composition of the frame showing Macbeth facing his enemy's army (*Manga Shakespeare Macbeth* 2008, p. 188) almost shamelessly echo Aragorn facing the Gates of Mordor in Peter Jackson's *The Return of the King*? And *Star Wars* comes to mind when Macbeth delivers the message of his promotion to his wife in Princess Leia fashion – it is only that R2D2 is missing as a projector.

*Manga Shakespeare Macbeth*, thus, uses more than an intense psychological representation to draw its young readers in. The series may financially profit from its use in education, which implies, as well, the goal to introduce young people to the Bard and Elizabethan theatre. Despite this added educational agenda, one should not forget that the series' major strategy to adapt the canonical text for a contemporary young audience is to explicitly graft the original text and the story onto a world of cultural images and icons the intended readers are likely to share. Shakespeare, the cultural icon, may be retrieved through its manga adaptation, yet it is also removed from its venerable, monolithic pedestal. If Shakespeare and his works are supposed to become popular with modern audiences, then they must partake in and merge with the icons of contemporary popular culture. The use of manga for this purpose is, in my opinion, a very appropriate device, because the visual conventions of the genre – despite their popularity – still signal a certain alterity. Manga, anime tradition aesthetics, samurai warriors and post-nuclear apocalyptic settings provide a spatial and temporal difference that, in a way, equals the alterity contemporary young readers will experience when being confronted with the topics, plot and text of Renaissance tragedies. As it retains the original text, the series also retains this idiosyncrasy and alterity of the Shakespearean text. By defamiliarizing Shakespeare's play visually, Manga Shakespeare paradoxically makes it possible to re-familiarize, for instance, *Macbeth* for readers who have grown up in a cultural context where four-armed mutant warriors may be more familiar than characters from Scottish or English medieval history.

# Conclusion

Let me end by drawing some tentative conclusions concerning adaptations of Shakespeare for young readers in a comic book format. First, in almost all the examples discussed in this chapter, the story of Shakespeare's play is foregrounded. With the exception of Marcia Williams, whose adaptation develops around the experience of an Elizabethan stage performance, the comic book adaptations take their cue from the story, which they either tell rather faithfully, visualizing a historical setting, or which they transport into a new setting. This observation corresponds to frequently voiced remarks that, when it comes to adaptations for children, the story is essential because children love stories. If a drama is adapted for children, the story told in the play is therefore the most crucial aspect. The abridgements and modernizations one encounters imply that no matter how much the immortal language of the Bard is celebrated, adaptations of Shakespeare can do without it if they target a young audience.[7] The story is what counts and what establishes the link of identity between Shakespeare's play and its adaptation in a comic book. Only the manga versions insist on Shakespeare's language as one marker of identity; Hayley explicitly links the perseverance of Shakespeare's popularity to 'the beauty of the language he uses' (2010, p. 269). Doing so, she is in company with Howard Marchitello, who hints at the paradox that, by focusing on the story instead of the language, adaptations of Shakespeare actually accentuate what is least 'Shakespearean'. After all, Shakespeare himself adapted stories he found in historiographical writings or in the works of other authors. The stories of Shakespeare's plays are themselves adaptations; the plays' originality (if one wants to use this term at all) rather resides in their language. Such an insight is not new in adaptation studies, which has long abandoned the search for fidelity as a criterion of quality and legitimation. Adaptations of canonical texts for children, however, have usually been treated differently. No serious scholar in adaptation studies would bother, with Marcia Williams, whether it is okay to 'mess with the Bard' or with any other canonical author. The fact that a connection to the 'original' (whose very existence would be questioned in state-of-the-art adaptation studies) seems to be an important issue, or that an adaptation of a canonical author for children ought to be faithful to the original text at least either in story or in language is definitely caused by the underlying educational agenda of such adaptations – even if this agenda may be ever so covert.

As Marchitello points out, adaptations of Shakespeare for young readers do not only intend to adapt individual works but also want to adapt 'Shakespeare' as a cultural icon. Marcia Williams' book is an excellent case in point, because her version illustrates (pun intended) what may belong to this cultural icon besides the play: reference to the time (e.g. Elizabethan costume), theatre conventions and the person himself, who features some cameo appearances in several panels of Williams' strips. It is no wonder that the Bard is also evoked in the titles of Williams' books: *Mr. William Shakespeare's Plays* and *Bravo Mr. Shakespeare*. This legitimating link back to the original also lurks behind the Classical Comics edition, with its chapters on the Bard's life and works, so as to situate the adaptation within a larger context identifiable as 'Shakespearean'. The preservation of Shakespeare's own text, as retained in the Classical Comics Original Text editions or in the manga versions, is arguably the closest tie established to 'Shakespeare'. The reference point of these adaptations is, thus, no point but a densely woven texture of works, manifestations, biographies or already existing adaptations of Shakespeare, each of which constituting the Bard as a cultural icon. Comic book adaptations of Shakespeare seek to integrate this canonical cultural icon into the plethora of icons of contemporary youth culture. Our appreciation of these adaptations should depend on the success of this integration. Fidelity to the original is secondary.

# Notes

1   Wetmore describes, for example, Fredric Wertham's scathing remarks on the U.S. Classics Illustrated series at large (2009, pp. 178–9).

2   Whether this is indeed the case or whether visual literacy should also be treated as a skill with different levels of complexity is an open question that cannot be settled in this chapter.

3   Similar to Williams, Amy E. Mathur also considers illustrations to be comparable to stage productions (2003, p. 146).

4   The Classical Comics series shares some of these features with the Classics Comics series, established in the United States in 1941, and later renamed Classics Illustrated (see Wetmore 2009, pp. 174–5). The 'making of' section of Classical Comics is, however, singular, and indicates the series' concern with what is presented as a proper, legitimate handling of an original text in an adaptation.

5   In fact, Sexton's preface seems to use the term 'manga' synonymously with 'comic', as he nowhere comments on the idiosyncrasies of Japanese comic art in comparison to its American or European 'relatives'.

6 The witches are portrayed as women of different ages: one young, lascivious and beautiful; one middle-aged and of fading beauty; and one old hag.

7 Such a tendency can also be found in German classrooms, where textbooks on canonical authors increasingly abandon the original text in favour of translations into a more modern language. This development is highly contested and heavily criticized as a denigration of the 'Classics'.

## List of works cited

Bouissou, Jean-Marie (2010), 'Manga: a historical overview', in Toni Johnson-Woods (ed.), *Manga: An Anthology of Global and Cultural Perspectives*. New York: Continuum, pp. 17–33.

Duncan, Randy and Smith, Matthew (2009), *The Power of Comics: History, Form and Culture*. New York: Continuum.

Hayley, Emma (2010), 'Manga Shakespeare', in Toni Johnson-Woods (ed.), *Manga: An Anthology of Global and Cultural Perspectives*. New York: Continuum, pp. 267–80.

Johnson-Woods, Toni (ed.) (2010), *Manga: An Anthology of Global and Cultural Perspectives*. New York: Continuum.

King, Douglas (2003), 'Mediating the supernatural in adaptations of Shakespeare for children: three unique productions through text and illustration', in Naomi J. Miller (ed.), *Reimagining Shakespeare for Children and Young Adults*. London: Routledge, pp. 129–37.

*Manga Shakespeare Macbeth* (2008), Robert Deas (ill). London: Selfmadehero.

Marchitello, Howard (2003), 'Descending Shakespeare: toward a theory of adaptation for children', in Naomi J. Miller (ed.), *Reimagining Shakespeare for Children and Young Adults*. London: Routledge, pp. 180–90.

Mathur, Amy E. (2003), 'Promoting the original: perspectives on balancing authenticity and creativity in adaptations of *The Tempest*', in Naomi J. Miller (ed.), *Reimagining Shakespeare for Children and Young Adults*. London: Routledge, pp. 147–52.

McCloud, Scott (1993), *Understanding Comics: The Invisible Art*. New York: Harper.

Miller, Naomi J. (ed.) (2003), *Reimagining Shakespeare for Children and Young Adults*. London: Routledge.

Sexton, Adam et al. (ed.) (2008), *Shakespeare's Macbeth: The Manga Edition*. Hoboken, NJ: Wiley Publishing.

Shakespeare, William (2008a), *Macbeth. The Graphic Novel. Original Text Version*. Litchborough: Classical Comics.

— (2008b), *Macbeth. The Graphic Novel. Plain Text Version*. Litchborough: Classical Comics.

— (2008c), *Macbeth. The Graphic Novel. Quick Text Version*. Litchborough: Classical Comics.

Wetmore, Kevin (2009), '"The amazing adventures of superbard": Shakespeare in comics and graphic novels', in Jennifer Hulbert, Kevin J. Wetmore and Robert L. York (eds), *Shakespeare and Youth Culture*. Houndmills: Palgrave, pp. 171–98.

Williams, Marcia (1998), *Mr. William Shakespeare's Plays*. London: Walker Books.

— (2000), *Bravo, Mr. William Shakespeare!* London: Walker Books.

— (2003), 'Messing with the Bard', in Naomi J. Miller (ed.), *Reimagining Shakespeare for Children and Young Adults*. London: Routledge, pp. 29–38.

# 7

# Adapting an Old English Epic: The Case of Rosemary Sutcliff's *Beowulf: Dragonslayer*

Łukasz Neubauer

Literary adaptation is a complex, purpose-led process whereby the source text that is being adapted undergoes a structural or sometimes even thematic transformation which, to a greater or lesser degree, affects its entire content. According to J. A. Cuddon, adaptation refers to 'the re-casting of a work in one medium to fit another, such as the re-casting of novels and plays as film or television script' (1991, p. 9). It may, however, also mean adapting a literary work within the same genre or medium, so as to accomplish a special purpose, for example, reworking a literary classic to suit the tastes of younger, though not necessarily less critical, readers.

This latter purpose has a long tradition that dates back to the eighteenth and nineteenth centuries, when the first abridged versions and retellings of 'adult' works eventually found their way into children's hands. There were obviously several reasons for this. First, it was assumed that the originals were not quite suitable for young and fragile minds. There were too many complex and frequently conflicting aspects of a moral and/or mocking nature in them that even grown-up readers could easily find baffling, to say nothing of those whose analytical faculties were not yet fully developed as a result of their young age. Second, by familiarizing young readers with some of the foremost works of the literary canon, one could make sure that they were introduced to what was believed to constitute the quintessence of the common European cultural heritage. In other words, by being acquainted with Homer or Shakespeare, children would get at least a taste of what was considered to be most influential in shaping Western culture.

Among those literary classics whose adaptability seems to have been questioned the longest was the anonymous Old English poem known under the editorial title of *Beowulf*. It must be admitted, though, that one of the major reasons for this was probably the fact that its literary – as opposed to historical – value had not been fully recognized prior to 1936 when J. R. R. Tolkien famously remarked in his now seminal essay 'Beowulf: The Monsters and the Critics' that 'so far from being a poem so poor that only its accidental historical interest can still be recommended, *Beowulf* is in fact so interesting as poetry, in places so powerful, that this quite overshadows the historical content' (Tolkien 2006, p. 7). Since then there has been a considerable rise in the interest in *Beowulf*, both academic and artistic with countless translations, scholarly editions, critical works, novelizations, graphic novels and film adaptations. It was only a matter of time before some modern retelling would find its way onto the teenage readers' bookshelves.

The aim of this chapter is to look into the book held by many to be one of the most successful (if not *the* most successful) of all beowulfian adaptations for the young reader: Rosemary Sutcliff's novelette *Beowulf: Dragonslayer*. I shall examine a number of features that contribute to its immense success and popularity (since it first appeared in 1961 it has never really been out of print). The chapter will thus concentrate on the book's plotline (with a particular emphasis on the narrative techniques employed by the author) and the numerous discrepancies (along with their possible explanations) that can be found between the two accounts of Beowulf's heroic exploits. These, of course, will include not only the rather obvious verse-to-prose transition, but also the adaptor's choice of vocabulary which, although notably modernized, does in several instances echo the style (as well as the actual wording) of the Anglo-Saxon *Beowulf*. Finally, it will delineate some of the most distinctive adaptational qualities and features which can be found in *Beowulf: Dragonslayer* and which may perhaps be universally employed in virtually any modern adaptation of early medieval literature.

## Earliest retellings of *Beowulf*

Before Sutcliff's novelette, there had been several attempts to adapt the story of Beowulf for adolescents. One of the earliest known retellings came in 1895 from the pen of Mara Louise Pratt-Chadwick whose short story 'Beowulf' appeared in her *Stories from Old Germany*. It was soon followed by Clara L. Thomson's *The Adventures of Beowulf* (1899) and Henrietta E. Marshall's *Stories of Beowulf Told to the Children* (1908). In 1933, Strafford Riggs published *The Story of Beowulf* 'decorated' with remarkable two-colour illustrations by Henry A. Pitz. After that, in the wake of J. R. R. Tolkien's essay, there were two major adaptations published in the 1950s – C. F. Bricknell Smith's *Beowulf* (1951) and Ian Serraillier's *Beowulf the Warrior* (1954), the latter re-cast in a well-wrought alliterative style. Finally, in 1960, there appeared Dorothy Heiderstadt's compilation of medieval tales under the collective title *Knights and Champions*. Among the short stories of St. George, El Cid and the Black Prince is also one about the famed Geatish warrior – 'Beowulf, Hero of the North'.

These are evidently not the only attempts to provide young readers with at least a few glimpses of the Old English epic. Certain beowulfian themes may also be found in a number of books published at the time, the most famous of them being, of course, J. R. R. Tolkien's *The Hobbit* (1937).[1] It must be observed, though, that many of them are either too sketchy – focusing on a subjective selection of episodes from the poem – or too simplistic and naïve to be enjoyed by a wider groups of readers.

The time for a complete and literarily satisfying retelling of *Beowulf* was clearly ripe in 1961 when English novelist Rosemary Sutcliff (1920–92), arguably one of the best-known twentieth-century authors of historical fiction for young people, published her novelette *Beowulf: Dragonslayer* (later also published as *Dragon Slayer: The Story of Beowulf*). Sutcliff had already made herself a name by writing the immensely popular *Eagle of the Ninth* series, set in second-century Roman Britain, as well as other works 'for children of all ages from nine to ninety' (Commire and Klezmer 2001, p. 29), and so appeared to be just the right person for the challenge. The gripping tale of Beowulf, a young Geatish warrior who comes to the aid of the Danish king Hrothgar, kills his otherworldly foes (Grendel and his hideous mother) and, 50 years later, dies in combat while defending his own people against the rage of a fire-spitting dragon, could ultimately receive the attention it well deserved from the young and old alike.

The task was quite hazardous, though. With its muddled narration and frequent textual ambiguities, this Old English epic of 3182 alliterative lines does not necessarily make it to everyone's favourite poem. There may be legions of enthusiasts all over the world, yet they are very likely to be more than counterbalanced by the likes of Alvy Singer, the phobic comedian in Woody Allen's *Annie Hall* who warns his girlfriend against taking 'any course where they make you read *Beowulf*' (Allen 1982, p. 50). In fact, the poem might easily constitute an insurmountable barrier to a great number of modern readers, regardless of their age. Adapting it would, therefore, require a great deal of alterations, deletions as well as narrative short cuts in order to make the poem more accessible.

Though, if an adaptation is to preserve at least some of the cultural ethos found in the Old English poem, it should not move away too far from the primary text. In other words, unless the writer has an entirely different concept in mind,[2] it should aim at a greater ease of understanding (bearing in mind the age group of the target readers), while at the same time staying as true as possible to the heroic–elegiac spirit (if not the actual plot) of the original.

It seems very likely that Rosemary Sutcliff must have taken all this (and more) into consideration while working on her own version of *Beowulf*. She does not only alter its entire composition by re-casting it in a far more accessible – though, at times, slightly archaized – modern English prose, but she also modifies a number of things in the story line. Both endeavours result in a fairly modern appearance of this more than a thousand-year-old tale. In no way, however, does she ever stray from its core, namely the veneration of the great Geatish protagonist, quite fittingly reported by the anonymous poet as being 'manna mildest ond mon-ðwærust,/leodum liðost ond lof-geornost' (*Beowulf* 3181–2) 'the mildest of men and most courteous, kindest to [his] people and most eager for fame', an authentic, if somewhat idealized, hero of his age.

## Narrative discrepancies

As far as the narrative structure of *Beowulf: Dragonslayer* is concerned, there appear to be no major alterations, no radical modifications to the poem's plotline and no dramatic reshufflings of its cast. There are, however, certain subtle changes which are doubtlessly meant to turn this complex, multi-layered account into a more accessible tale for young readers with not necessarily much knowledge of the Anglo-Saxon world. Needless to say, these comprise several inevitable, though not always plainly noticeable, narrative shortcuts which do not quite affect its main plot, but without which the book would not be as readable as it is today.

In comparison with the Old English poem, Rosemary Sutcliff's novelette has a more linear and compressed structure, which mainly focuses on the main character's heroic exploits in Denmark and Geatland. Gone are the many narrative detours – also known as 'episodes' or 'lays' – so that young readers are firmly guided along the main plot. Most medievalists may feel a sense of irreparable loss at the absence of Hildeburh (*Beowulf* 1114 ff), Finn (1068 ff), Ongentheow (1968 ff) or Herebeald (2434 ff). Likewise, there are no references to Beowulf's killing of the Swedish king Onela (2396 ff) and the predicted woes of Freawaru, Hrothgar's daughter betrothed to Ingeld the Heathobard (2022 ff). Nor is there any mention of Queen Modthryth whose early evil deeds are counterbalanced by her laudable conduct after she marries King Offa of the Angles (*Beowulf* 1931 ff). All in all, however, the idea behind writing *Beowulf: Dragonslayer* was to popularize the poem, make it more accessible to young readers, not merely translate it into Modern English prose. By reducing the narrative to the episodes that pertain directly to Beowulf's life, the author actually manages to achieve a far greater level of clarity, thus resulting in a more constant storytelling than in its Old English counterpart.

There are numerous ways of looking at the structure of the Old English poem, the majority of them focusing on the three monster combats (Grendel 662–835; Grendel's mother 1383–1569; the dragon 2510–2711) which actually provide the narrative spine for the 3182 lines of alliterative verse and propel the plot. An alternative way of looking at *Beowulf* proceeds along the three[3] funerals that are paired with the abovementioned battles. Apart from the poem's closing scene, when the hero's mutilated body is laid upon a massive pyre (*Beowulf* 3110–82), there are the highly evocative funerary descriptions when Scyld Scefing (1–52), Hildeburh's kin (1107–24) and those alluded to by the 'Last Survivor' (2247–66) leave this world of toil and trouble amidst the sorrow and grief of those who remain.

Unless one wishes to change the ending of *Beowulf* completely, there is no way of avoiding the funeral ceremony of its fearless protagonist who dies in battle, wounded by the venomous fangs of the dragon. Accordingly, Rosemary Sutcliff devotes a notable, though not substantial, part of the final chapter (2001, pp. 92–3) to a heart-rending farewell to the great Geatish champion. She mentions the 'worthy barrow . . . on the Whale's Ness' (Sutcliff 2001, p. 92) and its future function as a 'guiding-mark . . . for all who sail the sea' (2001, p. 92), perfectly corresponding to the respective passages in the poem when the grief-stricken Geats have their much-loved 'æþelinge boren/. . . to Hrones-næsse [hwær hie] him ða geg[yrwaþ]/ad on eorðan unwaclicne' (*Beowulf* 3135–8) 'leader borne to Whale's Ness [where they] make for him ready a not-too-badly-formed pyre on earth', 'weg-liðendum wide gesyne' (*Beowulf* 3158) 'widely visible to the sailors'. Interred with the hero are 'wrought gold and wondrous weapons of the dragon's hoard' (Sutcliff 2001, p. 93), while the barrow, which was built in ten days on the promontory, is big enough for as many as 'twelve chieftains of his bodyguard [to ride] sun-wise about it, singing [his] death song' (2001, p. 93). This is largely analogous to passages in the epic which allude to the beast's treasure as being 'swa unnyt swa hit æror wæs' (*Beowulf* 3168) 'as worthless as it was before' and to the fact that, following the funeral rites and the construction of a mighty barrow, 'ymbe hlæw riodan hilde-deore,/æþelinga bearn, ealra twelfa,/woldon ceare cwiðan, kyning mænan,/word-gyd wrecan ond ymb wer sprecan' (*Beowulf* 3169–72) 'round the burial-mound rode the battle-tried ones, chieftains' sons, twelve in all, who, in bitter grief, wished to mourn for their king, of the man speak and sing dirges'.

As Rosemary Sutcliff's *Beowulf: Dragonslayer* is principally concerned with the life and deeds of the title hero, the other three funerals appear to have been not significant enough to be included in the novelette. Even the poem's opening passage on the rise of the Scyldings (Danes) and their legendary ruler Scyld Scefing's 'ship of death' (Owen-Crocker 2009, p. 11) is deliberately omitted by the English novelist. Instead, Rosemary Sutcliff attempts to re-create some of the atmosphere of 'gear-dagum' (*Beowulf* 1) 'days of yore' when Anglo-Saxon *scopas* employ an impressive range of techniques to conjure up the right mood required for their gripping narratives: during a festivity in King Hygelac's mead hall, a sea captain tells the story about Grendel's havoc at Hrothgar's court. Contrary to the bards' traditional stories, however, the sea captain's story is said to be real. Apparently, the sea captain in *Beowulf: Dragonslayer* is such a gifted storyteller, because he can even silence King Hygelac and his favourite hearth companions, warning them that 'before even a King makes merry, it is as well that he should know who may hear the laughter in the dark outside' (Sutcliff 2001, p. 9). The Geatish audience (as well as some modern readers) are immediately all ears, their response triggered perhaps as much by nail-biting anticipation as by sheer fright of what might be lurking in 'the blue dusk that thickened beyond the foreporch doorway' (Sutcliff 2001, p. 9).

The fact that the characters of storytellers appearing in Rosemary Sutcliff's novelette – Angelm the Geat (2001, pp. 8–9), the nameless sea captain (2001, pp. 8–13), a Danish harper (2001, pp. 31–2; 42), Hrothgar (2001, p. 44), even Beowulf himself (2001, p. 67) – are given such attention evidently stems from the author's intention to introduce not only the story itself, but also the intricate cultural context of the age, thus recreating the atmosphere of the original performance for the modern reader. Though Sutcliff sometimes appears to give full rein to her vivid imagination by engaging those who would not, as a rule, take an active part in the singing (i.e. Hrothgar and Beowulf),[4] it is quite possible that in *Beowulf: Dragonslayer* the high status enjoyed by courtly poets in early medieval societies was presented in a most accurate, if evidently fictional, light. Yet although they are frequently mentioned, the storytellers in no way dominate the plot or spoil its skilfully built structure. Indeed, their little episodes are so subtly interwoven in the main narrative that there is absolutely no feeling of redundancy and dullness in them, as the action moves at a fairly brisk pace towards its dramatic conclusion in Beowulf's ultimate combat with the dragon.

As for the other, less evident discrepancies between *Beowulf* and its Modern English adaptation by Rosemary Sutcliff, when seen as a whole, they do not in the least alter the invariably heroic–elegiac tone of the original account. The author's specific motives appear to be wide ranging, largely depending on the character of each modification (lexical, narrative as well as contextual). There is, however, no denying that what actually made Sutcliff adapt this Old English epic was a wish to make it more accessible to young readers. It is for this reason, then, that Rosemary Sutcliff regularly tries to clarify, in the very narrative itself, the cultural concepts that are often heavily footnoted in the more scholarly editions of *Beowulf* where, depending on the approach (e.g. historical vs. literary), they may sometimes constitute the reading goal in themselves.

Not surprisingly, Sutcliff focuses only on those aspects that might seem ambiguous or even completely incomprehensible to young minds. One such aspect is the somewhat enigmatic idea of *Wyrd*[5] which Rosemary Sutcliff probably sees as the Anglo-Saxon equivalent of the Greek *Moirae* or Roman *Parcae* 'who weaves the fates of men' (Sutcliff 2001, pp. 12, 27) and, 'at [their] fated hour' (2001, p. 90), 'cuts the web of [their] living from the loom' (2001, p. 48). Even though her depictions do not differ considerably from those found in *Beowulf* – 'Wyrd ungemete neah,/se þone gomelan gretan sceolde,/secean sawle hord, sundur gedælan/lif wið lice' (*Beowulf* 2420–3) 'Wyrd was immeasurably near, that which should meet the old man, seek his soul's hoard and take life from the body' – it is not hard to get the impression that hers is a far more personalized *Wyrd*.[6] With the absence of the Christian God – unless He is disguised under the fairly syncretic name of 'All-Father'[7] (Sutcliff 2001, pp. 33, 88–9) – *Wyrd* is in fact the principal moving spirit of the tale, one who chooses (Sutcliff 2001, pp. 27, 53), decrees (2001, p. 68), touches (2001, p. 80) and cuts (2001, p. 48).

Bearing in mind that *Beowulf: Dragonslayer* is far more likely to be approached by younger rather than older minds, Rosemary Sutcliff also makes sure that the rivers of blood, which might sometimes seem to flow uncontrollably in the Old English poem, would not be an aesthetic obstacle to the youthful readers. This does not mean, of course, that the Geatish warrior suddenly adheres to the policy of peaceful negotiations with each of the three foes that happen to cross his path. Through a cautious selection of images, the author manages to illustrate Beowulf's combats in a way that eschews the more gruesome details while, at the same time, not losing much of its original flavour. A good example of this less gory approach is the passage in which the title character is literally locked in a deadly struggle with the 'Death-Shadow that fills [people's] nights with horror' (Sutcliff 2001, p. 12), Grendel himself. Necessarily violent, of course, the fight is noticeably less brutal in the well-selected words of Rosemary Sutcliff than in the corresponding passage in *Beowulf*. When the nerve-racking wrestling match nears its blood-spattered climax, the ghastly fiend

> gathered himself for one last despairing effort to break free. Beowulf's hold was fierce as ever; yet none the less the two figures burst apart – and Grendel with a frightful shriek staggered to the doorway and through it, and fled wailing into the night, leaving his arm and shoulder torn from the roots in the hero's still unbroken grasp. (Sutcliff 2001, p. 38)

It is obviously startling enough to distress some of the more sensitive readers, yet even this is nowhere near the terrifying words originally found in the Old English poem: 'lic-sar gebad/atol æglæca; him on eaxle wearð/syn-dolh sweotol; seonowe onsprungon,/burston ban-locan' (*Beowulf* 815–8) 'a horrible wound appeared in the monster's shoulder, sinews split, burst the bone-lappings'. And so, whereas the anonymous poet focuses – with a medical-like precision – on the very act of fighting and its immediate effect on Grendel's body, Rosemary Sutcliff clearly favours the 'long shot' approach with her 'verbal camera' without showing too many details. In other words, Sutcliff spares her young audience whenever there is an oncoming threat of violence and bloodshed by providing a more general notion of the scene instead of prying into gruesome details.

## Language and style

When it comes to the language used by Rosemary Sutcliff in her retelling of *Beowulf*, it seems worthwhile to take a closer look at the different textual aspects which, for a number of reasons, either were or were not transposed from the Old English epic to its twentieth-century adaptation.

It has already been observed that the author of *Beowulf: Dragonslayer* does her best to remain as close as possible to the ancient spirit of the poem. However, had she stayed true to the alliterative metre, she almost certainly would have risked not to be understood by the young readers she wished to address. Her way of dealing with this formal obstacle is to use the more straightforward language of prose and to embellish it here and there with archaic words or, at times, even complete phrases, the meaning of which could be easily deducted from the context. By doing this, she is able to re-create – through the words' association with the past – the very spirit and atmosphere of '*gear-dagum*' (*Beowulf* 1) 'days of yore'.

Rosemary Sutcliff does not go as far as, for instance, the two notable Germanic purists Lee M. Hollander and J. R. R. Tolkien, whose works are often crammed with obsolete terms the sense of which may not always be clear to the less philologically minded reader.[8] Nevertheless, she does manage to make her language noticeably more archaic, albeit in most cases not necessarily less accessible. Among the most apparent archaisms in *Beowulf: Dragonslayer* is the author's recurrent use of 'fire-drake' – a verbatim translation of Old English *fyr-draca* (*Beowulf* 2689) – as a synonym for 'dragon'. Despite the fact that 'drake' may nowadays easily invoke more anatine connotations, it is not difficult to see that the intended meaning is semantically as well as etymologically identical with, among others, Old English *draca* or Old Norse *dreki* (both, of course, akin to Modern English *dragon*). In other words, even if somewhat unfamiliar at first, the term 'drake' – additionally clarified by its constant association with fire – is not beyond the immediate recognition of a teenage reader, and so may well serve as a solid 'support' in the lexical 'bridge' between Old English *Beowulf* and its Modern English adaptation.

It must be admitted, though, that occasionally the meaning of certain words and expressions found in *Beowulf: Dragonslayer* may at first seem obscure to those modern readers whose historical awareness of the period is usually next to none. These necessarily rare words, however, are principally specialized terms typically used to denote those aspects of Anglo-Saxon culture that have no direct correspondence in contemporary reality such as: 'mead-hall' (Sutcliff 2001, p. 8, from Old English *medu-seld*, *Beowulf* 3065), 'battle-sark' (Sutcliff 2001, pp. 88, 91; from Old English *syrce* for 'shirt, corselet, coat of mail', *Beowulf* 334, 550 and 1111) or 'saex' (Sutcliff 2001, p. 88, more correctly *seax*, Old English for a 'long knife'). Still, none of these words ever appear out of context and, with this device, Rosemary Sutcliff keeps her text comprehensible without pulling down all lexical barriers between the past and the present.

Another aspect of her deliberately archaized style in *Beowulf: Dragonslayer* is the recurrent use of kennings. These figurative – sometimes highly abstract – expressions in which two or more words are combined to illustrate a concept which may otherwise be expressed by a simple noun once formed a highly distinctive feature of all Germanic poetry (English and Norse in particular), but have almost effectively gone out of use since the early Middle Ages. Prior to that, though, kennings constituted a crucial element of the pre-literate stage of alliterative verse whose chief functions were to add a much more expressive colour and suggest associations without diverting one's attention from the core of what was being communicated by the poet. They may vary considerably from fairly straightforward (e.g. Old English *heofon-candel* 'heaven's candle', meaning 'the sun') to far more complicated ones (e.g. Old Norse *hösvan serk hrísgrímnis* 'bush-grinner's [i.e. wolf's] grey coat', meaning 'wolf's skin'). Memorized and paraphrased, kennings were indeed a powerful lexical tool by means of which Germanic poets could capture the imagination of their noble audiences.

Trying to stay as close as possible to the ancient character of Old English verse (though at the same time bearing in mind that such a genre shift necessitates the omission of some structural devices), Sutcliff decides not to get rid of the kennings completely, but rather to embellish her prose here and there with some kenning-like metaphors of necessarily less complex nature. In this way, the reader could become easily acquainted with the imaginative language of the earliest English poetry without being frequently distracted from the main plot. These metaphors include direct translations from the poem as well as Sutcliff's own similarly evocative creations. The former incorporate, for instance, such vivid expressions as 'Sail-Road' (Sutcliff 2001, p. 93, cf. Old English *segl-rad*, *Beowulf* 1429) or 'Whale's Road' (Sutcliff 2001, pp. 18, 29; cf. Old English *hron-rade*, *Beowulf* 10), both of course meaning 'the sea'. The latter feature the equally suggestive 'Death-Shadow-in-the-Dark' (Sutcliff 2001, p. 46) and 'Wolf-Woman of the Sea' (2001, p. 53), both referring to Grendel's monstrous mother, or 'Terror-that-Flies/Flew-by-Night', which is used twice (2001, pp. 79, 92) as a synonym for 'dragon'. Other notable 'kennings' include 'life-place' (Sutcliff 2001, p. 29) for 'heart', 'House-Lord' (2001, pp. 74, 85) for 'king' and 'Night-Stalkers' (2001, p. 47) for Grendel and his mother.

As indicated above, none of the aforementioned kenning-like expressions appear to be particularly challenging. Indeed, Rosemary Sutcliff seems to have deliberately chosen to incorporate a number of these hyphenated figures in order to make her style look more contemporaneous with that of the Old English epic and to immerse her young readers in a particular use of language. In fact, the remarkable simplicity and straightforwardness of this particular type of metaphorical language make *Beowulf: Dragonslayer* a thoroughly good read from beginning to end, a successfully medievalized tale of the never-ending struggle between good and evil.

Sutcliff's meticulous efforts to balance the old and the new may also be seen in the way her characters' words echo those that were put to vellum more than a thousand years ago. Among the most striking examples are the uplifting words of Beowulf who, having heard about the sudden death of Aschere, one of King Hrothgar's most beloved men, at the hands of Grendel's mother, reminds the old king not to 'sorrow . . . so grievously [for it] is better that a man should avenge his friend than mourn him overmuch' (Sutcliff 2001, p. 48). This is naturally a direct word-for-word translation of the gnomic-like verses uttered by the Old English poem's hero: 'Ne sorga, snotor guma! Selre bið æghwæm,/þæt he his freond wrece, þonne he fela murne' (*Beowulf* 1384–5).

Perhaps equally expressive and well fitting are the words of Wiglaf, Beowulf's only living relative, who bitterly reproaches his faint-hearted companions, declaring that 'death is better for a warrior than a life of shame' (Sutcliff 2001, p. 91). Here again Rosemary Sutcliff draws from the Old English poem where the very same young warrior states that 'Deað bið sella/eorla gehwylcum þonne edwit-lif' (*Beowulf* 2890–1).

If one tries to acquaint young readers with an acclaimed classic by employing the exact words of the source text, a direct translation or at least a paraphrase is necessary, even if the author risks that his or her style may be regarded as awkward. This approach was used in 1807 by Charles and Mary Lamb, whose well-known *Tales from Shakespeare* were meant to serve as an introduction to the study of England's greatest playwright. As observed in their book's preface,

> his [i.e. Shakespeare's] words are used whenever it seemed possible to bring them in; and in whatever has been added to give them the regular form of a connected story, diligent care has been taken to select such words as might least interrupt the effect of the beautiful English tongue in which he [i.e. Shakespeare] wrote. (Lamb and Lamb 2007, p. 5)

There is, of course, no direct evidence that Rosemary Sutcliff actually pursues the same purpose in her book, but it can hardly be denied that without such easily discernible (though never pushy) references to the highly formulaic language of the original poem her novelette would lose some of its ancient flavour, and so turn out to be less inspiring in its linguistic surface. Her scrupulous choice of vocabulary at no point distracts the readers from the plot's brisk pace, but rather enables them to enjoy both the fascinating content and the necessarily modified style of the oldest English epic.

# Conclusions

These are only some of the techniques that Rosemary Sutcliff successfully used when adapting the Old English classic. It would by far exceed the scope of this chapter to name and classify all of them here. Nonetheless, there are certain easily discernible, adaptational qualities of *Beowulf: Dragonslayer* which can be listed as follows:

1. use of straightforward prose instead of the highly figurative language of poetry to make it more accessible to the young reader;
2. modernization of narrative techniques to make them fit contemporary standards and the genre of the novel;
3. exclusion of narrative digressions to make the plot considerably more linear;
4. deliberate use of slightly archaic words to achieve the effect of an ancient tale;
5. inclusion of short phrases or even complete sentences taken directly from the original to suggest a close cultural connection with the poem;
6. attempts to clarify or interpret certain ambiguities arising from cultural discrepancies;
7. noticeable reduction in the amount of bloodshed in the three major combat passages; and, above all,
8. retaining the spirit of the Old English poem as closely as possible.

Considering that to several modern readers *Beowulf* might easily seem to be a fairly distant, perhaps even profoundly bizarre work of ancient provenance, Rosemary Sutcliff has produced a highly successful adaptation which has never been out of print and continues to entertain successive generations of tale-thirsty teenagers. Although her *Beowulf* novelette is not entirely free from certain textual or factual weaknesses (such as occasional lexical mannerisms and anachronisms), it clearly ranks, in the eyes of many, among the most successful attempts to retell the greatest Old English poem for young readers.

There seems to be a widespread agreement that adaptations of canonical texts (or classics) may be highly beneficial in their didactic role. Written specifically with young readers in mind, such texts should be well adjusted to their readers' evolving educational needs, age and gender; they should be both stimulating and instructive, exciting and inspiring. Considering all this, Rosemary Sutcliff's *Beowulf: Dragonslayer* appears to be just the right book to fill the beowulfian void on young readers' bookshelves and satisfy the sudden need for early medieval tales triggered by the popular works of T. H. White or J. R. R. Tolkien.

Its compressed narrative (aptly stripped of superfluous digressions and other minor departures from the main plot), bowdlerized here and there of the blood that flows almost uncontrollably in the Anglo-Saxon *Beowulf* and richly adorned with the colourful expressions borrowed from or inspired by the language of the original poem, has proved to be a highly effective adaptation of the classic, far exceeding the aforementioned stories by Strafford Riggs or Ian Serraillier. Rosemary Sutcliff's *Beowulf: Dragonslayer* is not merely a successful retelling of England's oldest epic – it is a valuable creation in its own right, a fascinating journey into our modern reception of the world of Anglo-Saxon culture and its literary legacy with a particular emphasis on the pre-Christian worship of heroism, fame and honour.

# Notes

1  Arguably the most striking reminiscence of *Beowulf* in J. R. R. Tolkien's novel is Bilbo's theft of a golden cup from Smaug's hoard which leads to the latter's rage, near destruction of Lake-town and the dragon's eventual death at the hand of Bard.

2  Some of the most notable works inspired by the Old English epic, but not necessarily following the original plot and mood of the poem are John Gardner's parallel novel *Grendel* (1971, later adapted into the animated film *Grendel Grendel Grendel*) and Tom Holt's satirical book *Who's Afraid of Beowulf?* (1988).

3  Should we accept Gale R. Owen-Crocker's idea that the so-called Lay of the Last Survivor (2247–66) be counted as one, though, the number of funerals in *Beowulf* would amount to four (Owen-Crocker 2009, pp. 61–84).

4  Although they were not formally excluded from public storytelling, Scandinavian noblemen would not normally venture into the verbal area reserved for professional poets.

5  In Anglo-Saxon culture, the mysterious concept of *Wyrd* roughly corresponds to that of fate. In Old Norse texts, it is sometimes personalized as Urðr, one of the Norns who rule the destiny of all creatures, human as well as divine.

6  This is expressed, for instance, by the author's consistent use of the relative pronoun 'who'.

7  The term 'All-Father' is of course a direct translation of Old Norse *Alföðr*, one of the many epithetic names for Odin, the chief god of the Germanic pantheon. It may, however, also refer to the Christian God, 'our Father in heaven'.

8  Cf., for instance, Hollander's *mickle* 'large' and *eftsoon* 'forthwith' in his translation of *The Poetic Edda* (2000, pp. 80, 301) or Tolkien's *rune conner* 'reader of runes' in *The Legend of Sigurd and Gudrún* (2010, p. 269).

## List of works cited

Allen, Woody (1982), 'Annie Hall', *Four Films of Woody Allen*. London: Random House, pp. 3–112.

*Beowulf: A Glossed Text* (2000), Alexander, Michael (ed.). London: Penguin.

Commire, Anne and Klezmer, Deborah (2001), *Women in the World History: a Bibliographical Encyclopedia*. Waterford: Yorkin Publications.

Cuddon, John Anthony (1991), *The Penguin Dictionary of Literary Terms and Literary Theory*. London: Penguin.

Hollander, Lee M. (trans) (2000), *The Poetic Edda*. Austin: University of Texas Press.

Lamb, Charles and Mary (2007, 1807), *Tales from Shakespeare: Designed for the Use of Young Persons*. London: Penguin.

Owen-Crocker, Gale R. (2009), *The Four Funerals in Beowulf*. Manchester: Manchester University Press.

Sutcliff, Rosemary (2001, 1961), *Beowulf: Dragonslayer*. London: Random House Children's Books.

Tolkien, J. R. R. (2006), 'Beowulf: the monsters and the critics', in Christopher Tolkien (ed.), *The Monsters and the Critics and Other Essays*. London: Harper Collins Publishers, pp. 5–48.

— (2010), *The Legend of Sigurd and Gudrún*, Christopher Tolkien (ed.). London: Harper Collins Publishers.

# 8

# The Kids of the Round Table – Arthurian Legends Adapted for Children and Young Adults

Anne Klaus

*Hic jacet Arthurus, Rex quondam, Rexque futurus.* According to Sir Thomas Malory's account in *Le Morte Darthur*,[1] this Latin phrase – translated 'Here lies Arthur, King once, and King in future' – was carved upon King Arthur's tomb at Glastonbury (Malory 1996, p. 794). At the beginning of the twenty-first century, one can dare to claim that the messianic prophecy 'that he shall come again' (Malory 1996, p. 793) has undoubtedly come true: King Arthur has returned, repeatedly, in literature; and his reign in this realm does not seem to perish. Traces of the Arthurian legend not only run like a thread through fiction for adults, but also stories targeted at children and young adults are teeming with Arthurian material. What are the hidden values in these stories which seem to strike a common chord and which are obviously thought to still cater for a modern readership of children and young adults although the legends abound with violent scenes and overt sexual references? Are the less palatable aspects of the legendary pretexts muted for a contemporary juvenile audience in the process of adaptation, just as contemporary adaptations of Charles Dickens' *Oliver Twist* are 'sanitized' as Liz Thiel shows convincingly in her chapter 'Downsizing Dickens'?

At its core, this chapter will demonstrate that especially fantasy stories for children and young adults feed vampirically on elements of the Arthurian legends. Although the existence of historical fiction or science fiction that takes up Arthurian motifs should not be denied, the focus will be laid on Arthurian fantasy, which has flourished as a veritable subgenre of Arthurian literature as its wonders and supernatural occurrences seem to lend themselves most readily to a revival of Arthuriana. In 1985, Thompson detected the trend that the greatest growth of Arthuriana was shown in modern fantasy (cf. Thompson 1985, p. 87). This claim is certainly still valid and proves to be continuing. Although at first glimpse one could argue that these modern adaptations rely on a whole range of Arthurian legends rather than on a single individual text, one particular source, namely Malory's *Le Morte Darthur*, stands out among the numerous Arthurian pretexts as a 'canonical' text which has been drawn upon for the majority of adaptations as will be shown in this chapter.

Yet, as valuable distinctions would get lost if one lumped all fantasy works that are infused with aspects of the Arthurian legend together, a typological approach seems expedient. I propose a distinction of three different ways of reviving the existing Arthurian material in fantasy fiction for children and young adults:

1. Retellings
2. Variations
3. References/Allusions

In what follows, I will outline one example for each of the three categories, including the various mechanisms of adapting and reworking the legends of King Arthur and his Knights of the Round Table.

## Retellings

By definition, retellings, as updated or retranslated versions of a pretext, are 'strictly limited by what is included in their sources. Whenever they go beyond them they become more than a retelling' (Thompson 1985, p. 12). Thompson therefore awards only a minor contribution to the growth of the Arthurian legend to the pure retellings of the stories about King Arthur and his noble knights. Yet, retellings of these originally adult texts for children and young adults can – if not explicitly adding to the legends' growth – foster the readers' familiarity with the medieval legends that have come to be a crucial part of Britain's cultural heritage. The longevity and continuous popularity of retellings furthermore affirms the apparent topicality of the themes and values embodied in the legends. Roger Lancelyn Green's *King Arthur and his Knights of the Round Table*, originally published in 1953 and based on Sir Thomas Malory's prose romance *Le Morte Darthur* (1485), has been reissued ceaselessly by Puffin Books, the most recent edition in the Puffins Classics series being from 2008. A comparison of the medieval pretext and the retelling, which has come to be a 'standard version' for children (Lynch 2004, p. 28), should shed some light on the question of how faithfully and accurately the original pretext is taken up, and how useful the modern versions are as introductions to the canonical original.

Malory's famous *Le Morte Darthur*, which consists of twenty-one books altogether, has been repackaged by Green into four books, fairly maintaining the episodic character of the original. Yet, a process of rearrangement, abridgement and establishment of a thematic hierarchy is undeniable. 'Adapters always have to decide what to keep and what to cut, for no children's versions except those of Howard Pyle have approached Malory in length' (Lynch 2004, p. 2). As Green declares, his aim was to weave a 'fabric consisting of all the best-known adventures, exploits, and quests of the most famous knights of the Round Table, and a few lesser-known stories which fit into the whole' (Green, Author's Note 2008, p. xiii). Green certainly applies the method of telescoping and blending stories that had been told separately by Malory, yet, strikingly, there are hardly any notable broader thematic omissions. Apparently, the old stories of King Arthur and his fellow knights still encompass values that are deemed worth preserving in contemporary literature. Certainly, Malory's stories lend themselves for modern retellings for children because 'many of them feature aspiring male youths, determined to make good in the adult world' (Lynch 2004, p. 5). In her introduction to *Adapting the Arthurian Legends for Children*, Barbara Tepa Lupack acknowledges: 'When you're young, you respond to the story of the fellowship and the great deeds …' (2004, p. xiv) rather than to the romance and the tragedy. It has to be acknowledged that *Le Morte Darthur* 'is not much concerned with its heroes as children, but it returns repeatedly to their transition from youth to proven knighthood, often involving the assistance of experienced older figures' (Lynch 2004, p. 5). The medieval stories with their web of quests and tests find their perfect reverberation in retellings for children and young adults as the latter are often likewise concerned with the renegotiation of childhood, adolescence and maturity. Incidents like the acquisition of the sword or the discovery of the Holy Grail are rites of passage that mark the transformation of the knights (cf. Kellog 1993, p. 58). The presentation of apparent anti-heroes who are insignificant at the beginning of the stories but develop into courageous and persistent heroes in the course of their quests – Arden and Lorenz use the term 'Perceval pattern' (Arden and Lorenz 2002, p. 432) – is excellently suited for a target group of children and young adults. By depicting the knights as common or even detrimental, the texts offer to the readers a basis for identification with these ordinary characters who vicariously embark on various adventures. Furthermore, the quest itself 'does test the extent to which the protagonists are prepared to follow the standards of conduct that they hold dear' (Thompson 1985, p. 114).

Key scenes of questing, steadfastness and the finding of one's rightful place in society are adopted by Green most faithfully, such as the accounts of young Arthur's seizure of the sword in the stone which mark the beginning of the latter's kingship and ultimately his entrance into adulthood. Malory's wording

> there was seen in the churchyard, against the high altar, a great stone four square, like unto a marble stone; and in midst thereof was like an anvil of steel a foot on high, and therein stuck a fair sword naked by the point, and letters there were written in gold about the sword that said thus: Whoso pulleth out this sword of this stone and anvil, is rightwise king born of all England. (Malory 1996, p. 6)

is imitated almost verbatim by Green:

> for there was seen, though no man saw it come, a great square slab of marble-stone in the churchyard, and on the stone an anvil of iron, and set point downwards a great, shining sword of steel thrust deep into the anvil. . . . Round about the anvil they found letters of gold set in the great stone, and the letters read thus:
> WHOSO PULLETH OUT THIS SWORD FROM THIS STONE AND ANVIL IS THE TRUE-BORN KING OF ALL BRITAIN. (Green 2008, pp. 5–6)

The miraculous revelation of the aristocratic status in a 'kind of "blood will tell" move' is a typical feature of romance (Fuchs 2004, p. 6). Green fully takes up this episode of the royal heritage, hidden and unveiled, from the medieval original.

Not only is Arthur, at a moment's notice, transformed from the hitherto 'unknown boy' (Green 2008, p. 10) into the 'true and only son of the good King Uther Pendragon' (Green 2008, p. 11) by pulling out the sword. The recurring motif of the prophecy as a means to reveal and manifest a knight's special status can also be found in the foreshadowing of Sir Galahad's heroic deed. Long before the birth of Galahad, the Siege Perilous has been reserved by Merlin for the coming knight who is destined to win the quest of the Holy Grail. Again, Green sticks close to his pretext: In letters of gold it is written on the Siege Perilous that 'FOUR HUNDRED AND FIFTY AND FOUR YEARS AFTER THE DEATH OF OUR LORD JESUS CHRIST THIS SIEGE SHOULD BE FILLED' (Green 2008, p. 271), whereas Malory's text reads 'Four hundred winters and four and fifty accomplished after the passion of our Lord Jesu Christ ought this siege to be fulfilled' (Malory 1996, p. 565). When Galahad sits on the Siege Perilous the inscription changes in both versions into 'THIS IS THE SIEGE OF SIR GALAHAD THE HIGH PRINCE' (Green 2008, p. 274) or in Malory's case 'This is the siege of Galahad, the haut prince' (Malory 1996, p. 567).

Here again, when retelling the events of the destined Grail Knight, a straightforward questing topic, Green studies Malory's original wording meticulously. The comparisons reveal that Green mainly keeps modernizations and alterations in diction and a change of register to a minimum and that his work largely echoes the language of the original. Furthermore, if one was simply to list the characters and key events featured both in Malory and in Green, Green would certainly get a top score for faithfulness to the original.

Yet, while he remains close to the overall original storyline, more subtle aspects of Malory's accounts are muted in favour of the aforementioned focus on the quest patterns. Green has made obvious choices which episodes to cut within the borders of the individual Arthurian stories and which ones to keep – choices that speak volumes of the author's concept of his target group. Conscious omissions in retellings for children automatically reveal the idea of childhood and of what is suitable for children in the particular time and culture from which the retelling springs.[2]

In Green's case, clear deviations from the original can be detected in his tackling of the sexual implications inherent in Malory's text. Although with regard to plot coherence he cannot dodge the implications completely, the innuendos are downplayed on various occasions. While Malory devotes more than a chapter on Uther Pendragon's desire for the Dame Igraine and on '*how by the mean of Merlin he lay by the duchess and gat Arthur*' (Malory 1996, p. 2), Green settles the whole issue of Arthur's conception with merely three sentences:

> But Uther fell in love with Gorlois' wife, the lovely Igrayne, and there was battle between them, until Gorlois fell, and Uther married his widow. He visited her first in the haunted castle of Tintagel, the dark castle by the Cornish sea, and Merlin watched over their love. One child was born to Uther and Igrayne. (Green 2008, p. 4)

No child reader could possibly infer from this passage that Uther, disguised as Igraine's husband Gorlois, outwits the lady unabashedly to mate with her.

A similarly chaste omission can be found in Green's retelling of the story of Lancelot and Elaine. Malory's description of Lancelot who is deceived by the lady Elaine, whom he thinks to be his beloved Guinevere, is briefly mentioned, but even Malory's spare details are reduced to an ellipsis by Green: 'indeed Brysen the enchantress had made all things ready at the Castle of Case . . . . The morning dawned grey and ominous, and Launcelot awoke to find the Lady Elaine sleeping by his side' (Green 2008, p. 257).

And when Green retells the connection between Merlin and the Lady Nimue, no word is wasted on the fact that Merlin 'fell in a dotage on the damosel' (Malory 1996, p. 88), that he would not leave her side – indeed, Malory's descriptions of Merlin's lascivious advances border on stalking – and on his eager attempts at the lady's 'maidenhood' (Malory 1996, p. 89), not even stopping short of taking her unwillingly ('would have had her privily away by his subtle crafts' [Malory 1996 p. 88]). Consequently, the fact that Green's Nimue enchants Merlin and traps the wizard in a dark cave under the earth lacks any reasonable explanation in the retelling.

One has to admit that the fact that '[a]ll retellings imbue new value' (Stahlberg 2008, p. 210) obviously does not stop short of Green's work. His treatment of Arthurian sex scenes borders on censorship, an old-fashioned attitude that Andrew Lynch judges as the result of Green's former profession as a schoolmaster (cf. Lynch 2004, p. 28). No doubt the author has omitted this aspect not only because the passages seem discordant for decent heroic role models but also because he has to cater for a different target group. Nevertheless, Raymond Thompson rightly laments this noticeable trend of removing all traces of sexual immorality claiming that '[c]onsidering the amount of illicit sexuality in Arthurian tradition and how crucial it is to the meaning of certain key events, this effort to protect the innocence of young people cannot but rob the legend of much of its power' (Thompson 1985, p. 13). Sexual intricacies are faded out in order to place the quest stories and the knights' 'future roles in maturity' (Lynch 2004, p. 5) in the foreground. This subliminal thematic refocalization goes along with a refined change of tone when it comes to the portrayal of characters.

Retellings can effectively shape the overall colouring of the original pretext, as '[b]y including or omitting certain details, characterization may be subtly altered' (Thompson 1985, p. 14). This subtle process of change can be observed in Green's retelling as well, who to some extent approaches his pretext like Rosemary Sutcliff, who, in the author's note to her *The Sword and the Circle*, states in a straightforward manner that although she follows Malory 'in the main', she has not done so 'slavishly' because every minstrel 'adds and leaves out and embroiders and puts something of himself into each retelling' (Sutcliff 1981, p. 7).

Green adds moral evaluations of the set of characters to Malory's original. While readers of Malory are hardly provided with any insight into the emotional interior of King Arthur and the knights of the Round Table and their moral convictions have primarily to be inferred from their external actions, Green characterizes them in various scenes directly by means of subtle additions. Especially Green's treatment of the figure of the enchanter Merlin gives his retelling a new touch. Malory's neutral references to the wizard as 'Merlin' are adjusted by Green, who repeatedly talks of 'the wise Merlin' (Green 2008, p. 4), 'the good enchanter' (2008, pp. 5, 11, 72) and 'Merlin's wisdom' (2008, p. 17). Of course, one has to admit that Green stresses Merlin's wisdom and goodness at the expense of the wizard's initial appearance in the medieval pretexts as an ambiguous figure, a manipulative trickster sired by an incubus and possessing supernatural powers capable of destruction as well as welfare. Furthermore, as already pointed out, the lascivious nature of the wizard in his relationship to Nimue is simply muted.

Other key figures of the original legend receive additional characterizations by Green as well. For instance, when Sir Kay asks the young Arthur to ride for his sword, which he will need for the tournament in London, Arthur's reply in Malory is as follows: 'I will well, said Arthur, and rode fast after the sword' (Malory 1996, p. 7). Green, however, adds a subordinate sentence which clearly channels the readers' sympathies for the character: '"Certainly I will," said Arthur, who was always ready to do anything for other people, and back he rode to the town' (Green 2008, p. 7). While Malory does not 'plumb the depths or even scratch the surface of the character to explore feelings or motivations' (Spivack and Staples 1994, p. 61) and his characters tend to appear as archetypes rather than as individuals (cf. Spivack and Staples 1994, p. 1), Green already shows glimpses of the characters' inner feelings and motivations and shows a moralizing tendency which will find even greater attention in the variations of the medieval legends.

## Variations

This type of adaptation of the Arthurian legends is what Raymond Thompson calls going beyond what is included in the sources (cf. Thompson 1985, p. 12); however, the relationship to the original is still observable in these modern variations. In 'Why Do Some Stories Keep Returning?', Mary Frances Zambreno gives a convincing reason for the great suitability of the Matter of Britain to reappear moulded in various shapes: In reference to D. H. Green's *The Beginnings of Medieval Romance: Fact and Fiction*, she detects various 'windows of opportunity' in the legends, 'gaps that may be filled in by other stories, new stories, and perspectives omitted from or slighted in the original narrative' (Zambreno 2010, p. 119). These empty spaces contained in the framework of the Arthurian stories allow for subsequent authors to 'fill in the blanks' (Zambreno 2010, p. 121); and usually writers 'choose to develop one episode from the legend' (Thompson 1985, p. 121) instead of tackling the Arthurian myth as a whole. Open gaps in the Matter of Britain are, for example, the female perspective on the Arthurian legends and the closer examination of the background stories and motivations of figures like Guenevere and Morgan le Fay, as provided, for instance, by Marion Zimmer Bradley or Gillian Bradshaw, and also stories about the childhood and the coming of age of various characters can plug some of the existing holes in the legends.

To attract a young readership to the Arthurian legends and to allow for a greater identification, the early years of traditional figures like Arthur, Kay, Bedivere or Gawain are eagerly scrutinized (cf. Thompson 1985, p. 177). These stories remain available for the telling as they are – if at all – only briefly mentioned by the medieval authors; in fact, a sheer variety of gaps are filled, Nancy Springer's teen fantasy *I am Mordred: A Tale of Camelot* (1999) or T. A. Barron's *Lost Years of Merlin* (1996) being only two examples out of the immense field of variations.

T. H. White's classic *The Sword in the Stone* (1938), the opening instalment of his *The Once and Future King*, is still among the most famous and popular variations of King Arthur's story. The first volume of the series recounts the boyhood of Wart, who later becomes King Arthur. It takes place at the castle of his foster father, Sir Ector, and delineates the education for kingship that the young lad, who is still unaware of his destiny, receives from the magician Merlyn.[3] Thus, White devotes a whole book on incidents that are either completely neglected by Malory or are just depicted in a few paragraphs. This shift in the lifespan that is taken into focus automatically brings about a shift in themes that are discussed: Arthur's tense relationship to his foster brother Kay, his struggle with his orphan status, and especially his blossoming under the tutelage of the wizard Merlyn become core issues.

White, who brings the cast of Malory's *Morte Darthur* vividly to life, 'gives us an explanation of their psyches, their visions and ideals, the significance of their lives' (Mathews 2002, p. 113) and thus provides a personal colouring which exceeds the careful first steps in Green's retelling by far. By means of depicting the initially close but later diminishing friendship of the Wart (a name bestowed to the young Arthur by Kay 'because it rhymed with Art, which was short for his real name' (White 1998, p. 7)) and Sir Ector's 'proper son' (White 1998, p. 15), Kay, White weaves a thematic net which enables the author to insert topics of rivalry and identity crises which might capture his target group.

> Proportionately as the day became nearer, the two boys drifted apart: for Kay did not care to associate with the Wart any longer on the same terms, because he would need to be more dignified as a knight, and could not afford to have his squire on intimate terms with him. The Wart, who would have to be the squire, followed him about disconsolately as long as he was allowed to do so, and then went off full miserably to amuse himself alone, as best he might. (White 1998, p. 307)

The Wart's future prospects as an orphan seem limited as only Sir Ector's biological son can claim the title of knight. The Wart is assured of his ostensible inferiority to Kay whom he follows like a 'hero-worshipper' (White 1998, p. 15). When the two boys are caught by the witch, Madame Mim, he writes Kay's name on the goat's hoof to be seen by the rescuers because he considers Kay more important than himself (cf. White 1998, p. 90). Throughout the whole story, the Wart defends Kay's behaviour of superiority and submits himself to the future knight as his servant: 'As soon as he commands me, I will do exactly what he says. Honestly, I think Kay is a good person, and I am not sulking a bit' (White 1998, p. 313). Even when he pulls the sword out of the stone, he does not act for his own ends but for Kay who left his own sword behind in an inn: "'People,' cried the Wart. "I must take this sword. It is not for me, but for Kay. I will bring it back'" (White 1998, p. 343). The young boy remains unaware of his special status as the future king of Britain and of the truth about his royal heritage which is withheld from him until the very end of the book. Here again we find the issue of apparent anti-heroes and inconspicuous figures who will rise to perform great deeds, but this time the issue is enriched with manifold emotional insights.

The Wart's cluelessness about his special fate as depicted by White provides for a sanctuary of ignorance, a space in which the young boy can develop fully while remaining modest, prudent and unpretentious – each of them reflecting the four cardinal virtues of chivalry (prudence, justice, restraint or temperance and courage or fortitude). On the surface, these virtues will be of advantage in Arthur's future role as king, but on a subliminal level, they are, of course, also recommended to the young readers. This presentation of covetable traits and values definitely finds its peak in the tuition that the young boy receives from the magician Merlyn which lacks any equivalent in the medieval pretexts, but is put centre stage in White's variation. Merlyn's main aim is to widen the Wart's horizon by transforming his pupil into various creatures and thus letting the boy get an inside look into different concepts of life. In his extraordinary lessons, which are modelled on the still widespread idea of learning by doing, the Wart is taught useful worldly wisdom. When he is, for example, showing off as a fish, he is reminded that 'discretion is the better part of valour' (White 1998, p. 66). The animals that Wart encounters during his metamorphic adventures are rather 'shrewd caricatures of adults' (Lassen-Séger 2001) and the diverse interactions with them offer him various possible training grounds and thus can contribute to his learning about the world and his increasing self-confidence and responsibility: 'Education is experience, and the essence of experience is self-reliance' (White 1998, p. 64).

That a proper education and the respect for other creatures pays off is once again stressed in the final scene set in London: After the Wart fails twice to extract the sword from the anvil, a new creation of White's pen, he cries for help and is immediately surrounded by 'hundreds of old friends', animals and humans he has made friends with in the course of his education (cf. White 1998, p. 344). By enumerating all creatures that assemble around the chosen boy, T. H. White stresses how the Wart's respect, which he showed in the course of his life for these individuals, is rewarded with their joined power in times of need, a straightforward example of benefitting charity, and the importance of communal strength. The Wart's love for others is rewarded, for, in front of the stone, the creatures encourage him and thus support him to pull the sword out of the stone: '"Come along, *Homo sapiens*, for all we humble friends of yours are waiting to cheer." The Wart walked up to the great sword for the third time. He put out his right hand softly and drew it out as gently as from a scabbard' (White 1998, p. 345). The individualization of the hero and the insight into his inner world of insecurities as well as his moral concepts encourage identification with the young boy. The values of the old legends are renegotiated and partly updated by White, putting integrity, modesty, tolerance and stamina above mere physical strength, valor and martial prowess.

Apart from the targeted plotline, White also pays great attention at visualizing his medieval, slightly nostalgic setting for young readers by 'providing it with a rich supply of detail in order to recreate the Arthurian world' (Thompson 2004, p. 131). He supplies an abundance of details not only on the landscape and medieval castles but also on those fields of medieval activities, such as haymaking, with which his contemporary child readership might not be familiar. These affectionate depictions of the scenery combined with the delightful, comical side characters with which White peoples his story, such as the outlaws or the 'bumbling King Pellinore' (Thompson 1985, p. 126), 'make up the nuts and bolts of children's adventure stories' (Jackson 2009, p. 57).

Yet again we find a one-sided portrayal of the originally elusive Merlin whom White lifts from the traditions of the past, creates entirely anew (cf. Spivack and Staples 1994, p. 19), and 'lovingly idealize[s]' (Ibid.: 3). White's Merlin remains a 'credible character' (Ibid.: 19), but unfortunately his well-meant characterization of Merlyn with absent-mindedness and his reversed life span lays the ground for a hair-raising 1963 Disney rendition in which the wizard's power is diminished 'pitifully, making him a comic figure, an adult buffoon whose magic seems more playful and entertaining than mysterious or fearful. It underestimates children, for it doesn't give them anything difficult to work through, to imagine, to practice' (Kellog 1993, pp. 66–7):

> One wonders what Arthur has learned from such a bumbling and unfocused figure, as Merlin skids in at the end of the film, on a visit from the twentieth century in his beach-wear and sunglasses, offering moral support to the newly crowned, reluctant kid-king Arthur. (Kellog 1993, p. 67)

# References/Allusions

Until now, the focus lay on the works which I termed 'variations of the legends'; this terminology includes all adaptations which are either closely tied to the original plots, or which at least fill the gaps of the medieval pretexts and thus form complementary stories. The next category I aim to introduce comprises those works that are relatively detached from and merely include references and allusions to the Arthurian legends. Instead of providing an exhaustive recreation, the Arthurian elements in these works 'may constitute no more than a minor borrowing, like a name or an evocative situation' (Thompson 1985, p. 136). Examples are manifold and only a few will be taken up in the following paragraphs to illustrate this type of modern rendition.

Most strikingly, fantasy literature for children and young adults seems to be saturated with Merlin-avatars (Merlin is probably the Arthurian figure evoked most often in modern fiction, easily outranking Arthur or Lancelot). The wise mentor and his affiliation with the young Arthur in the Arthurian cycle of tales function as the most popular prototype for the presentation of many tutors in modern fantasy fiction. These figures are often elderly people who sublimate their experiences of life into nuggets of wisdom which they are ready to pass on to the young protagonists: Doubtlessly, Susan Cooper's Lyon Merriman in *The Dark is Rising*, a mysterious and ageless figure, incorporates the mythic wizard Merlin in his transcendence of the limitations of time and space as well as in his spiritual guidance and inspiration offered to the young protagonist Will (cf. Spivack and Staples 1994, p. 22). Merriman helps the young Will Stanton in his search for his identity and provides him with necessary information for his quest. In the other volumes of Cooper's series, such as in *Over Sea, Under Water*, he appears as Great-Uncle Merry and is a guiding figure for the Drew children, his name always bearing resemblance to his famous counterpart. Being tall and straight, 'with a lot of very thick, wild, white hair' and a fiercely curved nose (Cooper 2007, p. 3), he also comes very close to the stereotypical depiction of the wizard Merlin. It is noteworthy that neither Geoffrey of Monmouth nor Thomas Malory refer to Merlin's outer appearance. However, the general notion of the wizard as a bearded elder goes back to the early descriptions of Robert de Boron. Furthermore, the earliest paintings show him as an old man with a flowing white beard and a midnight blue robe, such as a French thirteenth-century miniature manuscript illustration in Robert de Boron's *Histoire de Merlin*, or the illustrations accompanying the Grail story *L'Estoire du Graal* from the fourteenth century, which certainly have fostered this popular image. Merlin's recognizable outward appearance is also assigned to the headmaster Professor Dumbledore in the *Harry Potter* series ('He had several feet of long silver hair and beard, half-moon spectacles and an extremely crooked nose' (Rowling 1999, p. 71)). Furthermore, Gandalf in Tolkien's *The Lord of the Rings* ('An old man' with a 'long white beard and bushy eyebrows that stuck out beyond the brim of his hat' wearing a 'tall pointed blue hat, a long grey cloak, and a silver scarf' (Tolkien 2002, p. 24)) resembles the model of the legendary magician. And Amanda Hemingway's cast in her *Sangreal* trilogy also includes a Merlin derivative, the ageless, 'fat and placid and kindly' (Hemingway 2006a, p. 17) wizard Bartlemy. Hemingway plays on his function as a Merlin figure in her stories by having him wear an 'enormous dark-blue dressing gown with stars on it' (Hemingway 2006b, p. 12), a clear jesting commentary on the popular image. Despite portraying Bartlemy as slightly eccentric, Hemingway – just like T. H. White, whose Merlin figure remains the culmination of peculiarity – retains an affectionate and ironic undertone when it comes to the wizardly tutor. Furthermore, in both cases, the mentors' wisdom is undoubtedly stressed and valued. Hemingway shows an obvious awareness of the tradition her Merlin-figure is built upon which borders on metafiction. By modelling her tutor playfully on the popular Merlin figure, Hemingway deliberately and ironically evokes a set of fixed associations and makes the reader reflect upon genre conventions.

It is conspicuous that in the majority of fantasy stories for children and young adults which include these old and wise Merlin figures, these characters are portrayed as superior human beings who offer guidance and inspiration to the saviours and serve as their role models. These aged figures usually form a contrast to children's innocence and naivety. As their careful considerations, their experience, and their reflective characters contrast with the children's unwise and naïve behaviour they are apt for the role as teachers which they often claim in the stories. The values that these figures transmit are naturally transmitted to the readership as well (cf. Kellog 1993, p. 58).

Other popular elements that are borrowed from the Arthurian legends and woven subtly into a completely new context are the legendary grail (e.g. it belongs to those items that the children in Cooper's *The Dark is Rising* series have to find to defeat the Dark, and the protagonist Nathan in Hemingway's *Sangreal* trilogy has to venture into parallel universes in his dream to retrieve the three grail relics – the cup, the sword and the crown), and the sword-in-the-stone episode, which, for instance, occurs in an altered form in Tamora Pierce's *Song of the Lioness* quartet (1983–88). In a scene that is highly reminiscent of King Arthur's claim of the sword, Pierce's female knight-to-be Alanna accompanied by her mentor Myles (yet another Merlin figure) finds her sword behind 'a great piece of stone' which nobody so far has been able to remove (cf. Pierce 2005, pp. 191–2). Surely some knowledge of the Arthurian elements is taken for granted to fully appreciate the intertextual reference here; if successful, a 'strong bond of complicity' (Malarte-Feldman 2003, p. 210) between readers and authors is forged. In any case, although the 'borrowings are largely removed from their Arthurian context, they do retain some of their traditional associations, and these associations do enrich the novels' (Thompson 1985, p. 114). Subconscious 'enrichment' is one of the reasons why some authors of fiction for children and young adults deliberately evoke associations with the Arthurian legends and incorporate elements of the latter in their otherwise independent plots, and why authors, who create pieces of literature that on the surface have no relation to Arthuriana whatsoever, deem it benefitting to decorate their works with Arthurian connotations. With their underlying Arthurian themes, these authors prove that 'despite recurrent efforts somehow to leave it behind, modernity continues to engage with romance, alternately embracing and rejecting it as a privileged mode of access to an idealized past, a vehicle for nostalgia, magic, and the imagination' (Fuchs 2004, p. 100). Those wishing to gloss over the allusions can do so without losing the thread of the narratives (cf. Latham 2008, p. 225), but for the readers who recognize the connections, an enhanced reading experience awaits and the intertextual insinuations make up a large part of the novels' attraction for a dual audience of both children and adults.

## Conclusion

As outlined above, the canonical Arthurian tradition is 'remythologized' in the modern works for children (Spivack 2004, p. 154), be it by omitting original aspects (e.g. sexual allusions) as to be found in the retellings, filling in existing gaps in the legends and thus illuminating new facets (especially the character's childhood, their inner life and their motivations) or by using the nostalgic Arthurian connotation as an ingredient, a background layer for completely new stories. It is exactly this protean nature, the 'mutability or plasticity of the legend', which offers the 'opportunity for later generations to remake the Matter of Britain into something relevant to their own needs' (Zambreno 2010, p. 118). The versions for children and young adults thus allow a determination of what the authors see as the essentials of the originals and provide a reading of the medieval material through the lens of writers in their respective time. The new versions automatically provide 'vital insights into the culture' (Lupack 2004, p. xiv) and the values from which they derive. Thus, in Pierce's sword-and-sorcery tetralogy, for instance, the episodic character of the chivalric legends is contained (each book ends with a cliffhanger which gives grounds to the readers' hopes for more knightly adventures), while the conventional male orientation is interrogated and twisted gender-wise (the destined knight is actually a girl). Pierce's work 'hence revalue[s] notions of the heroic, contributing towards the evolution of a contemporary female hero paradigm' (Stephens and McCallum 1998, p. 91).

Thus, new variations can surely acquaint readers with the original canon of Arthurian stories, but they exceed this look backwards by generating facets of the legends that might otherwise remain inaccessible and by transforming the legends into ever new, exuberant stories. They permeate, and thus help to construe a common cultural knowledge about the 'Matter of Britain' across the ages. '[I]t is apparent that the evolution of that story is not yet finished' (Lacy and Ashe 1988, p. 289).

## Notes

1 While most contemporary versions use *D'arthur*, the original spelling is *Darthur* as maintained in the Wordsworth edition used for this chapter.

2 A similar observation is made by Liz Thiel in 'Downsizing Dickens'. She claims that editorial decisions and sanitizations are 'inextricably linked with assumptions about the child reader, notions of suitability and an acute awareness of the moral implications of a text' (p. 154 in this volume).

3 '[S]ince the later books are for adult rather than younger readers' (Thompson 2004, p. 131) and the 'mood of the books grows increasingly somber and disillusioned as they move towards the tragic conclusion' (Thompson 1985, p. 127) – although here again we find characters, such as Gawain and Lancelot, who are enriched with an embellished childhood – the focus will remain on the first volume exclusively in this chapter.

## List of works cited

Arden, Heather and Lorenz, Kathryn (2002), 'The ambiguity of the outsider in the Harry Potter stories and beyond', in W. Wright and S. Kaplan (eds), *The Image of the Outsider in Literature, Media, and Society*. Colorado Springs: Society for the Interdisciplinary Study of Social Imagery, pp. 430–2.

Cooper, Susan (2007, 1965), *Over Sea, Under Stone*. New York: Margaret K. Mc Elderry.

Fuchs, Barbara (2004), *Romance (The New Critical Idiom)*. New York: Routledge.

Green, R. L. (2008, 1953), *King Arthur and his Knights of the Round Table*. New York: Puffin Classics.

Hemingway, Amanda (2006a), *The Greenstone Grail*. New York: Del Rey.

— (2006b), *The Traitor's Sword*. London: HarperVoyager.

Jackson, Aaron Isaac (2009), 'Writing Arthur, writing England: myth and modernity in T. H. White's *The Sword in the Stone*'. *The Lion and the Unicorn*, 33(1): 44–59.

Kellog, Judith L. (1993), 'The dynamics of dumbing: the case of Merlin'. *The Lion and the Unicorn*, 17(1): 57–72.

Lacy, Norris J. and Ashe, Geoffrey (1988), *The Arthurian Handbook*. New York: Garland.

Lassen-Séger, Maria (2001), 'Exploring otherness: animal metamorphosis of the fictive child', *15th Biennial Congress of the International Research Society for Children's Literature: change and renewal in children's literature*. Warmbaths, South Africa: 20–4 August 2001, viewed 7 September 2009, URL: www.childlit.org.za/ irsclpaplassenseger.html.

Latham, Don (2008), 'Empowering adolescent readers: intertextuality in three novels by David Almond'. *Children's Literature in Education*, 39(3): 213–26.

Lupack, B. T. (2004), 'Introduction', in B. T. Lupack (ed.), *Adapting the Arthurian Legends for Children. Essays on Arthurian Juvenile*. New York: Palgrave, pp. xiii–xxi.

Lynch, Andrew (2004), '*Le Morte Darthur* for children: Malory's third tradition', in B. T. Lupack (ed.), *Adapting the Arthurian Legends for Children. Essays on Arthurian Juvenile*. New York: Palgrave, pp. 1–49.

Malarte-Feldman, Claire (2003), 'Folk materials, re-visions, and narrative images: the intertextual games they play'. *Children's Literature Association Quarterly*, 28(4): 210–8.

Malory, Sir Thomas (1996), *Le Morte Darthur*. Ware: Wordsworth.

Mathews, Richard (2002), *Fantasy. The Liberation of Imagination*. New York: Routledge.

Pierce, Tamora (2005), *Alanna. The First Adventure*. New York: Simon Pulse.

Rowling, Joanne K. (1999), *Harry Potter and the Prisoner of Azkaban*. London: Bloomsbury.

Spivack, Charlotte (2004), 'Susan Cooper's "The Dark is Rising"', in B. T. Lupack (ed.), *Adapting the Arthurian Legends for Children. Essays on Arthurian Juvenile*. New York: Palgrave, pp. 139–59.

Spivack, Charlotte and Staples, Roberta L. (1994), *The Company of Camelot. Arthurian Characters in Romance and Fantasy*. Westport: Greenwood.

Stahlberg, Lesleigh Cushing (2008), *Sustaining Fictions. Intertextuality, Midrash, Translation, and the Literary Afterlife of the Bible*. New York: T & T Clark.

Stephens, John and McCallum, Robyn (1998), *Retelling Stories, Framing Culture. Traditional Story and Metanarratives in Children's Literature*. New York: Garland.

Sutcliff, Rosemary (1981), *The Sword and the Circle: King Arthur and the Knights of the Round Table*. New York: Dutton.

Thompson, Raymond H. (1985), *The Return from Avalon. A Study of the Arthurian Legend in Modern Fiction*. Wesport: Greenwood Press.

— (2004), 'The sense of place in Arthurian fiction for younger readers', in B. T. Lupack (ed.), *Adapting the Arthurian Legends for Children. Essays on Arthurian Juvenile*. New York: Palgrave, pp. 123–38.

Tolkien, J. R. R. (2002), *The Lord of the Rings*. London: HarperCollins.

White, T. H. (1998, 1938), *The Sword in the Stone*. London: HarperCollins.

Zambreno, Mary Frances (2010), 'Why do some stories keep returning? Modern Arthurian fiction and the narrative structure of romance'. *Essays in Medieval Studies*, 26. Illinois Medieval Association, 117–27.

# 9

# Downsizing Dickens: Adaptations of *Oliver Twist* for the Child Reader

Elizabeth Thiel

There are numerous adaptations of classic texts designed to appeal to the child reader. Browsing in bookshops or online is likely to yield a myriad of publications ostensibly derived from the classics, but reconfigured, re-presented and generally colourfully illustrated for a young market. There is a breadth of literature, from Sam Ita's pop-up version of *Moby Dick* (2007) to Marcia Williams' strip cartoons of *Mr William Shakespeare's Plays* (2000); there are retellings for a child of eight or nine and grittier graphic novels for an older readership. Among adaptations of the classics, Charles Dickens' *Oliver Twist* (1838) remains a popular choice, with editions ranging from early reader to young adult. Yet, examination of contemporary adaptations of Dickens' novel for a child reader exposes both the potential problems inherent to the adaptation process and the manner in which some texts can serve to diminish the validity of the source material. While adaptations necessarily reflect, to some degree, contemporary ideologies of the child, such emphases can seemingly result in a sanitization that significantly impoverishes the source text and simultaneously undermines its value as a socio-historic artefact of relevance to a contemporary reader.

Adaptation of the classics has long been a controversial issue. Orion publishers, launching a range of compact editions of classic texts three years ago as 'great reads in half the time', allegedly met 'howls of indignation' from literary purists, according to a report in *The Times* newspaper, and were accused of patronizing readers (Hoyle 2007, n. p.). In contrast, and in response to Orion's publications, Peter Briffa, writing in the online daily newspaper, *The First Post*, declared: 'Face the facts: too many of these ancient texts are just plain tedious' (Briffa 2007). While Orion's texts were not specifically intended for the younger reader, adaptation of the classics for children has been, and remains, a similarly contentious subject and is rendered additionally complex by those who laud such literature, in its entirety, as suitable for children and those who perceive it as culturally elite and accessible only to A grade students. Adult texts have made the transition into the children's market for many years, most notably, perhaps, with *Aesop's Fables*, *Gulliver's Travels* and *Robinson Crusoe*, while Charles and Mary Lamb's *Tales from Shakespeare* was marketed to a child audience over two hundred years ago. But adaptations of the classics for children are now abundant, while concerns about children's literary knowledge also appear to have expanded. In the UK, a survey by supermarket chain Asda asserted that seventeen percent of primary school children surveyed thought Fagin was a Manchester United footballer, while forty percent believed Moby Dick to be a pop star (Wallop 2010); in fact, the footballer is Craig Fagan and the singer Moby. However, Asda, launching their Big Read selection of cut price classics, suggested that many children had little or no knowledge of classic literature and predicted that should the decline in classics continue, authors such as Brontë and Dickens could be extinct within a generation (Wallop 2010).

While Asda's conclusions might appear somewhat alarmist and were concurrent with a product launch, it would, nevertheless, seem a valid exercise to introduce children to classic literature and for them to comprehend that in Dickens' nineteenth-century tale of *Oliver Twist*, Fagin is a thief and the head of a gang of pickpockets in London, and that Moby Dick is the white whale in Herman Melville's 1851 novel. Indeed, acquisition of such details might be perceived as general knowledge and classic texts have created specific signifiers that have subsequently permeated British life and the English language. For example, 'Dickensian' is used freely to describe conditions of poverty and, perhaps somewhat confusingly, traditional images of Christmas. As children's literature scholar Nicholas Tucker asserts, the word Dickensian is 'pretty meaningless if you haven't read any Dickens' (quoted in Enfield 2010, n. p.) and many of those who use the term may have no real knowledge of the author from whom it is derived. However, as Tucker also comments, 'The Victorians did tend to write in long, convoluted sentences and never used a short word where they could use a long one. Their pages are scattered with nonchalance and balefulness, which all seem rather out of place now' (quoted in Enfield 2010, n. p.).

The notion that writers of the classics present prose that is problematic for today's young readers appears to dominate discourse on adaptations for children. Publishers Usborne produce the Young Reading Series, which includes adaptations of Dickens' work, and Claire Cowling, reviewing Usborne's version of *A Christmas Carol* (Cowling 2008, n. p.), claimed that such texts gave young children the opportunity to experience classic literature, making it accessible to all ages and ability ranges. Familiarization with the icons of English literature at a young age and reading these works for pleasure in interesting, colourful books, would, hopefully, instil a love for the full and unabridged novels, she suggested. She further commented that Dickens' stories could certainly be off-putting for older children, including teenagers and even adults, but that 'Dickens's plot lines and characters are so exciting, robust and unforgettable that everyone should be able to enjoy them' (Cowling 2008, n. p.). Cowling's emphasis is, in part, on the cultural value of such texts and the idea that children should be familiar with the classics, an emphasis that flourishes in much of the British education system. There is a sense that authors like Dickens are a part of the common consciousness, the national or international heritage, and so should be available and accessible, albeit in truncated form.

However, there is a contrasting view that was encapsulated by children's literature scholar Perry Nodelman, writing nearly thirty years ago. Reviewing *Once Upon the Classics*, an American television series of adaptations, Nodelman commented that while Dickens, Eliot and Scott were 'pretty good storytellers' who invented interesting, suspenseful plots, 'none of them were as good at inventing things to write about as they were at finding interesting ways to write about those things' (Nodelman 1982, p. 28). They were, he said, dealers in words, not inventors of action-filled scenarios. And, for Nodelman, in Classic Comic versions of texts or in *Once Upon The Classics*, the events the novelists described were divorced from their descriptions and became 'just scenarios'. The worst thing, he said, was that scripts based on these scenarios deprived Dickens and Eliot and Scott of their wonderful, distinct styles and made them all come out the same (Nodelman 1982, p. 28).

There is, assuredly, often a homogeneity in the various adaptation series in terms of style, illustration and narrative voice; publishers may utilize the same writers and illustrators for their series. But events as described by Dickens and re-created in these publications are not always entirely divorced from the 'distinct styles' of the source materials.

In the Classics Illustrated version of *Oliver Twist* (above), first produced by the Classic Comic store in the 1950s and still in print today, there is clearly a dearth of description in comparison to Dickens' tale. But there is, nevertheless, descriptive material contained within the illustrations that, to some degree, reiterates the essence of Dickens' prose – the worldly demeanour and confident

**Figure A** *Oliver Twist*, Classics Illustrated (2008, pp. 8–9). ©2013 First Classic Inc. All Rights Reserved. By Permission of Jack Lake Productions Inc.

swagger of the Dodger as he confronts the exhausted Oliver, the overcrowded room where the boys live, smoke their pipes and drink their alcohol and the predatory nature of Fagin. The text above the illustration is largely concerned with plot: 'They had supper. Oliver ate his share and Fagin then mixed him a glass of hot gin-and-water. Immediately afterward, Oliver felt himself gently lifted on to one of the sacks. He sank into a deep sleep' (2008, p. 9). But much more is evident in the final illustration. A smiling young thief lurks in the background while Fagin, scrawny and clad in a dressing gown, looms over Oliver and considers his newest recruit. Although this version may not fully echo the power of the written word as provided by the source text, it nonetheless strives to achieve more than simply plot and does so through extensive and detailed imagery that extends the basic narrative.

Indeed, while many children's adaptations of Dickens' *Oliver Twist* have the subtitle 'retold by', which locates the creative power in the hands of the text's author, they may similarly incorporate fragments of Dickens' narrative through illustration or narrative description. Adaptation is, in such texts, a non-specific term for abridgement, revision and sometimes re-creation of the source text and Graffex's graphic novel of *Oliver Twist: Charles Dickens* (2006b) explicitly incorporates elements of Dickens' material throughout, such as Fagin's greeting to Oliver and his accusation when the old man suspects that Oliver has spied his hoard.

The speech in each of these bubbles is drawn from the source text – 'We are very glad to see you Oliver', 'Clever Dogs! Fine Fellows!', 'What have you seen? Speak out boy!' (2006b, p. 12). It is a technique that effectively supplements the information contained within the central narrative, and, in addition, recognizes the historical nature of the source text. Terms such as 'pocket book' and 'handkerchief', which subsequently appear in the narrative's speech bubbles, may be unfamiliar to the reader, but are explained in footnotes and, in this way, the Graffex version declares its allegiance to Dickens' text and its historicity. In fact, the publication opens with a direct quote attributed to Dickens, which replicates the source text:

> After a few struggles, Oliver breathed, sneezed and proceeded to advertise to the inmates of the workhouse the fact of a new burden having been imposed on the parish, by setting up as loud a cry as could reasonably have been expected. (2006b, p. 5)

The muted, sepia-like tones of the illustrations further align the text with the past and with the dark emphasis of Dickens' tale of destitution and criminality

# MEETING NEW FRIENDS

We are very glad to see you, Oliver.

Jack led Oliver upstairs to a room at the back of the house. Inside was a shrivelled old man cooking sausages over a fire, and four or five boys.

The man with the villanous-looking face was Fagin. He gave Oliver, Jack and the others their supper. Then he poured Oliver a glass of water and hot gin.[1]

Clever dogs! Fine fellows![2]

What have you seen? Speak out boy!

The gin made Oliver tired. He was soon fast asleep in Fagin's den, on a rough bed made of old sacks.

Next day, as Oliver awoke to the sound of Fagin muttering, he saw the old gentleman take a gold pocket-watch from a box full of jewellery.

Fagin had thought that Oliver was sleeping, but when his dark eyes saw that the boy had been watching him, he slammed the lid down on the box.

All I have to live upon in my old age.

What have you got, Dodger?

A couple of pocket-books.[3]

Oliver admitted he'd seen the pretty things, and Fagin, saying they were his, hid the box.

The Dodger entered the room with Charley Bates, another of Fagin's lads. As they talked about some sort of work, Fagin gave Oliver a sly look.

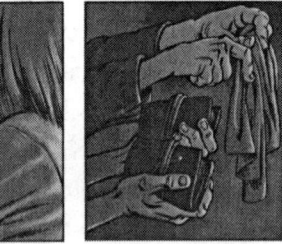

Dodger handed the pocket-books over to Fagin, and Charley gave him four silk handkerchiefs.[4] Fagin was very pleased.

1. Gin: A strong alcoholic drink. Oliver drank it diluted with water.
2. Clever dogs! Fine fellows!: Fagin is talking about the boys who work for him.
3. Pocket-books were what gentlemen carried their money in.
4. Handkerchief: A large square of expensive silk carried by Victorian gentlemen; their initials were sewn into them.

12

**Figure B** *Oliver Twist: Charles Dickens*, Graffex (2006b, p. 12). Copyright © 2006 Penko Gelev, John Malam. From OLIVER TWIST: CHARLES DICKENS retold by John Malam & illustrated by Penko Gelev. Reproduced by permission of The Salariya Book Company, Book House, 25 Marlborough Place, Brighton, BN1 1UB www.salariya.com

and so, perhaps, appear more sympathetic than the primary colours evident in the illustrations of many other versions.

Other adaptations of *Oliver Twist* are much more akin to re-creation; the author may draw on the source plot and characters to tell the story, but the language is contemporary and there is widespread use of what might be considered poetic licence in terms of correlation with Dickens' plot. For example, in the Real Reads version of *Oliver Twist* (2007), Fagin meets Oliver for the first time: "'Fagin – this is Oliver Twist,' said The Dodger. "Glad to see you, young Oliver," sneered Fagin. "You'll like it 'ere, won't 'e boys! Ha ha ha." His laugh sent cold shivers down Oliver's spine' (2007, p. 14). In the Penguin classics edition of Dickens' text, Fagin *does* comment, 'We are very glad to see you, Oliver – very' (2003, p. 66), but the sneering is absent, as are the shivers down Oliver's spine. In the Real Reads version, Fagin is immediately characterized as a frightening, threatening individual, which entirely simplifies Dickens' portrait of the miserly criminal and denies the reader the opportunity to gradually assess Fagin's character and thus emulate Oliver's own dawning awareness of Fagin's nature. Moreover, this instant appraisal of Fagin disregards Oliver's initial trust in his new home, which is pivotal to the events that follow. Oliver innocently follows the Dodger and Charley as they prepare to pick pockets, is appalled when he realizes the truth of their trade and is consequently arrested, which, in turn, leads to his rescue by Mr Brownlow.

Not all adaptations revise characters or episodes so markedly, but the Real Reads version is what publishers Usborne might classify as 'easy reading', a term they utilize about their own Young Reading series, which, they state on the rear cover of *Oliver Twist* (2006a), 'combines good stories with easy reading text'. An 'easy reading text' might also be translated as a simplification that distils events from source text material to present a précis of what the writer selects as the most significant episodes. This distillation is, however, a variable, and comparison of the opening paragraphs of different versions demonstrates the breadth of such selectivity. For example, the first chapter of the Penguin classics edition of *Oliver Twist or The Parish Boys Progress* (2003), titled 'Treats of the place where Oliver Twist was born and of the circumstances attending his birth', opens:

> Among other public buildings in the town of Mudfog, it boasts of one which is common to most towns, great or small, to wit, a workhouse; and in this workhouse there was born on a day and date which I need not trouble myself to repeat, inasmuch as it can be of no possible consequence to the reader . . . the item of mortality whose name is prefixed to the head of this chapter. For a long

time after he was ushered into this world of sorrow and trouble by the parish
surgeon, it remained of considerable doubt whether the child would survive to
bear any name at all. (2003, p. 3)

There is much emphasis on both the nineteenth-century world and the social
attitudes within this brief passage; every town in England had a workhouse, the
pauper child's birthday is of no consequence, and an item of mortality, a baby,
has been born. The term "an item of mortality" objectivizes the as-yet-unnamed
child; he is a 'thing' within the workhouse system, 'ushered' into a gloomy world
by an implicitly impatient surgeon. It is doubtful whether the child will survive
and the detached, unemotional narrative voice – 'it remained of considerable
doubt whether the child would survive to bear any name at all' – consolidates
the image of a child about whom no one cares. Dickens' opening paragraph
was explicitly a political statement criticizing the Poor Law amendment act of
1834, which renewed and re-emphasized the importance of the workhouse as a
means of relief for the poor and it is, perhaps, this political thrust that rendered
it so powerful.

At the opening of her comic strip retelling of *Oliver Twist* (2002) (below),
Marcia Williams echoes the information and sentiments of the same episode:

Among other buildings in English Victorian towns, there often stood a house
for the poor, known as the workhouse. On the night this story begins, a young
girl collapsed in the street and was carried into one. Her shoes were worn with
walking and she was heavily pregnant. The next day, in the presence of a parish
doctor and a drunken nurse, she gave birth to a baby boy. Oliver breathed,
sneezed and let out a cry. (2002, p. 6)

Williams' text references much of Dickens' opening narrative with its historical
information of the workhouse and Victorian England, its unemotive depiction
of the circumstances surrounding Oliver's birth and those present, and the
lack of celebration as Oliver enters the world. The appalling conditions of the
workhouse are represented in the illustration, which is made additionally harsh
with its jagged frame and numerous rats. The baby, violently red and dangled
over a candle as the unshaven doctor slaps him, is the only bright colour within
the otherwise dingy scene and is thus metaphorically separated from all that
surrounds him. He is visually identified as Other and so clearly does not belong
to this destitute world; as the tale unfolds, it becomes apparent that Oliver is
genetically aligned to the middle-class world and that his wider family is both
respectable and wealthy. Thus Williams' illustration, with its red baby amidst the
gloom, foreshadows the events to come.

*Treats of Oliver Twist's Birth and Board*

*Where she came from, or where she was going to, nobody knows.*

*Let me see the child, and die.*

OLIVER TWIST

Among other buildings in English Victorian towns, there often stood a house for the poor, known as the workhouse. On the night this story begins, a young girl collapsed in the street and was carried into one. Her shoes were worn with walking and she was heavily pregnant. The next day, in the presence of a parish doctor and a drunken nurse, she gave birth to a baby boy. Oliver breathed, sneezed and let out a cry.

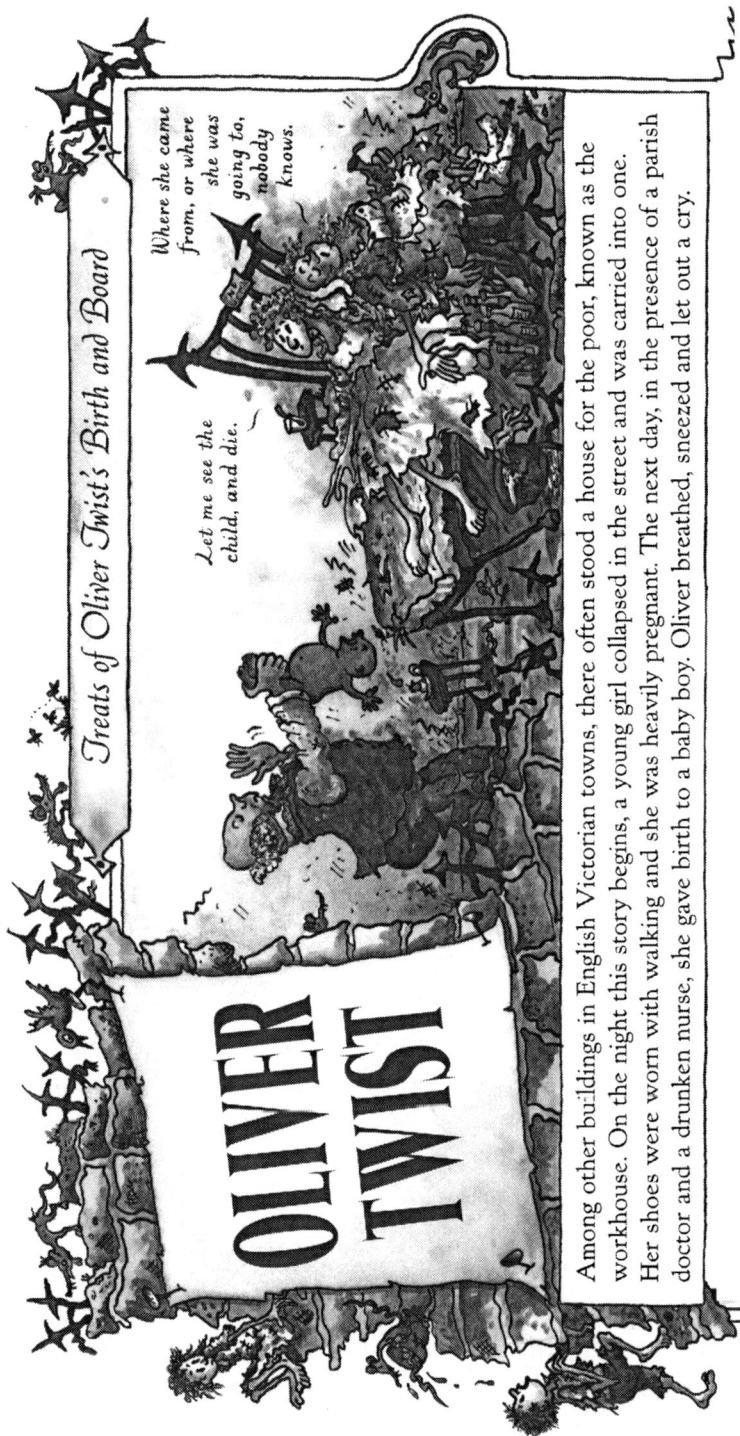

**Figure C** *Oliver Twist and other great Dickens stories*, (2002, p. 6). Copyright © 2002, 2007 Marcia Williams. From OLIVER TWIST AND OTHER GREAT DICKENS STORIES retold & illustrated by Marcia Williams. Reproduced by permission of Walker Books Ltd, London SE11 5HJ. www.walker.co.uk

The Ladybird Classics retelling (1995), like Williams' text, opens by contextualizing its story and also provides additional, educative information:

> In the first half of the nineteenth century, there existed in most English towns a grim building known as the workhouse. This was where the parish authorities sent the aged, the homeless and the poor who could not work and had nowhere else to go. (1995, p. 4)

The child reader immediately learns what workhouses were, the profile of inmates and how extensively such institutions operated in nineteenth-century England.

In contrast, however, the Real Reads version of *Oliver Twist* (2007) begins:

> Oliver Twist didn't know who had named him. It wasn't his father, who had never seen him, and it certainly wasn't his mother, who died giving birth to him. It was probably someone in the cold, grey workhouse in which he lived with hundreds of other orphaned boys. (2007, p. 7)

Within these first few lines the scene is established: Oliver is an orphan and lives in a workhouse, as do hundreds of other similar boys. The sense of historicity so evident in Williams' and the Ladybird text is absent and Oliver is distinguished only by his likeness to other orphan boys. His father is unknown to him, his mother died in childbirth and, overall, his entry into the world is vaguely drawn.

The contrast between these opening paragraphs exposes the plot-driven nature of some adaptations for children, although Dickens' text might also be perceived as plot-driven to some degree. The story was first published as a serial in monthly parts from 1837 to 1839 and, as Julie Sanders points out in *Adaptation and Appropriation* (2005), '[m]any [nineteenth-century] novels were published in instalments, encouraging readerly addiction to plotlines and characters and honing the authorial skills of creating suspense by means of the "cliffhanger" ending' (2005, p. 122). Dickens' fiction was no exception. However, an overall emphasis on plot in adaptations for children might be considered reductive and, taken in conjunction with what might also be perceived as the sanitization of Dickens' story, suggests that simplified and abridged adaptations can serve to impoverish Dickens' work.

The criminal underworld of early nineteenth-century London provides much of the setting for Dickens' novel, and in his introduction to the Penguin Classics edition of *Oliver Twist*, Philip Horne extends this focus on criminality to describe the world of the text as 'gallows-haunted' (2003, p. xv). He comments that '[b]etween 1801 and 1835, 103 death sentences were passed on children under the age of 14 for theft (although sensibilities were changing and not one was carried out)' (Horne 2003, p. xv). In Dickens' *Oliver Twist*, Fagin casually asks Dodger and Charley whether there had been much of a crowd at the execution – the boys have returned after picking pockets and, presumably, taking advantage of the crowd who had gathered to watch – and there are other notable hangings in the source novel. Murderer Bill Sykes, trapped on a rooftop trying to escape capture, loses his balance and the loop of rope intended for his waist becomes a noose at his neck: 'He fell for five and thirty feet. There was a sudden jerk, a terrific convulsion of the limbs and there he hung... lifeless against the wall' (Dickens 2003, p. 428). Fagin too is captured and hanged: on the morning of his execution, writes Dickens,

> a great multitude had already assembled; the windows were filled with people smoking and playing cards to beguile the time; the crowd were pushing, quarrelling and joking. Every thing told of life and animation, but one dark cluster of objects in the very centre of all – the black stage, the cross-beam, the rope, and all the hideous apparatus of death. (Dickens 2003, p. 450)

The emphasis on capital punishment, or in Bill Sikes' case a quasi-hanging, is evident throughout Dickens' text, as is the notion that a disastrous end awaits those who immerse themselves in the criminal underworld. The martyr-like Nancy, girlfriend of Sikes, is beaten to death by Sikes with a gun and a club; he batters Nancy as she raises her hands towards Heaven: '[He] seized a heavy club and struck her down' (Dickens 2003, p. 397). However, he supposedly shoots her in the Usborne, Ladybird and Real Reads retellings in an apparently altogether less bloody finale. In the Classic Starts adaptation, published in 2006 by Stirling, the text pertaining to this particular episode is largely devoid of violence:

> Bill said nothing as he walked towards Nancy. She backed her way around a corner as Bill followed her and a few moments later, a terrible scream was heard. People standing in the street ran toward the sound. They turned the corner to see Bill Sikes running away from Nancy's lifeless body. (2006c, p. 129)

In this way, the event is cleansed of its more gruesome emphases. As the cover of the Classic Starts version comments, each novel in the series is 'filled with all the magic and excitement that made the original story a beloved favourite' and the details of Nancy's murder are presumably neither magical nor exciting in the manner that the quote would seem to propose.

If the manner of Nancy's death varies in children's adaptations, the denouement for Bill Sikes and Fagin appears equally subject to variation. In the Real Reads and Classic Starts versions, Bill simply falls to his death from the roof, and rather than confronting the hangman's noose, Fagin meets an undisclosed end in Real Reads –'he already looked more dead than alive as he awaited his punishment' (2007, p. 53) – and, in what might be seen as a somewhat extreme measure, is merely sentenced to many years of hard labour by Classic Starts, a rewriting that suggests hanging may be too sensitive a subject for a young reader.

It would, perhaps, be inappropriate to present young readers with the unexpurgated horror that is often evident within Dickens' text, but editorial decisions to reduce the severity of these villains' deaths are indicative of a sanitization of the text, a desire to render Dickens more seemly for a contemporary younger reader. Such sanitization is inextricably linked with assumptions about the child reader, notions of suitability and an acute awareness of the moral implications of a text. As literary theorists John Stephens and Robyn McCallum point out, there are, of course, ideological and cultural functions at play in retold stories for children, as there are in children's texts generally, and retellings 'serve to initiate children into aspects of a social heritage, transmitting many of a culture's central values and assumptions and a body of shared allusions and experiences' (1998, p. 3). They continue:

> The major narrative domains which involve retold stories, all, in the main, have the function of maintaining conformity to socially determined and approved patterns of behaviour, which they do by offering positive role models, proscribing undesirable behaviour and affirming the culture's ideologies, systems and institutions. (Stephens and McCallum 1998, p. 3)

Stephens and McCallum are concerned primarily with traditional tales here, not the classics, but their comments would seem particularly pertinent to a discussion of classics for children, and various adaptations of *Oliver Twist* would seem to conform to many of the characteristics they identify. Dickens' story of an orphan who resists the corruption of Fagin and his gang and is ultimately rescued and rehomed by a benevolent philanthropist is a tale that, on its simplest level, champions rectitude and moral strength and invites disdain for those who steal and lie. Ostensibly bad characters are punished and the good survive and are rewarded; Fagin is hung, the Artful Dodger is arrested and sentenced and Oliver, the epitome of the Romantic child, is relocated to a life of love and relative luxury. The social and moral mores of the nineteenth century, which frequently equate to those of the twenty-first, are reiterated in the most basic of adaptations, while the adaptation itself represents a further ideology, acknowledging the text as a classic and thus reaffirming its identity within the literary canon. However, as Sanne Parlevliet comments:

> [I]n the case of adaptations, the selection of literary items also gets manipulated, adapted to the norms and values of the new context in which stories are to function as stories for children. Besides transmitting culture, both the selection and the manipulation of the selection bring about cultural change; old values are replaced by new values and new ideas about the child as reader and as a human being influence the way the old stories are retold. (Parlevliet 2009, p. 382)

She then importantly asserts:

> This gives adaptations a thoroughly contemporary character; they only suit a particular time and place ... [and] this contemporary character can provide us with a great deal of information about the period in which the texts came into being and the context within which they functioned. (Parlevliet 1998, p. 382)

As she concludes, adaptations of historical literary texts consequently have a dual function. The text lives on as literature but the adaptations can illuminate cultural constructions of the child, the child reader and children's literature (Parlevliet 1998, p. 383).

Parlevliet's comments succinctly identify how contemporary adaptations of *Oliver Twist* might be viewed in relation to their production. While gauging fidelity to the source text can expose where and how changes are wrought, such comparison additionally invites examination of the child reader or, more precisely, the concept of childhood envisaged by the publishers of these adaptations and, by implication, the way in which society generally may perceive the contemporary child.

To present a young reader with a version of Dickens that is merely a moral tale of good versus bad and innocence triumphant suggests an agenda of over-protection, censorship and a denial of the enduring validity and complexity of Dickens' work. Such an approach may patronize the child, situating him or her as incapable of engaging with a historic text and its implications and insisting on the child reader's innocence to the extent that distasteful material must be thoroughly expunged. There are both innocent and degenerate children in Dickens' text, but the character of Oliver invariably predominates within adaptations while, in many versions, the Dodger is depicted as little more than a bad boy in overly large clothes.

Furthermore, although Oliver's name may provide the title for Dickens' text, the supporting characters are significant components of the source novel. The tension between the Dodger as the degenerate child and 'spawn' of Fagin and Oliver as innocence personified is fundamental to Dickens' exploration of early Victorian childhood, but these contrasts cannot be explored within the confines of a slender adaptation insistent on a retelling that is primarily a moral tale. So Oliver remains the central force of many of these adaptations while the Dodger and Fagin are relatively peripheral.

However, a certain diminishing of Fagin, as depicted by Dickens, is endemic in adaptations for children. When he is introduced in Dickens' text, he is described as 'a very old shrivelled Jew, whose villainous looking and repulsive face was obscured by a quantity of matted red hair' (2003, p. 64). He is metaphorically the devil incarnate as he cooks his sausages and prepares his flock for a hell-fire roasting and Dickens' image is seemingly redolent with anti-Semitism. As Susan Meyer comments in her study, 'Antisemitism and social critique in Dickens's *Oliver Twist*' (2005), Dickens' portrayal of the Jewish underclass villain has perturbed some readers almost since the novel's first publication:

> Not only does Dickens pointedly and repeatedly term him "the Jew", but he emphasizes character traits familiar from the anti-Semitic tradition, namely his miserliness, his greed, his exotic and strange appearance, his effeminacy, his obsequiousness, his cowardliness – and the size of his nose. (Meyer 2005, p. 239)

Criticized by a Jewish acquaintance about Fagin's characterization, Dickens never admitted that his portrait was problematic, but later edited out many references to Fagin's ethnicity, substituting his name instead (Meyer 2005, p. 239). However, Meyer also asserts that Fagin is part of a symbolic schema in which the categories Jew and Christian play interconnected roles; thus Fagin's Jewishness might be considered an important element of his characterization in the source text.

It is unsurprising, perhaps, that textual references to Fagin's ethnic identity are absent from contemporary adaptations for younger readers. Historic literature marketed for children has often been edited to avoid any potential for a text to be read as racist, classist or sexist and Fagin is generally referred to by his name in the adaptations discussed here. But, and paradoxically, in many texts he is illustrated in accordance with Dickens' depiction, with long matted red hair and miserly joy as he gloats over his jewels and gold, while animalistic facial features characterize him as Other in the Usborne illustrations below.

A child reader may or may not be aware of the concept of anti-Semitism and its attendant implications, but an adult might well perceive the ideologies inherent to such an image. Stylistically similar portraits of Fagin are common

The next morning, waking in the pale half-light of dawn, Oliver saw Fagin open a chest and run his hands over necklaces, sparkling rings and shining gold coins.

Fagin turned to face Oliver's gaze. He thrust the chest back under the floor, seized a knife and pressed the blade into Oliver's neck.

"What did you see?" he hissed.

"Nothing," stammered Oliver, terrified.

**Figure D** *Oliver Twist*, Usborne (2006a, p. 30). Reproduced from Oliver Twist by permission of Usborne Publishing, 83–5 Saffron Hill, London EC1N 8RT, UK. Copyright © [2009] Usborne Publishing Ltd.

in adaptations of *Oliver Twist* for children and are equally evident in screen and stage versions of Dickens' text, such as Lionel Bart's stage and film musical, *Oliver!* But the characterization of Fagin as a re-creation of a traditionally anti-Semitic paradigm demonstrates how stereotypes can be normalized, perpetuated and so remain unexamined: images of Fagin are frequently threatening and bestial. And bringing such images of Fagin forward into the present day highlights one of the fundamental problems facing writers and illustrators as they attempt to re-create a historic text and to do so for a contemporary and sensitive market.

What might be perceived as the attitudes and prejudices of a historic novel are intrinsic to that novel, whether those prejudices are racial, sexist or classist. Such perceptions existed when the novel was produced, informed the author and his readership and, may have been, as Meyer suggests, a vital component of the entire work. Material that invites discrimination is assuredly problematic when considering a child reader, but recognition of a past in which poverty, discrimination, classism and racism existed is surely vital in comprehending why they should no longer be tolerated. These are enduring issues and all are pertinent to Dickens' text, but they are also intrinsic to a more extensive discourse surrounding the editing of historic books for children and the eradication of what might today be deemed unacceptable attitudes. Numerous texts, ranging from Pamela L. Travers' *Mary Poppins* to Enid Blyton's *Noddy* books, have been adapted for a contemporary market and thus their perceived elements of racism have been deleted. The discussion about such editing continues. While the removal of potentially offensive original material may seem necessary if a text is to be republished and remain available for child readers, the rewriting of a historical text might also be perceived as the rewriting of history.

Moreover, retelling *Oliver Twist* in order to capture, as Classic Starts suggest, 'the magic and excitement that made the original story a beloved favourite' demonstrates an adherence to the notion of Dickens as a storyteller, when he was, essentially, an amalgamation of novelist and social commentator. To overlook the specific historic and social implications of Dickens' text and to prioritize story is implicitly to disregard the novel as an artefact. For example, the opening paragraph of the Classic Starts retelling states: 'This particular story opens in a workhouse. There was a time – the same time that our story takes place – when too many cities and towns were home to these large, cold buildings' (2006c, p. 1). Contained within the paragraph is information about the condition of the poor, yet the phrase 'there was a time' undermines any sense of historical veracity and is reminiscent of the language of fairy tale. However, this absence of historical positioning appears uncommon; many of the texts explored here explain that

Dickens' text is evidence of an earlier period, an acknowledgement that would seem to be a most salient point if a text is to represent cultural knowledge.

Significantly, adaptations acknowledging the historicity of the source tale may also explicitly invite the child reader to engage with and discuss the numerous socio-historic questions raised by *Oliver Twist*. The penultimate pages of the Real Reads version, for example, contextualize Dickens' work and briefly offer the details of sub-plots erased in adaptation; the editorial comments: 'The loss of so many of Charles Dickens original words is a sad but necessary part of the shortening process. The points below will fill in some of the gaps, but nothing can beat the original' (2007, p. 55). The appendix also suggests secondary reading and web sites, ranging from the Dickens Museum in London to a site on the history of workhouses. In addition, as well as actively encouraging the reader to turn to the full-length version and lose himself in Dickens' 'wonderful storytelling' (2007, p. 61), it also offers what is termed 'Food for Thought', suggesting questions about how society might have been seen to fail the poor and the differences between the rich and those in poverty, subjects that might be deemed pertinent to a contemporary world.

If a classic text is to endure in popularity, it must remain relevant to subsequent generations and for children's author Michael Morpurgo, *Oliver Twist* offers such potential. In his foreword to the Collins 1996 illustrated version of *Oliver Twist* he writes:

> There is a temptation with all Dickens's novels to be comforted by the distance between his world and ours. We so easily say to ourselves, "Yes, but things aren't like that anymore". So with *Oliver Twist*. Certainly our inner-city squalour today is not the squalour of Dickens's time, but it is squalour all the same. We do not have workhouses anymore, but there are still young children on our streets, growing up amongst criminals, their young lives corrupted and twisted, and they are led, often irretrievably, into evil. (Morpurgo, 1996, p. 6)

Here Morpurgo explicitly emphasizes the importance of a historic text for a modern generation, recognizing Dickens' novel as a social document, but one with relevance and perhaps implications for the present day. The version that Morpurgo first read as a child was, coincidentally, the Classics Illustrated version, which was discussed at the outset of this chapter, and he explains that he progressed to read the complete text. His comments encapsulate how adaptations might be considered valuable additions to the children's market by drawing on the preoccupations of a former period, promoting engagement with the source text and so fostering an interest in both history and classic literature. Adapting the classics for children can undoubtedly diminish the source text and invalidate the historicity of the work. However, adaptations can also invite extensive contemplation of the past, the present and the importance of the written word, ultimately eliminate any likelihood of such classic texts being forgotten and assist in perpetuating knowledge and some understanding of the young reader's cultural heritage. Moreover, they can also serve to confirm that Fagin is not a footballer and that *Moby Dick* has nothing to do with music.

# List of works cited

Briffa, Peter (2007), 'Are the classics abridged too far?', *The First Post*, June, viewed 1 April 2010, <http://www.thefirstpost.co.uk/5575,news-comment,news-politics,are-the-classics-abridged-too-far>.

Cowling, Claire (2008), 'How to get children reading Dickens', *Suite 101*, 11 November, <http://childrensbooks.suite101.com/article.cfm/how_to_get_children_reading_dickens>.

Dickens, Charles (2003), *Oliver Twist*, Philip Horne (ed.). Penguin Classics. London: Penguin.

Enfield, Lizzie (2010), 'Classics are not relics children', *Telegraph*, 5 April 2010, viewed 7 April 2010, <http://www.telegraph.co.uk/culture/books/books-life/7545909/Classics-are-not-relics-children.html >.

Hoyle, Ben (2007), 'Publisher makes lite work of the classics', *Times Online*, 14 April, viewed 1 April 2010, http://entertainment.timesonline.co.uk/tol/arts_and_entertainment/books/fiction/article1652629.ece>.

Ita, Sam (2007), *Moby Dick*. New York: Sterling.

Meyer, Susan (2005), 'Antisemitism and social critique in Dickens' *Oliver Twist*'. *Victorian Literature and Culture*, 33: 239–52.

Morpurgo, Michael (1996), Introduction to *Oliver Twist*. Illustrated by Christian Birmingham. London: Collins.

Nodelman, Perry (1982), 'Not much more than once upon a classic'. *Children's Literature Association Quarterly*, 7(3): 27–30.

*Oliver Twist* (1995). Retold by Brenda Ralph Lewis and Ronne Randall. Illustrated by John Holder. London: Ladybird Books.

— (2006a) Retold by Mary Sebag-Montefiore. Illustrated by Barry Ablett. London: Usborne.

*Oliver Twist: Charles Dickens* (2006b). Retold by John Malam. Illustrated by Penko Gelev. Brighton: Graffex.

*Oliver Twist* (2006c). Retold from the Charles Dickens original by Kathleen Olmstead. Illustrated by Dan Andreason. New York: Sterling (Classic Starts).

— (2007). Retold by Gill Tavner. Illustrated by Karen Donnelly. Stroud: Real Reads.

— (2008) Classics Illustrated. Thatcham: Classic Comic Store.

*Oliver Twist and Other Great Dickens Stories* (2002). Retold and illustrated by Marcia Williams. London: Walker Books.

Parlevliet, Sanne (2009), From *Masterpieces With Donkey Ears: Adaptations of Literary Classics for Children 1850–1950*. Summary of Dissertation, University of Groningen, <http://irs.ub.rug.nl/ppn322567998>.

Sanders, Julie (2005), *Adaptation and Appropriation*. London and New York: Routledge.

Stephens, John and McCallum, Robyn (1998), *Retelling Stories, Framing Culture: Traditional Story and Metanarratives in Children's Literature*. London and New York: Garland.

Wallop, Harry (2010), 'Children think Fagin is man u player', *Daily Telegraph*, January, viewed 1 April, <http://www.telegraph.co.uk/education/educationnews/7018534/Children-think-Fagin-is-Man-U-player.html>.

Williams, Marcia (2000), *Mr. William Shakespeare's Plays*. London: Walker.

# 10

# *The Nutcracker* from ETA Hoffmann to Matthew Bourne: Adaptation of a Children's Story with Adult Messages

Jan Keane

## Introduction

Any consideration of the evolution and adaptation of narratives in children's literature must raise the question of the moral and didactic content of those narratives, and the messages which the originators of the successive versions seek to convey. This chapter traces the evolution of what is perhaps one of the most widely known narratives – *The Nutcracker* – through changes to plot and character from the original children's story of Ernst Theodor Amadeus (ETA) Hoffmann, *Nussknacker und Mausekönig* (1816) down through Alexandre Dumas père's revision, *Histoire d'un Casse-Noisette* (1844) and nineteenth- and twentieth-century ballet versions, to Matthew Bourne's contemporary interpretation for the stage (1992).[1] It is the contention of this chapter that these adaptations of Hoffmann's story have become, in effect, works in their own right.[2]

The methodology employed in undertaking this research has involved a close analysis of the original stories on which the ballet in question was based, consultation of secondary sources, and for the ballets themselves attendance at live performances as well as close scrutiny of visual recordings, and consultation with a former member of the Royal Ballet Company.[3]

Three propositions are explored: (1) that historical context affected perceived messages; (2) that early versions of the narrative and Bourne's ballet contain differing messages of a social, cultural, political and gender nature; (3) that the narratives are intended for both children and adults, and reach them in different ways. The focus is on the isolation of themes relating to the individual's duty to authority, ideas on loyalty and on justice, the individual as victim and as rebel and lastly love and sexuality. I intend to show that not only do the adaptations of *The Nutcracker* discussed in this chapter respond to and reflect changing historical contexts for a child audience, but also that the messages they contain concern the values and behaviour of children as future adults. Finally, the opportunity will be taken to reflect briefly on the ability of these messages to transcend national boundaries.

## Fairy stories

There is a substantial literature on fairy stories. In particular, Jack Zipes speaks of the civilizing mission of the fairy tale, which 'assumes great importance because it reveals how social mores and values were induced in part through literature and constituted determinants in the rearing of an individual child' (2006, p. 48). Elsewhere Zipes suggests that, from the eighteenth century, intellectuals have appropriated fairy tales and have consciously turned them into a discourse about mores, values and manners. In other works, he writes about the historical transformation of individual fairy tales (Zipes 1997), international conceptions of the fairy tale (Zipes 1999) and the ways in which fairy tales and other children's literature have been drafted into the acculturation of American children (Zipes 2002).

Bruno Bettelheim was instrumental in raising awareness of the importance of fairy tales for children in the twentieth century. Citing Mercia Eliade, he speaks of myths and fairy tales as 'models for human behaviour [that], by that very fact, give meaning and value to life' (Bettelheim 1991, p. 35). Max Lüthi sees the fairy tale as 'a poetic vision of man and his relationship to the world – a vision that for centuries inspired the fairy tale's hearers with strength and confidence because they sensed the fundamental truth of this vision' (1970, p. 19). In his ten essays, he goes on to elucidate various dimensions of the genre.

A number of significant fairy tale narratives were transposed to the stage in the form of ballets. Because the medium of expression is different, the nature of critical comment has also been different. It has tended to focus on the presentational aspects of this performance art and the way it has evolved: choreography and dance technique, music, sets and costumes, and of course the virtuoso performances of the principal dancers who are the stars of the genre. Only relatively recently more analytical work has begun to appear, which addresses symbolism and meaning in ballet, and the nature of the messages it may convey.

In this genre, Jennifer Fisher's excellent investigation of the history of *The Nutcracker* ballet as a 'New World phenomenon' is of particular interest for the present study (2003). In addition, there is the work of Susan Foster (1998), Sally Banes (1998) and Jane Desmond (2001). Foster's work is concerned with understanding messages about desire and sexuality, which have been conveyed through dance over the past three centuries. Desmond takes up the same theme, and maintains that dance is a prime medium for the expression of messages about gender and sexuality. Banes points to the common theme of the marriage plot in many romantic ballets.

Somewhat surprisingly, still relatively little serious analytical writing of any kind exists on Matthew Bourne's ballets. However, a major source of insight is the long series of interviews with Bourne conducted and edited by his former tutor, Alastair Macaulay, and published in 1999.

## *The Nutcracker*: Successive synopses

Of all the stories that have ultimately been transformed into ballets, *The Nutcracker* is perhaps one of the most complicated.[4] The original nutcracker story, written in 1816 by the German Romantic and polymath ETA Hoffmann, was a novella published in a Christmas collection for children.[5] In this version, the central character Marie Stahlbaum is given a Nutcracker doll for Christmas by her Godfather, Herr Drosselmeier. At night, the Nutcracker doll comes to life and leads his forces in battle with the main protagonist in the form of the seven-headed King of Mice and his soldiers. Marie intervenes and saves Nutcracker by throwing her shoe at the Mouse King. At this point, the battle and everyone taking part in it disappear. Marie is found in the toy room by her mother, her arm badly cut by glass from the toy cupboard.

During Marie's recuperation, Drosselmeier tells her a long story ('The Story of the Hard Nut') which explains why Nutcracker and the Mouse King are old enemies. The story recounts the fate of beautiful Princess Pirlipat, previously rendered grotesque by the curse of Dame Mouserink, the mother of the seven-headed King of Mice, for wrongs done to her family by the King and Queen – Pirlipat's parents. This curse can only be reversed when the hardest nut in the world is cracked by an innocent youth and the Princess eats its kernel.

Drosselmeier's nephew is this young man. Although he breaks the spell on Pirlipat, he accidentally kills Dame Mouserink. As she dies, she transfers the curse to the nephew and he becomes a wooden nutcracker. Dame Mouserink's son, the seven-headed King of Mice, vows revenge on Nutcracker. Thus, the story within a story accounts for the dynamics of the main plot which can ultimately only be resolved when someone (who turns out to be Marie) falls in love with Nutcracker and turns him back into human form.

After her recuperation, Marie is visited at night by the Mouse King who demands successively bribes of sweets and other items in order to leave Nutcracker alone. After acquiescing a third time, she is asked by Nutcracker for a sword with which to despatch the Mouse King once and for all. Marie obtains the sword, Nutcracker kills the Mouse King, and returns to bring her the good news. Together they pass through a wardrobe[6] into a magical kingdom of sweets, where Nutcracker is revealed as a prince, and a feast takes place at Marzipan Castle. When Marie opens her eyes again she is in her own bed. Her family believe her stories to be dreams. A little later Drosselmeier arrives with his nephew. Marie realizes he is the flesh and blood Nutcracker; he proposes to her, a year and a day later they marry, and they return to Marzipan Castle to live happily thereafter.

In the version of *The Nutcracker*, as translated and revised by Alexander Dumas père in 1844, the story elements, the length and the construction are essentially the same as in the Hoffmann version, but with some of the more disturbing elements of the original story removed. These were passages that could be construed as being of an overtly sexual or horrific nature.[7]

The first ballet version of *The Nutcracker*, staged in St. Petersburg in 1892 to music by Piotr Tchaikovsky and choreography by Lev Ivanov,[8] was broadly based on the Dumas revision, but lacked entirely the story within the story, which had served to explain the plot in the written versions (Wiley 1985). Essentially, this was a ballet in two acts separated by a linking scene. The first Act presents the family at Christmas, the battle between Nutcracker and the Mouse King and Clara (as Marie is called in this version) throwing her shoe at the Mouse King. In the linking scene, Clara travels through the land of snow with Nutcracker. Act Two takes place in Confiturembourg, the Land of Sweets, where the Queen, the Sugar Plum Fairy and her partner, the Prince, reward Clara for her bravery and loyalty with a series of divertissements[9] and a signature *pas de deux*. In this ballet, Clara never returns from the Land of Sweets to the everyday world, and some of the moral force of the original tale is lost.[10] This was not true for later versions of the ballet, such as that of Peter

Wright, which take Clara back to the world from which she has come and thus resolve the story more completely.

Matthew Bourne's *Nutcracker* of 1992 retains the coming-of-age story, and still relies on Tchaikovsky's music.[11] Here, however, the setting is an orphanage in England, probably in Edwardian times, though some licence is taken with the precise period. Bourne forsakes the conventional structure of two acts to present a series of scenes, which are linked to make up a coherent narrative. The focus in this ballet is on Clara and Nutcracker, two orphans. The ballet opens on Christmas Eve as the children, under the watchful eye of their hard-hearted Matron, decorate their dormitory with a few tattered streamers and a 'Christmas tree', which is nothing more than a dead, leafless house plant in a small pot. The orphanage is visited by the head of the governors, Dr Dross, his spoilt children Sugar and Fritz, and by other dignitaries. Each of the orphans is given a Christmas gift – Clara's is a ventriloquist's doll with a moving mouth, reminiscent of the jaws of a nutcracker – but these are all taken away and locked in a cupboard later by the matron after the dignitaries depart.

Sugar wants Clara's doll. As she goes to open the cupboard door, the doll, now the size of a man, breaks out and walks stiffly and menacingly towards her, whereupon she flees. Cracks appear in the walls of the orphanage as Nutcracker and Clara leave the scene, while the remaining orphans rise in revolt against Fritz, Sugar and Matron. Dr Dross evades capture. Clara watches as Nutcracker casts off his doll-like appearance and turns into an attractive young man. They dance a romantic *pas de deux*. At this point, the scene changes to a frozen lake,[12] where Nutcracker is knocked unconscious by a snowball. When he comes to, Sugar is the first person he sees and he mistakenly believes himself to be in love with her, leaving Clara in abject misery.

The following scenes trace the route to the wedding of Nutcracker and Sugar, and Clara's attempts to win Nutcracker back, aided by two bespectacled cupids in striped pyjamas. They manage to change Clara's shabby nightdress into a stylish polka-dot frock, although their efforts to fire love's arrows at the correct person go wildly amiss. Here, the divertissements, unlike those in the traditional ballet, appear in the guise of sweets.[13] Clara remains hopeful, yet all seems lost when Nutcracker and Sugar are married in front of an enormous wedding cake. During the wedding celebrations, Clara appears again wearing her shabby nightdress, holding her ventriloquist's doll. She dances briefly with Nutcracker before he runs off the stage. Sugar, in all her wedding finery, stares triumphantly at Clara, and departs. Defeated, Clara takes out her frustration on the doll by throwing it to the floor, then, alone and in despair, she cries herself to sleep.

When she wakes, she is back in the orphanage. Has it all been a dream? Clara walks dejectedly towards her bed, and pulls back the covers. Suddenly her Nutcracker is revealed, a poorly dressed orphan, but now on the verge of manhood. The climax comes as they escape to freedom by means of knotted sheets through the orphanage window.

## The impact of historical context on perceived messages

The historical setting for each version of *The Nutcracker* (by which is meant the context of the time in which it is being told) is significant to an understanding of the story's intended messages, and to the analysis of plot and characterization. Moreover, as we trace the metamorphosis from a fairy story to a live performance, it is necessary to consider how the respective audiences may have changed, for instance, in terms of nationality, social attitudes and class. There is, therefore, a complex pattern of influences on the story according to the period and the format in which it is being retold, and which reflects the contemporary local or national concerns.

Both the fact that Hoffmann was from Königsberg, and the date of his *Nutcracker*, 1816, may be seen as significant. Europe had achieved peace only one year before the story's publication. While Prussia had been a powerful adversary of Napoleon (and an ally of Britain), the degree of mobilization necessary for the war effort, and the loss of life, had taken their toll. Moreover, East Prussia felt particularly exposed, surrounded as it was by Russian-dominated Poland – which had been invaded by Napoleon – and was completely physically separated from the rest of Prussia.

The violence in the story may well owe something to the traumas of the previous decades. Could the seven-headed Mouse King have been Napoleon? Could the land of sweets be seen as Europe at peace, and the love story with the happy ending be the triumph of individual humanity over the horrors of warfare?

For Dumas, in 1844, the audience would, for the most part, have been French middle-class readers, many of whom would still have recalled the troubled times before 1816. His version saw few changes in plot or in character, although the more gothic aspects of the story were no longer present, making it more palatable for children.

The first ballet version was produced in Russia in 1892.[14] In its new format as a ballet, *The Nutcracker* was simplified, and lost its 'story within a story'. What remained were two Acts – the first containing an unexplained fight scene, and the second a series of divertissements. While in the first Act the violence remained, its impact may have been reduced for Russian audiences by the relatively long period of peace that Russia had enjoyed in the decades immediately prior to the 1890s. Moreover, the ballet gave full play to costume and the other visual possibilities of the story – the actual performance of the various acting and dancing parts and the visual representation of the fantasy elements. Thus, for the Russian audiences of the time, the ballet may have seemed much more like the performance version of an entertaining fairy tale.

Yet this was its undoing. Critics complained that the plot no longer made any sense, and that the fine music was wasted on such a flimsy libretto.[15] It is ironic that *The Nutcracker* went on to become such an iconic ballet worldwide in the twentieth century.

Bourne, by contrast, mixes fantasy with social realism. Setting his *Nutcracker* in an Edwardian orphanage, he evokes the grim austerity of many such institutions in England at the time, including the cruelty bordering on abuse, which characterized some. Class divisions are portrayed through the contrast between Clara and the other orphans on one hand, and Fritz and Sugar, the children of Dr Dross, on the other. The theatrical conceits used (e.g. the large mouth on stage at one point) and other presentational aspects date the 'production itself' firmly in the last decades of the twentieth century; gestures of homage to Andy Warhol and the influence of advertising on art would not have been understood at any other time. Moreover, Bourne's interpretation of the story, his focus on social injustice, and especially his concern for the abuse of children, introduces subject matter which has only very recently become acceptable for public discussion. There are clearly still many elements of fantasy in his production, and the divertissements that feature in the classical versions are retained, although reinterpreted, this is after all a ballet, and the display of technical virtuosity remains an essential part of the art form – but Bourne's *Nutcracker* is in every other way very much a product of its time.

## Didactic messages of a social, cultural, political and gender nature

As previously noted, close scrutiny of the primary sources revealed six themes that can be identified as present in all the different versions: duty to authority, loyalty, justice, the plight of victims, rebellion, love and sexuality.

## Duty to authority

Messages about a citizen's duty to authority are not a major element in Hoffmann's novella, Dumas' story, or in the traditional ballet, but are nonetheless present in an oblique way. Hoffmann adopts a confidential tone in his narrative, rather like a benevolent uncle – 'I appeal to you, kind reader (or listener)' (Hoffmann 1967, p. 132) – and takes care to remind the young reader especially of how children ought to behave, albeit in the gentlest of tones. For example, on Christmas Eve, when the story begins, Marie and Fritz sit 'together in a corner of the back parlour' having been told that they 'were not allowed on any pretext whatever at any time that day to go into the small drawing-room, much less into the best drawing-room into which it opened' (Hoffmann 1967, p. 130). They do not attempt to peek into the forbidden room where the Christmas celebrations are being prepared. Although their parents are not portrayed as repressive, obedience was nonetheless expected.

Dumas, more mindful of his child audience, provides clearer signposts regarding respect for authority. Of Marie he writes, 'She was very obedient to her mother and never contradicted her governess', whereas it is the father, Judge Silberhaus, who deals with Fritz's extremes by 'raising his forefinger [saying] "Fritz!" This was quite enough to make Fritz wish that the earth would open and swallow him up' (Dumas 1976, p. 1).

In the Ivanov/Tchaikovsky ballet, we are presented with a thoroughly civilized and happy household in which there seems to be no domestic tension. The Stahlbaum parents appear genial and untroubled, having no need to exercise their authority in anything other than the most gentle way. If there is a distinctive authority figure in either the novellas or this ballet, it is the godfather, Drosselmeier, a man of talent and mystery who inspires the fear and respect of his godchildren. In the background of the story, there are the traditional authority figures of the King and Queen. Nutcracker himself is ultimately revealed to be a prince. The Mouse King is a commanding figure in his own way, exercising authority over his own realm. The plot of the stories and of the classical ballet proceeds in the context of a world in which certain individuals exercise power and authority, and others are expected to obey.

In Matthew Bourne's *Nutcracker*, Dr Dross, the Head of the Governors, clearly is someone whom the orphans are expected to obey, as is the Matron. Even so, the orphans, in the absence of these authority figures, act out fantasies of rebellion. Moreover, ultimately Dr Dross and the Matron are defeated, and Clara and Nutcracker make their escape. In Bourne's ballet, authority is challenged and overcome.

## Loyalty

In both the Hoffmann and the Dumas versions of the story, Marie is totally devoted to Nutcracker. From the moment she sets eyes on him under the Christmas tree, there is an instant attraction. 'As Marie kept looking at this little man, whom she had quite fallen in love with at first sight, she saw more and more clearly what a sweet nature and disposition were legible on his countenance' (Hoffmann 1967, p. 134). In the Dumas revision, Nutcracker is about to be taken prisoner by the King of Mice. Marie is beside herself with anxiety – 'Oh, my poor nutcracker!' she exclaims. 'I love you with all my heart and cannot bear to see you die!' (Dumas 1976, p. 20). She acts quickly and instinctively by throwing her shoe at the Mouse King, saving Nutcracker in the process. Marie's loyalty is further tested when the King of Mice reappears, demanding over three nights her sweets, sugar dolls and treasured books in return for not eating Nutcracker. She complies, but on the final night manages to get Nutcracker a sword with which he dispatches the Mouse King.

In both the stories and the classical ballet versions, therefore, loyalty is held up as an important virtue. In a perverse way, moreover, it is the Mouse King's loyalty to the memory of his mother that gives rise to the feud in the first place.

In Bourne's ballet, Clara's loyalty to Nutcracker is similarly central to the plot, though it could be said that as with much of Bourne's work, the moral message is ambiguous. Here, Clara's loyalty can be seen as a device which enables the visual presentation to be played out, rather than as carrying an injunction to the audience to behave in a certain way.

## Justice

In both versions of the story and in the ballets, justice is established. In the stories and the classical ballet, the death of the King of Mice seems richly deserved in view of his violent and vengeful behaviour. Nutcracker is ultimately returned to his human form, a reward for his virtue and determination in conquering the Mouse King. Moreover, he regains his rightful place as the Prince of Marzipan Castle (or of Confiturembourg in the Dumas' revision). For her part, Marie is an honoured guest in the magic world of sweets. An unspecified time later, she marries her Nutcracker prince there and becomes Queen of that realm, where 'all kinds of miraculous and wonderful things may be seen by those who have eyes sharp enough to discover them' (Dumas 1976, p. 74). The Ivanov/ Tchaikovsky ballet is simpler, in that the narrative ends at the end of Act One with the killing of the Mouse King. Clara is commended for her actions by the Queen of Confiturembourg, the Sugar Plum Fairy and her consort, the Prince. Thus, bravery and virtue are rewarded, and justice prevails. Bourne's *Nutcracker* preserves the main outcomes of the earlier versions. Clara ultimately gets her Nutcracker, Nutcracker regains his human form, Dr Dross is defeated, and Clara and Nutcracker in the end manage to escape from the orphanage – justice for them as individuals, as they have both suffered, and by implication a victory for the poor and neglected over the establishment.

Thus, in all versions of the narrative, justice is the ultimate outcome.

## Victims

In 'The Hard Nut', the story within the story of *The Nutcracker*, there are several victims, not obviously determined by gender or class. Princess Pirlipat, through no fault of her own, is a victim of Dame Mouserink's curse. Dame Mouserink is a victim, too, losing all her relatives because of the King's harsh overreaction to the tasteless sausages. In this story, court mathematician Drosselmeier and young Drosselmeier are also victims, the former because the King needed someone to blame, the latter because of an accident.

In Bourne's ballet, however, it could be said that Clara, and some of the other orphans too, are victims of fate, and perhaps too of their class origins in a class-ridden society. Dr Dross and Matron victimize the children in their care as they have an unchallenged position of power over them. What is striking is that neither in the earlier versions nor in the Bourne ballet is there a strong gender implication to victimhood; both misfortune and persecution may affect people of either sex, and there is no negative gender message for girls in this respect.

## Rebels

In both the stories and the earlier ballet versions, Marie/Clara is presented as a strong female character. Independent of mind, she rebels against what might be regarded as the conventional expectations for her sex, although she is eventually appropriated by the system through marriage. In Bourne, however, Clara is portrayed in a less proactive way; that she eventually gets and keeps her Nutcracker is through no particular determination of her own. Thus, the gender message about the expectations of women would seem to be more radical in the case of the earlier versions than in the case of Bourne.

**Love and sexuality**

In all versions except Bourne's, love is the means through which Nutcracker is made human again. Love means supporting your partner (Nutcracker) in battle if necessary. Love is the 'Land of Sweets', in which deserving people may live happily ever after.

In Bourne, Clara, deprived of parents, transfers her love to Nutcracker. In doing so, she is forced to confront competition in the form of Sugar's determined rivalry, and treachery in the form of Nutcracker's betrayal. Love is replaced by sexual gratification – the pleasures of 'Sweetie Land'. Love may appear to triumph in the end, but we are not told what this may mean in the long term. The message in Bourne's *Nutcracker* with respect to the power of love is ambiguous at best.

## Messages for both children and adults, reaching them in different ways

Peter Hunt observes that, in literature for children, 'there is... a long – and far from dead – tradition of didacticism, which holds that children's books must be moral and educational' (2001, p. 5). In Hoffmann's story, the ballet derivatives, and ultimately *The Nutcracker* of Matthew Bourne, such a compelling undercurrent of didactic intent is obvious. In the present chapter, I have sought to explain the way in which plot and character may communicate messages, notably about authority, society, gender roles and other issues. In this sense, works of children's literature, fairy tales and performance art have much in common.

Does this suggest that Hoffmann's fairy tale on which the ballets were based was really meant for adults? According to Zipes, Hoffmann himself approached Fouqùe and Contessa regarding the joint publication of a book of fairy tales for children (2007, p. xx). However, it is my contention that the answer to this question is not clear-cut. Perhaps the most important point is that adults influence, to a large extent, the reading choices of children. They also participate in the transmission of the messages inherent in the work – every time the story was rehearsed, the adult would have been conveying and reinforcing a set of shared values, a sense of justice and attitudes to duty, loyalty, fidelity, authority and other expectations of the culture prevailing in the community. The process might best be described as affirmation for adults, and initiation for children into what Stephens and McCallum call their 'culture's central values' (1998, p. 254).

Each time the story of *The Nutcracker* is taken as the plot for a ballet, new dimensions are opened up. The performance on stage has an immediate impact: it is intensely visual with its often elaborate costumes and sets, is accompanied by a strong musical score and may have a plot which moves easily back and forth between fantasy and reality, just as children do themselves.

In the past fifty years *The Nutcracker* has indeed become above all an entertainment for children.[16] An animated Disney film, countless illustrated books, and a plethora of promotional products related to the story have ensured that this is so. For many English-speaking children and families, attendance at a professional or amateur performance of *The Nutcracker* is a Christmas pilgrimage. This cannot be said of the Bourne version of the ballet. Bourne's concern to present works that reflect some of the social and psychological dilemmas contemporary to his own time, or to the recent past, means that the plot and characterization in his ballets may be much less accessible to children. It could be argued that the social problems he deals with often involve children – the plight of the orphans in the case of his *Nutcracker*, for example, which may have become less recognizable when translated into the more modish particular of child abuse in orphanages. It may be that Bourne's messages at first sight appear less accessible to children than the earlier narratives, but is this to say that his ballet is not for children? Not precisely, as the visual, dance and musical spectacle are still there. To sum up, therefore, one conclusion may be that the stories, and more particularly the ballets, work at different levels for children and adults.

## Messages which transcend national boundaries

What can the experience of *The Nutcracker* tell us of the ability of the values expressed in the story to transcend national boundaries? Theorists have suggested that national identity may be primarily a cultural phenomenon (Smith 1991, 1999), a complex structure of knowledge, beliefs and feelings (Barrett 2007), that the nation is an imagined community with a 'mythologized past' (Anderson 2006), which may be 'constructed and conveyed through discourse, predominantly in narratives of national culture' (Wodak et al. 2009, p. 22). How then, can a story such as that which inspires *The Nutcracker* come to appeal across national frontiers, enjoying success with audiences in France, Britain, the United States and other Western societies around the globe?

The answer to the question may lie with the imagination of common values and ethics – a Western meta-ethic, as John Stephens and Robyn McCallum put it. Stephens and McCallum speak of the retelling of stories through diverse genres, raising social issues which are 'always dealt with in relation to or in dialogue with an overarching central or moral perspective, or assumed bundle of values' (1998, p. x). They maintain that the 'values, attitudes and conceptualization of individual subjectivity which inform (children's) literature are firmly grounded in the Western humanist tradition' (Stephens and McCallum 1998, p. 18). Bullock (1985), too, sees Western humanism strongly in evidence in narratives for children, which tend to be focused on

> themes of conscience, conflicts of loyalty, rebellion and authority, the ambiva-
> lence of feelings, the search for identity, the power of art and myth, passions and
> compassions … this complex of themes, aspirations and values, which is such
> a precise description of the dominant processes in retelling stories. (quoted in
> Stephens and McCallum 1998, p. 20)

The implication here, judging by the example of *The Nutcracker*, must be that despite distinct national variations, there are, after all, shared experiences and common values which are not confined by national boundaries, and indeed are almost certainly not exclusive to Western cultural traditions. This is a hopeful message on which to close, and one which suggests possibilities for further work beyond the scope of this chapter.

# Notes

1  Sanders points out that Kristeva's idea of intertextuality need not be confined
   to literature, but may equally encompass art, music, drama, dance and other
   forms – 'a living mosaic, a dynamic intersection of textual surfaces' (see Sanders
   2006, p. 3).

2  Hutcheon has noted that 'there are many and varied motives behind adaptation
   and few involve faithfulness' (2006, p. xiii).

3  Julie Bowers, BA Hons, ARAD, former first artiste with the Royal Ballet Company,
   is now a senior administrator for the Royal Academy of Dance, and the Artistic
   Governor of Elmhurst School for Dance in association with the Birmingham
   Royal Ballet. I had a number of face-to-face meetings with Ms Bowers,
   whose insights into the aesthetic and technical aspects of performance were
   enlightening, and have been most useful to me in the preparation of this chapter.

4   In each of the various incarnations of *The Nutcracker*, names and spellings are changed. In Hoffmann's version, the principal characters are Dr and Mrs Stahlbaum, their children Louise, Fritz and Marie, Godfather Drosselmeier, Princess Pirlipat, Dame Mouserink, and the seven-headed King of Mice. In Dumas père's version, we have Judge and Mrs Silberhaus, Fritz and Marie, Dr Drosselmeyer, Princess Pirlipatine, Madame Souriçonne and the King of Mice, whereas in the original ballet the names are Dr and Mrs Stahlbaum, Fritz and Clara, Herr Drosselmeyer and the Mouse King.

5   First published in 1816, as volume one of a two-volume Christmas collection of children's fairy tales (Kinder-Märchen) 1816/1817. See Hoffmann (1816).

6   This passage predates C S Lewis's *The Lion, the Witch and the Wardrobe*, first published in 1950, by one hundred and thirty four years.

7   See Hoffmann (1967, pp. 167, 178).

8   This was a double premiere; Tchaikovsky's opera, Iolanthe, opened the same night. See also endnote 11.

9   These are: The Spanish Dance, The Arabian Dance, The Chinese Dance, The Cossack Dance, The Dance of the Mirlitons (Reed Flutes) and The Waltz of the Flowers.

10  The ballet was not well received at the time, principally because the actual narrative finishes at the end of Act 1, and Act 2 is just the series of divertissements, to demonstrate the skill of the dancers. However, the reviews were not all negative. For example, the scene that links the two acts, known as The Waltz of the Snowflakes, was praised. See Fisher (2003, pp. 13–14).

11  The premiere on 26 August 1992, at the King's Theatre, Edinburgh, together with Opera North's Iolanthe, celebrated the centenary of the original Tchaikovsky double bill of 1892 at the Maryinsky Theatre, St Petersburg. See entries in Warrack and West (1992, p. 773) and Craine and Mackrell (2002, p. 351).

12  This is the link scene between reality and fantasy, and thus serves the same narrative purpose as the Waltz of the Snowflakes in the traditional Nutcracker ballet. See endnote 10 above.

13  Now the divertissements are Liquorice Allsorts, Marshmallows, Gobstoppers and the lascivious Knickerbocker Glory. The overwhelming emphasis in these dances is decidedly oral. In this world, the inhabitants communicate by licking and tasting.

14  Pleshcheyev, a writer on Russian theatre, remarked 'towards the beginning of the twentieth century ballet was the best loved entertainment not only of high

society but also of the broad public' (Wiley 1985, p. 10). Wiley also outlines the social make-up of people who attended the ballet:

> There was, first of all, an element of nobility in that audience. From here, moving down the social ladder, we work our way through the ranks of ambassadors, military officers and the rich commercial class. Moving up the theatre – and still further down the social ladder – we would have found lesser officials, students, and, on matinee days, children (Wiley 1985, pp. 10–11).

15  See Peterburgskaya gazeta, 8 December 1892, p. 4, cited in Wiley (1985, p. 221).

16  Not only for children, but with children; the original Nutcracker ballet contained a large number of roles for children, principally students of the Imperial Ballet School, whose presence did not always enhance this new production's reputation. See Fisher (2003, p. 15).

## List of works cited

Anderson, Benedict (2006), *Imagined Communities*, 2nd edn. London: Verso.

Banes, Sally (1998), *Dancing Women: Female Bodies on Stage*. London and New York: Routledge.

Barrett, Martyn (2007), *Children's Knowledge, Beliefs and Feelings about Nations and National Groups*. Hove, East Sussex: Psychology Press.

Bettelheim, Bruno (1991), *The Uses of Enchantment: The Meaning and Importance of Fairy Tales*. Middlesex: Penguin Books.

Bourne, Matthew (choreographer) (1992), *Nutcracker*. Performed by Alan Vincent, Etta Murfitt, and the cast of New Adventures 2002. DVD, Warner Vision International, released 2003.

Bullock, Alan (1985), *The Humanist Tradition in the West*. New York: Norton.

Craine, Debra and Mackrell, Judith (eds) (2002), *The Oxford Dictionary of Dance*. Oxford: Oxford University Press.

Desmond, Jane (ed.) (2001), *Dancing Desires: Choreographing Sexualities on and off the Stage*. Madison: University of Wisconsin Press.

Dumas, Alexandre (1976), *The Nutcracker (Histoire d'un Casse-Noisette)*, Douglas Monroe (trans). London: Oxford University Press.

Fisher, Jennifer (2003), *Nutcracker Nation: How an Old World Ballet became a Christmas Tradition in the New World*. New Haven and London: Yale University Press.

Foster, Susan Leigh (1998), *Choreographing Narrative: Ballet's Staging of Story and Desire*. Bloomington and Indianapolis: Indianapolis University Press.

Hoffmann, ETA (1967), *The Best Tales of Hoffmann*, E. F. Bleiler (trans). New York: Dover Publications Inc.

— (1979, 1816), 'Nussknacker und Mausekönig', in C. W. Contessa, F. de la Motte Fouquè and E. T. A. Hoffmann (eds), *Kinder-Märchen*, vol. 1. Berlin: Realschulbuchhandlung. Hildersheim: Georg Olms Verlag.

Hoffmann, ETA and Dumas, Alexandre (2007), *Nutcracker and Mouse King, The Tale of the Nutcracker*, Joachim Neugroschel (trans). London: Penguin Books.

Hunt, Peter (2001), *Children's Literature*. Malden, MA: Blackwell Publishing.

Hutcheon, Linda (2006), *A Theory of Adaptation*. New York: Routledge.

Ivanov, Lev and Wright, Peter (1985), *The Nutcracker*. Performed by Lesley Collier, Anthony Dowell, and the cast of the Royal Ballet. DVD, Warner Vision International and NVC Arts.

Lüthi, Max (1970), *Once Upon a Time: On the Nature of Fairy Tales*, Lee Chadeayne and Paul Gottwald (trans). Bloomington and London: Indiana University Press.

Macaulay, Alastair (ed.) (1999), *Matthew Bourne and his Adventures in Motion Pictures*. London and New York: Faber and Faber.

Sanders, Julie (2006), *Adaptation and Appropriation*. Abingdon, VA: Routledge.

Smith, Anthony David (1991), *National Identity*. Reno and Las Vegas: University of Nevada Press.

— (1999), *Myths and Memories of the Nation*. Oxford: Blackwell.

Stephens, John and McCallum, Robyn (1998), *Retelling Stories, Framing Cultures: Traditional Story and Metanarrative in Children's Literature*. Abingdon: Routledge.

Warrack, John and West, Ewan (eds) (1992), *The Oxford Dictionary of Opera*. Oxford: Oxford University Press.

Wiley, Roland John (1985), *Tchaikovsky's Ballets*. Oxford: Clarendon Press.

Wodak, Ruth, de Cillia, Rudolph, Reisigl, Martin, and Leibart, Karin (2009), *The Discursive Construction of National Identity*. Edinburgh: Edinburgh University Press.

Zipes, Jack (1997), *Happily Ever After: Fairy Tales, Children, and the Culture Industry*. New York and London: Routledge.

— (1999), *When Dreams Came True: Classical Fairy Tales and their Tradition*. New York and London: Routledge.

— (2002), *Sticks and Stones: The Troublesome Success of Children's Literature from Slovenly Peter to Harry Potter*. New and London: Routledge.

— (2006), *Fairy Tales and the Art of Subversion*. New York and Oxford: Routledge.

— (2007), 'The merry dance of the Nutcracker: discovering the world through fairy tales', in Introduction to ETA Hoffman and Alexandre Dumas, *Nutcracker and Mouse King, The Tale of the Nutcracker*. London: Penguin Books, pp. vii–xxx.

# 11

# *Pinocchio* in English

Iain Halliday

It is a truism to state that very nearly all children's literature is written and published by adults, but stating the obvious can sometimes be useful. When we consider adults in contrast to their non-adult counterparts, we tend to give to our categories a unity that they simply and objectively do not have, and can never have given the nature of human beings. We expect that adult writers, adult publishers and adult adapters of books will share a common outlook on the nature of the work they are engaged in when they prepare literature for children, but the reality is that such a common outlook is impossible given the myriad variety of concerns that these adults necessarily have; one adapter may have been commissioned by a publisher to produce a text suitable for a 32-page picture book, another may have a brief that includes a more philologically rigorous concern and respect for the original text, yet another may have received instructions to maintain an overriding concern with keeping the language basic, which necessarily means considerable changes to what Linda Hutcheon prefers to call the adapted text rather than the source or original text (2006, p. xiii). Here, Hutcheon herself is an adapter, changing language to suit her purpose and thus manifesting another reading, another approach.

I hope in this chapter on Pinocchio's adventures in the English language, adventures that continue at a distance of some 120 years since their first appearance, to show that every republication of *Pinocchio* is to some extent an *adaptation*. The fact that Pinocchio as a character and *The Adventures of Pinocchio* as a text have been in the public domain for many years (and in any case first appeared in an age when application of copyright rules was haphazard to say the least) is significant because those who have adapted the text have had completely free rein in terms of authorial and editorial control. And in merely quantitative terms, we shall see later in this chapter that even a praiseworthy attempt made in the 1980s to catalogue existing editions (including all adaptations) of the character and the story in English in North America proved impossible. For my purposes here, I have limited my choice of texts to some seven editions that span the publishing history of *Pinocchio* in English, a selection that includes the very first translation into English and one theatrical adaptation. I have never seen a theatrical production based on this last, so it remains for me a printed text, just like the other texts analysed here. Nevertheless, while not offering examples of audiovisual adaptation, which is today the most widespread form of adaptation, the texts of the seven editions do provide some interesting material for analysis.

Indeed, the textual adventures of Pinocchio since 1892 contain illuminating evidence of the fact that publishers and adapters carry out their work with very specific goals in mind, with precise purposes guiding their editorial interventions. Literature for children, despite an adult tendency to reduce it to a monolithic category – in the same way that many adults tend to view childhood as a homogenous – is just as heterogeneous as literature for adults. Adaptations, which are expressions of intralingual translation, constitute confirmation of the ambivalent and subjective nature of reading and publishing.

So, adult exponents and users of children's literature – writers, publishers, purchasers and readers – do not constitute a unitary category and this fact is reflected in the great variety of published children's literature that is now available. Another, positive phenomenon of recent times is a change in the way children's literature is perceived. There is now less of a tendency among adults to dismiss all writing for children as kids' stuff that is by definition inferior to writing for adults. Philip Pullman's success in 2002 in winning the Whitbread Book of the Year with his novel *The Amber Spyglass* is indicative of this change, and indeed he himself in a 2003 article in *The Times* said: 'I've been arguing for a long time that children's books belong in the general literary conversation' (Pullman 2003). But, of course, the general literary conversation is in itself a conversation that contains many different points of view regarding authors, styles, themes and genres; even the canon is open to constant discussion in the literary schemes of things.

In 1980, the Israeli scholar Zohar Shavit published an article titled, 'The Ambivalent Status of Texts: the Case of Children's Literature.' In it she states:

> At a given point, in a given period, a text normally has a univocal status in the system it has entered. This is the case with most of the literary texts. However, some texts maintain a status which cannot be seen as univocal, but rather as diffuse ... Children's literature read primarily by adults is a typical example of a class of texts whose status is not univocal. (Shavit 1980, p. 75)

I would like to suggest, using some examples from various English editions of Collodi's *The Adventures of Pinocchio*, that it is precisely this ambivalence which lies in large part behind the motivations for the various adaptations and abridgements of the work across the 120 years since its first publication in English in a translation by Mary Alice Murray. The other major point I intend to make is that in the ambit of children's literature even canonical texts ostensibly written for children are not above adaptation within the genre and indeed are sometimes adapted to make them apparently more appropriate for specific child readers, to suit the purposes of whoever is carrying out the adaptation.

That children's literature is also (if not 'primarily') read by adults is another truism that often remains unacknowledged; before becoming autonomous readers, children are generally aided in their reading by adults and many adults will maintain an interest in their children's reading even when they are autonomous. Certainly it is a fact of life that adults have always reviewed, bought or somehow provided and often participated in or guided the reading of children. Another useful point to recall is that very few works of literature in any genre immediately have or are immediately guaranteed canonical status. Here are the words of an anonymous reviewer of the first edition of *Pinocchio*, published in *The Bookman* in 1892: 'Children are at once so independent and so conservative in their literary judgments, that we hesitate before recommending books to them that are not sanctified by custom and tradition' (1892, p. 148). Such was the novelty of Collodi's work that the reviewer approached it with some trepidation, but then with a considerable dose of (adult) irony he or she proceeded to provide the stamp of approval:

> It is with their elders we have to deal, and with them we are on more certain ground. Children seeking gifts, therefore, for their sober-minded elders might do worse than choose this "Story of a Puppet." Pinocchio is the most fascinating creature we have met with for a long time. (1892, p. 148)

Pinocchio's systemic ambivalence (children's/adult literature) has been present since the very beginning of his life in English, as his narrative ambivalence (boy–puppet/well-behaved–delinquent) continues to be one of the driving forces behind the text's continued success. Shavit's use of the word 'diffuse' in the quotation above, with its suggestion of an amorphous, changeable status for children's literature, also affords some reflection on the fact that in the denotative meaning of 'diffuse', *Pinocchio* must certainly be, and has been since the early twentieth century, one of the most widely distributed and widely read children's stories in the Anglophone world and beyond.

To return momentarily to *The Bookman* review, its very last sentence goes thus: 'The translator's part has been skilfully carried out, and never for a moment hinders us from recognizing that the story of Pinocchio is a work of genius' (1892, p. 148). I have no wish, in this context, to enter into any detailed discussion of the matter of the interlingual translation of *Pinocchio* – for the most part I will be looking more at the matter of intralingual translation, which is what adaptation is – but it does seem appropriate to join with the anonymous reviewer in complimenting M. A. Murray for the effectiveness of her work as translator and to compliment the reviewer on his or her foresight in identifying the text as a work of genius. Canonical status for *Pinocchio* would not be long in coming: *Pinocchio*'s publication in London in the Everyman's Library edition of 1911 (in Murray's translation) is a useful marker of this event.

The illustrated title pages of the Everyman's Library edition of *Pinocchio* carry an epigraph from Shakespeare's *The Winter's Tale*: 'This is fairy gold, boy, and 'twill prove so' (*WT*: III 3).[1] The decision by the publisher to include this epigraph does indeed provide heady and prestigious company for a work that had been published barely two decades previously. Similarly, the work and its author are also granted the status of a dedicated introduction; at the very end of this laudatory piece, however, we find an example of some shoddy editorial work – evidently a sort of copy and paste mix-up – where the writer of the introduction blithely states, 'The following are the chief editions of *Pinocchio*' (Lorenzini 1911), as prelude to a long list of many of Lorenzini's works, none of them actually editions of *Pinocchio*. As mentioned above, this first Everyman's Library edition makes use of the Murray translation and certainly in the few passages I have compared word for word, the texts are identical, but I have not undertaken the painstaking job of attempting the close reading necessary to root out any editorial changes made in its preparation.

Some two years previously, *Pinocchio* had been published in the United States and in England by Doubleday in an edition with a translation by A. G. Caprani, edited by Mary E. Burt. Here, too, there is a biographical introduction to Lorenzini – much more detailed and accurate than in the Everyman's Library edition. Burt's preface to the work is also very interesting in the way it grants prestige to the work and tells us much about the circulation of books in general and *Pinocchio* in particular at the beginning of the twentieth century:

> While travelling in Italy in 1902, I found the book, Pinocchio, in Naples. I was told that many hundred thousand copies of it had been sold in Italy and that it was regarded as the greatest Italian juvenile ever written. I had never seen the

book before and I presume [*sic*] that no English translation of the story had been made in America although one existed in England, I was told, made by some English scholar. When I came to the city of Florence, I went to the publishers who agreed to sell me the right to bring out a translation in America, and so this book is not pirated.

Pinocchio, like "Alice in Wonderland," or "Robinson Crusoe," or "Rikki-tikki-tavi," or "Howell's Pony Engine," or "Gulliver's Travels," is an immortal, a classic, a landmark in the world of letters. It is a child's book, a teacher's book, a parents' assistant, a guide to common sense, a book of fun, a serious book, a fairy-tale, a treatise on ethics. (Lorenzini 1909, p. xvii)

Burt's concern to emphasize that her edition is not pirated is indicative of the extent to which piracy must have been a problem at that time. Interesting also is the transatlantic dismissal of M. A. Murray's translation as a job done 'by some English scholar', an attitude we might expect of someone who 'found' the book in its native Italy and who, as editor of the translator's work, gets her name on the title page: the proprietary instinct is often a strong one in anyone who edits, let alone in anyone who consciously sets out to adapt.

These two editions, though both extremely close to the original interlingual translation process, do provide us with an opportunity to compare two coeval English texts of the story – there are some interesting linguistic points to consider that do not derive from the question of the translation from Italian into English. The episode I have chosen to analyse comes at the end of Chapter XIX and is Pinocchio's famous courtroom appearance.

The judge was a big Monkey of the Gorilla species. He was much respected for his great age and his white beard, and especially for his gold spectacle frames which he wore without any glasses in them. These he was obliged to wear on account of weak tear ducts which had given him weeping eyes for many years. Pinocchio related to the Judge every detail of the fraud of which he was the victim. He gave the names and a description of the rascals and ended by asking for justice. (Lorenzini 1909)

The judge was a big ape of the gorilla tribe—an old ape respectable for his age, his white beard, but especially for his gold spectacles without glasses that he was always obliged to wear, on account of an inflammation of the eyes that had tormented him for many years. Pinocchio related in the presence of the judge all the particulars of the infamous fraud of which he had been the victim. He gave the names, the surnames, and other details, of the two rascals, and ended by demanding justice. (Lorenzini 1911)

Leaving aside all open-class words, which can obviously differ in the two texts due to the fact that they are distinct translations of the same source text, it is obvious that Burt (Lorenzini 1909) has a penchant for capitalization: several simple nouns are granted the status of proper nouns or names, while Murray (Lorenzini 1911) has a 'down' style. Murray, on the other hand, has a preference for 'that' as relative pronoun before a defining clause, while Burt prefers 'which'. It is easy to dismiss these as minor differences, saying that such matters simply regard style, but the point is that style is in itself, *in nuce*, a manifestation of adaptation. Another possible way of explaining these relatively minor differences is to suggest (quite reasonably) that they derive from the differences between British and American English. Having worked during the 1980s in the editorial department of a leading British children's book publisher for whom American co-editions of works were particularly important from a sales and a prestige point of view, I know that the Americanization of British texts is an adaptation activity that regularly takes place. Indeed, in more recent times, the publication of the *Harry Potter* series in the United States brought this type of adaptation to the limelight. In a 1999 *New Yorker* article by Daniel Radosh, which appeared shortly after the publication of *Harry Potter and the Prisoner of Azkaban*, Arthur Levine, editor at the American publishers Scholastic, had this to say about his work:

> I wasn't trying to, quote, "Americanize" them. What I was trying to do is translate, which I think is different. I wanted to make sure that an American kid reading the book would have the same literary experience that a British kid would have. A kid should be confused or challenged when the author wants the kid to be confused or challenged and not because of a difference of language. (Radosh 1999, p. 56)

Once again, adaptation appears in the form of an intralingual translation. Radosh also points out that at least one British expression was translated in such a way as to remove any possible confusion or challenge and to make the language sound even more British: 'cracking' became 'spanking good'. The process is evidently a sophisticated one that requires some considerable attention and thought – Levine indicates that he consulted frequently with the book's author, J. K. Rowling and sums up his work in this way, 'I wouldn't say it was done haphazardly – I'd say that it was not done mechanically' (Radosh 1999, p. 56).

But to return to our 1909 and 1911 editions of *Pinocchio*, two original texts – or rather as close to English-language originals as we can come in the case of Collodi's work – it will be interesting to take a look at the same two paragraphs as published in editions of *Pinocchio* from 1938 to 2003, the former being an acknowledged 'ABRIDGED EDITION'.

| | |
|---|---|
| The judge was a big ape of the gorilla tribe—an old ape respectable for his age, his white beard, but especially for his gold spectacles without glasses that he was always obliged to wear, on account of an inflammation of the eyes. | The judge was a venerable old monkey, with a venerable white beard and a very venerable pair of gold-rimmed spectacles, with no lenses, which he was forced to wear on account of an infection that had been troubling him for years. |
| The judge listened with great benignity, and, when the puppet had nothing further to say, he stretched out his hand and rang a bell. (Collodi 1938) | When Pinocchio came before the judge, he explained the despicable trick that had been played on him. He gave the names and descriptions of the two villains and ended by asking for justice. (Collodi 2003) |

Immediately obvious is the fact that the 1938 abridged version is based on Murray's translation and its second paragraph bears neither relation to the second paragraph of that text nor to the text of the unabridged 2003 edition, for the evident reason that the entire paragraph in which Pinocchio's speech before the judge is described has been suppressed. Abridgement, as a form of adaptation, is often simply a brutal reduction of a text to make it fit within the confines of a publishing format – in this case, a small, illustrated hardback edition. While such work is not mechanical, it does come close to it. The briefest of glances at the book, with illustrations by Esther Friend, is enough to let us realize that here we are dealing with a text that can only be, is indeed intended to be, reductive. A look at the simple stylized lines of the front cover illustration and the fact that Pinocchio carries a spelling book under his arm further explains what type of Pinocchio is on offer here. The title page shows Pinocchio himself proudly presenting 'AN ABRIDGED EDITION'. Some forms of adaptation are simply governed by the contingencies of deciding to publish in particular sectors of the book market; and the children's book market has as many if not more typologies of books from which to choose, from colouring books to picture books, to staged readers and complete texts. These typologies reflect the fact that for children reading is a learning process spanning some years.

In the above extract from her 2003 'translation' of *Pinocchio* for Walker Books, Emma Rose introduces in the very first sentence a technique that is appropriate in texts for young readers: repetition. The word 'venerable', itself a high-register addition, is repeated three times adjectivally. Her use of 'monkey', rather than 'ape' does recall Collodi's original, in which the judge is a *scimmione*, literally a 'big monkey'. From a diachronic point of view, our more modern 'lenses' appears instead of 'glasses', which, of course, in contemporary English has come to be a much more widely used word for 'spectacles'; the stronger, more serious 'infection' replaces the more generic 'inflammation'. 'Despicable trick' leads us away from the legal status of the word 'fraud'; and while it is more apparently reassuring and perhaps appropriately less alarming in the context of children's literature, it does detract somewhat from the exaggerated absurdity of Collodi's scene in the supposed formality of the courtroom. But then 'rascals', as used in the 1909 and 1911 editions, becomes 'villains' – surely a weightier, more serious piece of vocabulary.

To continue with this comparative analysis, here is a further extract from the 1938 and 2003 editions, continuing from the courtroom scene:

The judge listened with great benignity, and, when the puppet had nothing further to say, he stretched out his hand and rang a bell. At this summons two mastifs immediately appeared dressed as gendarmes. The judge, pointing to Pinocchio, said to them: 'That poor devil has been robbed of four gold pieces; take him up and put him immediately into prison.'

The puppet was petrified on hearing this unexpected sentence and tried to protest; but the gendarmes stopped his mouth and carried him off to the lockup.

And there he remained for four months—four long months—and would have remained longer still if a fortunate chance had not released him. For I must tell you that the young Emperor who

The venerable monkey listened with interest. He nodded sympathetically, and even wiped away a tear. Then, when the story was over, he reached out and rang a bell. Two mastiffs in constable's uniforms came into the courtroom.

'This poor devil has had four gold coins stolen from him,' the judge said to them. 'Take him to the cells.'

When Pinocchio heard this, he was dumbfounded. He was about to protest, but the policemen avoided any pointless time-wasting by covering his mouth and dragging him off to jail.

Which was where he remained for four whole months. It would have been longer, except that he had a stroke of luck: the young emperor who ruled over Swindleton, having won a great victory against his enemy, ordered public celebrations, including illuminations, fireworks, races and, as a final grand gesture, freedom for all the villains in the city's prisons.

reigned over the town of 'Trap for Blockheads,' having won a splendid victory over his enemies, ordered great public rejoicings. There were illuminations, fireworks, horse races, and velocipede races, and as a further sign of triumph he commanded that the prisons should be opened and all the prisoners liberated. (Collodi 1938)

'If they're being let out, I should be too,' Pinocchio said to his jailer.

'No, not you,' the man replied. 'You're not a villain.'

'I am, I really am,' insisted Pinocchio. 'I'm an incorrigible scoundrel.'

'I do beg your pardon,' said the jailer. 'My mistake.'

He opened the door of Pinocchio's cell, doffed his cap and bade him a polite farewell. (Collodi 2003)

Rose avoids the word 'benignity', certainly a legacy of the first translations with their literal use of the cognate (and synonym) of *benignità*, which the *OED* quotations show has much declined in use throughout the twentieth century. 'To listen with interest', 'to nod sympathetically' and above all 'to wipe away a tear' are very adept ways of expressing the concepts in the original description of the judge's behaviour, but above all they are expressions of our time, expressions we are familiar with as early twenty-first century Anglophones. The relative elegance and rarity of 'dumbfounded' rings much better to our ears than 'thunderstruck' (Burt/Caprani) or 'petrified' (Murray). The noun form 'time-wasting' is certainly an improvement (and would have been even in the early twentieth century) of a 'waste of time' (Burt/Caprani) or 'losing time' (Murray). A 'stroke of luck' is a much more natural form than either 'a lucky circumstance' (Burt/Caprani) or 'a fortunate chance' (Murray/Rand, McNally). The name of the town, *Acchiappa-citrulli*, is certainly better conveyed with 'Swindleton' than the more literal 'Fools' Trap' (Burt/Caprani) and 'Trap for Blockheads' (Murray/Rand McNally) simply because it reads morphologically as a plausible name for an Anglophone town while maintaining the semantics of the original. The 'velocipede races' become simply races, perhaps because today even children's parents would have difficulty with the archaic 'velocipede', which we now know as a bicycle. The Barbary horse races disappear completely, perhaps considered a cumbersome detail, perhaps in order to gain a line in the page layout. Very effective is the high register, the almost-pomposity – which is, of course, absurd coming from such a stupid creature as Pinocchio is – of, 'I'm an incorrigible scoundrel'. In a similar vein is the formula, 'doffed his cap'. But these features, too, constitute stylish writing from Rose, an embellishment in her adaptation.

Another two editions of *Pinocchio* I think worthy of some discussion here are Adams T. Rice's theatrical rendition published by Samuel French in the United

States in 1931 and *Pinocchio . . . Put into Basic by Margaret Bottrall,* published by Kegan Paul & Co. in London in 1940.

Basic is an acronym for British American Scientific Commercial. Anyone who wants to go beyond the acronym and learn more about Charles K. Ogden's fascinating scheme need do no more than point their browser to URL http://www.ogden.basic-english.org where they will find the following presentation:

> If one were to take the 25,000 word Oxford Pocket English Dictionary and take away the redundancies of our rich language and eliminate the words that can be made by putting together simpler words, we find that 90% of the concepts in that dictionary can be achieved with 850 words. The shortened list makes simpler the effort to learn spelling and pronunciation irregularities. The rules of usage are identical to full English so that the practitioner communicates in perfectly good, but simple, English.
>
> We call this simplified language Basic English, the developer is Charles K. Ogden, and was released in 1930 with the book: *Basic English: A General Introduction with Rules and Grammar.* He founded the Orthological Institute to develop the tools for teaching Basic English. His most famous associate, I. A. Richards, led the effort in the Orient, which uses the techniques to this day. (*Ogden Basic English*)

Ogden's introduction to the 1940 Basic edition of *Pinocchio* tells us a lot not only about Basic English, but also about his attitude towards the job of adapting the text (entrusted to Mrs. Bottrall) for basic purposes. The first point to make is a contextual one: this 1940 edition of *Pinocchio* represents a synchronized film tie-in with the release of what perhaps remains the most famous adaptation of Collodi's work: Walt Disney's animated version. Again, it is important to remember that an added benefit for Ogden as publisher was the fact that the original text was, even then, conveniently out of copyright.

The story itself begins immediately with a travesty of the original text, where 'Once upon a time' is replaced with the Basic, 'There was at one time . . .' and, '"A king!" my little readers will instantly exclaim,' with, '"A great ruler!" my little readers will say', – which truly is wishful thinking on the part of Mr Ogden and Mrs Bottrall (Collodi 1940, p. 11). The travesty continues with a paragraph dedicated to explaining what a 'marionette' theatre is – the rules of Basic English eliminate the word 'puppet' from the vocabulary of the language – before we learn that Geppetto decided to make Pinocchio because in this way he will 'get some money' (Collodi 1940, p. 11). This really is very basic entrepreneurial stuff and I found myself turning to the originals to verify Geppetto's venal credentials, which in M. A. Murray's 1892 translation are presented thus: 'With this puppet I would travel about the world to earn a piece of bread and a glass of wine' (Lorenzini 1892, p. 6). Geppetto, in truth, was simply a man of subsistence-level ambition, but by 1940, although he was speaking in extremely plain English, he was also expressing an extremely plain enthusiasm for capitalist realities. And it is also worth noting that we are well into Chapter Two at this stage in the original: the Basic edition appears to be a serious reduction with serious embellishment, too.

The prestigious theatrical publishers Samuel French produced an edition of *Pinocchio* in 1931 and here again we find that the appropriation of the work is so violent that no respect at all is shown for the integrity of Collodi's story, indeed the provenance of the story is reduced to the status of 'Dramatized from the Translation of The Italian Fairy Tale by Hezekiah Butterworth', with no mention at all of Carlo Collodi, while Samuel French's copyright notice in fine legalese, including a long extract from US statutes, warns transgressors about possible prosecution. To provide an idea of how the story is altered, the first scene brings us a convenient visit to Geppetto by the character of Fire-Eater, the puppeteer, to commission a new puppet.

I was curious to see whether Samuel French still had *Pinocchio* on their list, and a brief catalogue search on the internet (http://www.samuelfrench.com) shows that it is no longer in print, while the catalogue provides us with two currently available stage versions, one by John Morley, which appears to be a musical, and one by Blanche Marvin, which appears to be thoroughly confused in that it is 'Based on Pirandello's Six Characters in Search of an Author' – evidently publishers, writers, editors can reach a point in the adaptation and appropriation process where one classic is not enough and two can be amalgamated while retaining only the title of one of the works.

The observations and analyses above (particularly the textual analyses) show clearly the attention to detail, the close reading that is required in any thoughtful consideration of a text and in any thoughtful discussion of any adaptation of a text. They also show us, however, that the nature of a text illuminates the purpose behind any adaptation that text has undergone. The layers of reading behind the preparation of texts for publication and for adaptation manifest themselves in the textual variations we find from one edition to another and from one adaptation to another. All of the layers of reading undertaken for this project, all of the analysis, brings to mind what

George Steiner posited in the first chapter of his seminal book, *After Babel*, 'Understanding as Translation':

> Any model of communication is at the same time a model of translation, of a vertical or horizontal transfer of significance. No two historical epochs, no two social classes, no two localities use words and syntax to signify exactly the same things, to send identical signals of valuation and inference. Neither do two human beings. (Steiner 1992, p. 47)

And neither does an editor and his or her reader. We are all necessarily translators, all of the time. Readers of *Pinocchio* (and this category includes publishers) have always made use and will always continue to make use of the text for their own, particular, purposes: whether that purpose be something as ordinary (and as rewarding) as reading a story with a child, something as noble as providing a philologically valid text or something as perverted as writing and filming a pornographic version of the story. This last undocumented reference of course (and thankfully) is certainly not within the ambit of children's literature and is perhaps of more pressing and useful interest to behavioural psychologists than to scholars of language and literature.[2] The root meaning of 'to adapt', after all, means to physically alter something so that it fits a purpose. Indeed, as Linda Hutcheon puts it in the first chapter of *A Theory of Adaptation* in which she eschews the notion of fidelity as being a paramount criterion in the study of adaptations: 'If the idea of fidelity should not frame any theorizing of adaptation today, what should? According to its dictionary meaning, "to adapt" is to adjust, to alter, to make suitable. This can be done in any number of ways' (Hutcheon 2006, p. 7).

*Pinocchio* in English, *Pinocchio* the text, exemplifies that 'any number of ways'. And then, fittingly, Pinocchio himself, Pinocchio the character, begins his life as a log, before his own transformation at the hands of Geppetto into a puppet and then, through his experiences in the world, into a boy; he is an adaptation.

The genesis of *Pinocchio* in English as a posthumous, translated work published in a period of rampant piracy meant that the text was fair game for appropriation, adaptations, abridgements. The plethora of adaptations of the text mean that inevitably there are some that constitute distortions (even perversions) of the original story and they remain so even when those adaptations are successful in terms of their own purposes. *Pinocchio* in Basic English, for example, respects the linguistic strictures of its own scheme, but reduces and condemns the text and the character to a linguistic stasis that is the antithesis of Collodi's story. This said, Ogden's *Pinocchio* is in itself an expression of a particular concern from a particular time and as such is valuable as an adaptation, as all adaptations, as all readings are, precisely because they help us understand texts and their reception by readers.

Richard Wunderlich had this to say in the introduction to his admirable, though as he himself admits, ultimately incomplete, *The Pinocchio Catalogue*:

> *Pinocchio* in English rendition tells us about North American society, its changes over time, and the changes in its perception of children. In this regard *Pinocchio* offers a unique and almost archaeological record: it provides an original alongside a very full series of reasonably dated adaptations of various types. And if adaptations are dated, the approximate dates of particular kinds of change become known; and when these are known, the social conditions prompting them can be better disentangled. Hence *Pinocchio*, the original, designed to tell us something about ourselves individually, in adaptation over time, tells us something about ourselves collectively. (Wunderlich 1988, pp. vii–viii)

In this chapter, we have seen that the seven versions of *Pinocchio* selected for analysis represent considerable variety in their approaches. I have argued elsewhere that the 1892 translation of Collodi's work by Mary Alice Murray is the 'definitive' and most effective translation, partly because of its fidelity to the source text (it is evident that fidelity was and still is a paramount criterion in interlingual translation).[3] Murray's translation is the starting point for many subsequent adaptations. The 1909 and 1911 editions – American and English respectively – represent *Pinocchio*'s entry into the canon of Anglophone children's literature. The linguistic differences between the texts evidently and inevitably reflect the slight differences in the two forms of the language; the differences in the publishing contexts and the presentations of the work show us (particularly with regard to the American edition) how adaptation can also be a form of appropriation. The 1931 theatrical edition published by Samuel French, the abridged Rand McNally edition of 1938 and Ogden's Basic English edition of 1940 are all versions in which, due to the contingencies of the type of adaptation required, *Pinocchio*, for better and for worse, becomes something other than Collodi's original work. Walker Books' 2003 edition completes the diachronic spread of the selected works and was chosen deliberately because it is a complete version of the text in which we can see the English language being adapted to suit contemporary usage.

It is the reason why works are adapted that is the key to understanding adaptations. Close consideration of the contexts in which the works are collocated, in time and in space, together with close reading of the language used in them can reveal much about the processes, the products and the people who create them.

I would like to end this chapter with the words of Nancy Banks-Smith, someone who has spent much of her working life as a journalist reviewing television programmes, a medium not mentioned in this chapter, but a medium now of immense cultural importance. It is interesting that this quotation, though deriving from consideration of the medium of television, brings us back to the place where all texts in all media find their initial expression: 'You cannot put pen to paper or finger to keyboard without confessing something' (Banks-Smith 2007). Banks-Smith's observation is as true of anyone engaged in any form of adaptation as it is of any creative writer.

# Notes

1   While writing, in what I might realistically call a nostalgic moment, I actually pulled *The Oxford Dictionary of Quotations* from the shelf above my computer in the hope of showing that real reference books are still useful resources, even though it may take minutes, rather than seconds find the source of a quotation. In fact, two or three minutes of searching were enough to show me that the quotation in question simply is not there in the 1999 fifth edition of the dictionary: a Google search provided the exact provenance almost immediately.

2   The fact of the existence of pornographic versions of *Pinocchio* was brought to my attention by Roberto Fedi of the Università Italiana per Stranieri di Perugia in the context of a small conference on the work held in Catania in April 2010. During my presentation I had thought I would inject some shock value by citing a 1996 English-language horror movie inspired by Collodi's story (*Pinocchio's Revenge*, written and directed by Kevin Tenney, two stars out of five on IMDB), but Prof Fedi trumped me by describing some pornographic comics based on the story. A summary search on Google confirms a shocking abundance of such material, much of it audiovisual, that could prove to be a considerable resource for anyone wishing to carry out research into adaptations of children's literature into works with 'adult' content.

3   Halliday, Iain (2009). *Huck Finn in Italian, Pinocchio in English: Theory and Praxis of Literary Translation*. Madison/Teaneck: Fairleigh Dickinson University Press.

# List of works cited

Banks-Smith, Nancy (2007), 'Last Night's TV: Coronation Street', *The Guardian*,
  1 November, viewed 5 January 2012, <http://www.guardian.co.uk>.
Collodi, Carlo (1938), *Pinocchio*, an abridged edition, Esther Friend (ill). Chicago: Rand
  McNally & Company.
— (1940), *Pinocchio*, put into Basic by Margaret Bottrall, James Forsyth (ill). London:
  Kegan Paul, Trench, Trubner & Co., Ltd.
— (2003), *Pinocchio*, Emma Rose (trans), Sara Fanelli (ill). London: Walker Books.
Halliday, Iain (2009), *Huck Finn in Italian, Pinocchio in English: Theory and Praxis of
  Literary Translation*. Madison/Teaneck: Fairleigh Dickinson University Press.
Hutcheon, Linda (2006), *A Theory of Adaptation*. New York: Routledge.
Lorenzini, Carlo (1892), *The Story of a Puppet; or, the Adventures of Pinocchio*, M. A.
  Murray (trans). London: T. Fisher Unwin.
— (1909), *Adventures Every Child Should Know: The Marvellous Adventures of Pinocchio*,
  Mary E. Burt (ed.) from an original translation by A. G. Caprani (trans). London,
  New York: Doubleday, Page & Co.
— (1911), *Pinocchio*, M. A. Murray (trans). London: Everyman's Library.
*Ogden's Basic English*, viewed 5 January 2012, <http://www.ogden.basic-english.org>.
Pullman, Philip (2003), 'The Big Read', in *The Times*. London, December 20.
Radosh, Daniel (1999), 'Why American kids don't consider Harry Potter an insufferable
  prig', in *The New Yorker*, September 20: 54–6.
Rice, Adams T. (1931), *Pinocchio: A Fantastic Comedy in Eight Scenes*, Dramatized from
  the Translation of the Italian Fairy Tale of Hezekiah Butterworth. New York, Los
  Angeles: Samuel French.
Samuel French, Inc., The House of Plays and Musical Plays for Over 175 Years. Online
  catalogue, viewed 4 January 2012, <http://www.samuelfrench.com>.
Shavit, Zohar (1980), 'The Ambivalent Status of Texts: The Case of Children's Literature'.
  *Poetics Today*, 1(3), Special Issue: *Narratology I: Poetics of Fiction* Spring, 75–86.
Steiner, George (1992), *After Babel: Aspects of Language and Translation*, 2nd edn.
  Oxford: Oxford University Press.
*The Bookman* (January 1892), 'The Story of a Puppet', p. 148.
Wunderlich, Richard (1988), *The Pinocchio Catalogue: Being a Descriptive Bibliography
  and Printing History of English Language Translations and Other Renditions
  Appearing in the United States, 1892–1987*. New York: Greenwood Press.

# 12

# To Be or Not to Be a Canonical Text of Children's Literature: Polish and Italian Translations of *Winnie-the-Pooh*

Monika Wozniak

With regard to translations of children's literature, Emer O'Sullivan distinguishes three kinds of texts:

- adults' classics assimilated by children's narrative;
- fairy tales and other traditional narratives, often originated from oral culture and mythological tales;
- works created and written explicitly for children. (O'Sullivan 2005, p. 132)

These types are usually associated with three main procedures: adults' classics are adapted, fairy tales and myths are retold and children's narratives are translated. While we approve of or at least understand the necessity of simplifying adult classics in order to make them accessible to children, children's canonical works seem to be given a more solid literary status. That is not to say that they are not subject to alterations and interventions of all sorts in the process of being transferred into other languages. However, these changes are examined carefully and are often frowned upon by the scholars who opine that a canonical work of children's literature should be granted the same respect and the same rights as any literary classic; adaptations should therefore not deviate from the original. In view of the undeniable mutilations some children's masterpieces have suffered in the process of linguistic transfer into new cultural contexts, this approach seems irreprehensible from an ethical as well as a strictly literary point of view. I will argue, however, that the problem is by no means as simple as that, and it is, in fact, still open to debate.

Take, for example, Carlo Lorenzetti's *Pinocchio*. Collodi's novel is doubtlessly a classic, a canonical work of children's literature. Nevertheless, the Italian original has undergone numerous transformations in different countries. Iain Halliday's contribution to the present volume has illustrated Pinocchio's various fates in English translations. The American *Pinocchio*, and Disney's *Pinocchio* in particularly, thus have become rather distant cousins of the original Italian puppet. But the case of *Pinocchio* appears even more complicated if we shift our attention to Eastern Europe. In Russia, where *Pinocchio* was also translated (1908, 1924 and 1959), Aleksey Tolstoy rewrote Collodi's work in 1936, claiming that he had read the original novel only once, in his childhood, and therefore he decided to write a new story based only loosely on the Italian book. This new version, called *Golden Key or the Amazing Adventures of the Puppet Buratino*, gained more popularity than Collodi's translations, became a classic work of the children's literary canon in Russia, and successively also in Belarus and Ukraine. When, in the 1990s, political transformations made direct contacts between the Western and Eastern book markets possible, some editors published new translations of Collodi's *Pinocchio*, but the audience did not accept them: as it turned out, Tolstoy's work was already too deeply embedded in the national culture to be displaced by its Italian model. It means that several millions of Russian, Ukrainian and Belarusian children have never read the original *Pinocchio*.

But let us move to the main topic of this chapter, the case of *Winnie-the-Pooh*. Both *Winnie-the-Pooh* (1926) and *The House at Pooh Corner* (1928) are undoubtedly canonical works of English Children's Literature, becoming classics almost as soon as they were released. The first English edition of *Winnie-the-Pooh* exceeded 30,000 copies, an impressive number by the standards of that period,[1] while in the United States 150,000 copies were sold by the end of 1926. By 1968, the English editions alone exceeded 1.5 million copies. Even more importantly, Milne's books were hailed by critics as 'full of delights for all children under seventy' (Thwaite 1992, p. 99) and that they 'are and should be classics' (Connolly 1995, p. 14). Winnie-the-Pooh found enthusiasts among adult readers: 'Adults loved him first... Every intellectual knew the books by heart' (Thwaite 1991, p. 318). An article from 1931, saying that Milne 'may be said to have already won immortality in the nursery' (Thwaite 1992, p. 129) was expressing a general opinion. By the 1930s, the novels had already acquired the status of a cultural icon and the Pooh industry was flourishing, offering toys of various kinds, board games and even paper dolls. The following decades consolidated the prestige and the status of Milne's creation. Translations in Esperanto (*Winnie-la-Pu* 1972) and in Latin (*Winnie-ille-Pu* 1958, the first foreign-language book to be featured on the *New York Times* Best Seller List), both of course products of and mainly for an adult readership, conferred to the Bear of the Very Little Brain an almost mystical aura of uniqueness and nobility, unparalleled by any other children's classic. Of course, since the 1960s *Winnie-the-Pooh* has also become one of the most profitable fictional characters to be copyrighted by Walt Disney Company Franchises, grossing billions of dollars every year.

> The case of Winnie the Pooh is in many ways different from other examples of Disney's literary acquisitions; the company has completely absorbed the character, right down to the original conceptual design, spitting out only the hyphens in its original name. No other source material for a Disney animated film has undergone the total corporate integration of Milne and Shepard's work. (Taylor 2005, p. 183)

However, Disney's aggressive appropriation of Milne's work and the subsequent replacement of the original visuals with their disneyfied simulacra in the imaginations of children do not necessarily need to be seen as a threat to the canonical status of the original text. One can even argue that the Disney Company enhanced – for their own commercial purposes – the prestige of Milne's novels, and 'part of [the Disney] films' success may be attributed to a perceived faithfulness to their source material' (Taylor 2005, p. 184). Therefore, as O'Sullivan notes: 'To the present day the book enjoys an almost cult status among young adults in America and … is one of the most quoted children's books in British culture' (1993, p. 112).

But if this may be true in English-speaking countries[2] it does not automatically mean that the same patterns apply to the countries where the *Winnie-the-Pooh* books had to be mediated by a linguistic and cultural transfer. In fact, the reception of Milne's novels and their resulting literary status in the two countries constituting the object of my study could not be more different: whereas in Poland, Milne's novels have become truly beloved classics that defend their privileged status in the face of Disney's insistent marketing action, in Italy, the original *Winnie-the-Pooh* has not so much been erased by Disney's version, but rather never had a chance to truly take an eminent role in Italian children's literature. I will try examining the reasons behind such a striking contrast, in order to understand better the dynamics and the various factors deciding on a successful or failed entrance of a literary work into a target literature and culture. I will consider issues that inhere directly to Milne's translations or adaptations in both languages, as well as the influence of multiple extratextual factors in Italy and Poland.

The first, obvious difference is the number of translations of Milne's books: four in Italy versus only two in Poland. In Italy, *Winnie the Pooh* first arrived in 1936, translated by Lila Jahn and published in Milan by Genio as *L'orsacchiotto Ninni Puf, traduzione dall'americano. Con numerose illustrazioni di Edward H. Shepard* (*Teddy bear Ninni Puf, translation from American [sic!]. With numerous illustrations by Edward H. Shepard*). This version was never reprinted and today is completely forgotten.[3] After World War II, Elda Zuccaro[4] translated both *Pooh* books, curiously first *La casa nei paraggi di Puh* (*The House in the vicinity of Puh* 1948) and then *Uini il Puh* (1949), all published by Genio.[5] In 1960, yet another translation arrived, *Winny Puh l'orsetto*[6] (*Winny Puh teddy bear*) by Maria Cristina Gaetani and Ida Omboni,[7] who translated the poems. These translations were published by Garzanti in Milan and issued again in 1967, while in 1979 they were reissued by Vallardi. The last Italian translation of the *Pooh* books so far – *Winnie Puh* and *La strada di Puh* (*Puh's road*) – was published in 1993 by Salani. The author of this new version, Luigi Spagnol, a novelist and scriptwriter for theatre and television, is by far the most eminent of Milne's translators in Italy. His versions of the *Pooh* books were reissued twice,[8] but since Spagnol is also the chairman of Salani publishing house, it is hard to tell whether these new editions were motivated by a literary need or rather by economic factors.

All Italian versions can be considered reasonably decent attempts to deliver in Italian the warmth and humour of the English original. Jahn's old translation is probably the most naturalized and the most flawed, due to the translator's imperfect knowledge of the English language and culture, while Spagnol's recent offering seems the most satisfactory and intelligent. To compare in which way the different translators dealt with the problems of conveying linguistic and stylistic dimensions of the English books in a new context is a pleasant academic exercise, but apparently none of these translations managed to conquer the Italian audience as it were. The Winnie-the-Pooh that is best known to Italian children is his Disney incarnation in films and books alike.

In Poland, both *Pooh* books were first published in 1938 by Przeworski, two years after the first Italian edition. Unlike the Italian translation, however, the Polish versions – entitled *Kubuś Puchatek*[9] and *Chatka Puchatka* (*Puchatek's Hut*), both executed by Irena Tuwim (1900–87), – were an immediate success. After the editorial gap of World War II, numerous new editions followed. *Kubuś Puchatek* had its first post-war edition in 1946, and it was reissued no less than 26 times between 1948 and 2007 by Nasza Księgarnia, with the number of copies ranging from 10,000 to 100,000 for each edition; it became also recommended reading for elementary schools. The other *Pooh* novel, *Chatka Puchatka*, had almost as many post-war editions, even without being part of the obligatory curriculum.[10] Up to the present day, Milne's novels remain among the most beloved texts of Polish children's literature, as evidenced by numerous fan websites and entries in internet forums.

However, *Kubuś Puchatek* conquered the hearts of Polish adult readers, as well. In 1946, the influential critic Kazimierz Wyka called *Pooh* 'an honorary chairman of the Pickwick Club'. Other reviews and essays followed; mentions of *Pooh* can be found in the prose and poetry of famous Polish authors such as Zbigniew Herbert, Wisława Szymborska or Czesław Miłosz, who wrote a moving epitaph of Christopher Milne in the form of Winnie-the-Pooh's monologue included in volume *Road-side Dog*. In 1956, Kubuś Puchatek's name was given to a street in Warsaw; today many such streets exist, not to mention primary schools and children's clubs named after Milne's protagonist. Several terms from the books have become idiomatic expressions in everyday Polish language: 'już czas na jakieś małe conieco' ('it's time for a little something'), 'krewni-i-znajomi królika' ('rabbit's friends and relations'), 'coś, co Tygrysy lubią najbardziej' ('what Tigers like best'), 'umówiona kryjówka' ('established hiding place' – an expression that actually does not appear in the original text, but was invented by Tuwim). There is also a very popular, if apocryphal, saying 'na mój Puchatkowy rozumek' ('according to my little Puchatek's brain').[11]

Interestingly, on two occasions it was actually possible to verify just how deeply *Pooh*'s novels had been appropriated by the Polish culture. In the 1980s, a young scholar, Monika Adamczyk-Garbowska, influenced by early Western Children's Translation Studies, especially Göte Klingberg's works, criticized Irena Tuwim's translation in a few essays. She pointed out, and correctly so, some linguistic blunders and errors, but above all she objected to the style of Tuwim's *Puchatek* as too infantile and therefore not appropriate for the double audience the original books imply. Subsequently, Adamczyk-Garbowska proposed her own translation of the *Pooh* book in 1986. This version, based on very rigid theoretical premises and called *Fredzia Phi-Phi*,[12] was rather disappointing from a literary point of view, but what was really remarkable was the furious reaction it stirred. A heated debate in the media engaged not only many distinguished literary critics, but also average readers; even today several debates and critics' opinions about the *Fredzia Phi-Phi* translation continue to appear in internet forums. Apart from the critics' debates concerning the style and translation strategy chosen by Adamczyk, there was an emotional response to what had been perceived by many as an 'infamous' (Fordoński 2011) attempt against a canonical text of Polish children's literature. A vast majority of the opponents of the new *Pooh* translation were not really interested in debating its fidelity or adequacy in comparison to the original text, because through decades Irena Tuwim's version had acquired the position of an autonomous work embedded deeply in the Polish literary system.

A further confirmation of *Kubuś Puchatek*'s status as a part of Polish cultural heritage was given by a heated protest against Disney's franchise appropriation of Winnie-the-Pooh's rights (both literary and to the character). In the 1990s, the Disney Company, unhappy with the Polish name *Kubuś Puchatek,* proposed that it should be abolished in favour of the original *Winnie-the-Pooh.* This claim was met with a general indignation, bordering on national riot: there were even proposals to bring the question to the attention of the European Court of Justice. Eventually, Disney's representatives decided to adopt names taken from Irena Tuwim's version for their *Winnie-the-Pooh* films and books distributed in Poland. This astonishing victory of the translation of a literary work over the global power of Disneyfication is certainly worth further scrutiny.[13]

The question I am going to pursue in the second part of my chapter is: Why? How to explain the fact that whereas in Poland *Winnie-the-Pooh* is a beloved children's (and adult's) book, in Italy literary *Pooh* leads a comparatively marginal life? There are three possible factors that may have contributed to such a situation: the compatibility or non-compatibility of the original work with the target culture, the quality and the strategy of translation(s) or adaptations and extratextual circumstances. Let us examine them one by one.

The *Winnie-the-Pooh* books are undoubtedly a product of English culture. The idealized, idyllic rural setting of the five-acre wood is not only reminiscent of typical English landscape representation, but is also a metaphor 'for the middle-class insulation of the nunnery' (Connolly 1999, p. 202). Milne's novels embody values and attitudes towards life that the English hold dear: understated humour, cheerful optimism and nostalgia for a simple life. However, their cultural context surfaces far less obviously than it does in other English classics such as *Alice in Wonderland, Mary Poppins* or even *Wind in the Willows.* The double appeal of the books to children and to adults captivated by the subtle irony and the serenity of a long-lost childhood paradise can be easily understood and shared across national borders.

It is significant, indeed, that *Winnie-the-Pooh* did not raise objections of Italian fascist censorship, who were generally very hostile towards English and

American children's classics.[14] Similarly, in communist Poland, *Winnie-the-Pooh* not only survived the ideological scrutiny of suspicious censors, but had also been officially included in the mainstream of Polish children's literature as an obligatory reading at school.

The vision of 'a world where characters may adventure but come to no harm, a place where companionship and the simple enjoyment of the nature mark the day' (Connolly 1999, p. 201) has all the premises to be universally alluring. However, the true Englishness and therefore difficulty of transferring Pooh's world into other languages seems to lie in the books' style that combines subdued, tongue-in-cheek humour and an amusing and insightful imitation of children's logic of speech with the long-established tradition of nursery rhymes in numerous verse interludes. A clever rendition of all these characteristics of the original text in a target language can therefore be considered a crucial factor for the books' success with new audiences.

In fact, a first general overview of the Italian and Polish versions of the *Winnie-the-Pooh* novels reveals that they all follow the plot of the original texts rather faithfully.[15] The main difference between the translations consists in the way they approach the question of style. With the exception of Lila Jahn and Irena Tuwim, the translators tried hard to remain as close to the original as possible, and they did their best to reproduce Milne's language and to find exact equivalents of his puns and wordplays. There is no place here for an in-depth comparative study of each translator's proposals. Suffice it to look at the translation of proper names, as they appear to be fairly representative of the general strategy of each *Winnie-the-Pooh* version.

A quick comparison of these choices makes it clear that Zuccaro, Gaetani and Spagnol struggled to find the most adequate equivalents of English names. Their translational priorities are particularly evident when it comes to more difficult cases. The wordplay in the protagonist's name is not comprehensible to a foreign child who will also stumble on its pronunciation; however, the translators limited their effort to a phonetic simplification of the spelling of 'Winnie-the-Pooh'. Similarly, they tried to replicate the mechanism proposed by Milne in the division of Kangaroo in two parts, Kanga and Roo, to the rather poor effect: neither 'Kangù' nor 'Kan' sound natural in Italian and, above all, do not seem an adept name for a female and maternal figure of Milne's Kanga.[16] The same problem applies to Eeyore, which becomes an unpronounceable 'Ih-Oh' in Gaetani's translation, and a rather inadequate biblical 'Isaia' in Spagnol's version.[17] Particularly unconvincing are Zuccaro's proposals, based on the (approximate)

**Table 1** Names in *Winnie-the-Pooh* in Italian and Polish Translations

| Original | Jahn | Zuccaro | Gaetani | Spagnol | Adamczyk | Tuwim |
|---|---|---|---|---|---|---|
| Winnie-the-Pooh | Ninni Puf | Uini Puh | Winny Puh | Winnie Puh | Fredzia Phi-Phi | Kubuś Puchatek |
| Christopher Robin | Pino Robino | Robin | Robin | Christopher Robin | Krzysztof Robin | Krzyś |
| Piglet | Porcellino | Piglet | Porcellino | Porcelletto | Prosiaczek | Prosiaczek |
| Owl | Gufo | Aol | Gufo | Gufo | Sowa | Sowa Przemądrzała |
| Eeyore | Pipporaglio | Ijor | Ih-Oh | Isaia | Iijaa | Kłapouchy |
| Rabbit | Coniglio | Rebit | Coniglio | Coniglio | Królik | Królik |
| Kanga | Cangura | Kenga | Cangù | Kan | Kanga | Kangurzyca |
| Roo | Rino | Ru | Ro | Guro | Gurek | Maleństwo |

English pronunciation of names. The same tactic can be observed in Adamczyk's Polish version and the effects are similarly unimpressive. The name 'Gurek', for example, produced an unhappy connotation with a cucumber, rather than with an animal, since the Polish word for cucumber is *ogórek*.[18]

The only Italian translator who approached the question from a different angle was Lila Jahn. While she, too, searched for the names close to the original, she took care to make them sound natural and funny in Italian. Her proposals, to begin with cosy and likeable 'Ninni Puf', are decidedly more persuasive than other Italian versions and, in fact, if it were not for too many errors due to her faulty knowledge of English and rather insipid rendering of rhymes, Jahn's translation in many points could be considered the most resourceful and amusing of them all.

While the artistic effects of Zuccaro's, Gaetani's, Spagnol's and Adamczyk's translations vary in proportion to each translator's individual skill and talent, their main limitations derive from the factor that can be noticed already in the example of the translation of proper names given above: namely, the loyalty to the source text on its linguistic level prevails over the ambition to create a coherent stylistic proposal in the target language. Even Luigi Spagnol, without doubt the most daring and innovative in his translational choices, often wavers in face of the necessity of introducing some radical alterations and chooses a solution that is less satisfactory but closer to the original. As a result, none of these translations was able to gain the status of a fully independent, original work in the target culture.

Let us now have a closer look at Tuwim's *Kubuś Puchatek*, the only translation that has achieved such an accomplishment. Of all Italian and Polish translators, Irena Tuwim had undeniably the best literary credentials. She was a sister to famous poet Julian Tuwim, a major figure in Polish literature of the twentieth century, author of masterpieces of Polish poetry for children and also a brilliant translator of Pushkin. Irena, a gifted poet herself, was also the author of some charming picture books and a translator of several children's classics.[19] While she evidently did not intend to rewrite the *Winnie-the-Pooh* books, she approached the translation with a liberal spirit, which is clearly discernible in her treatment of the protagonists' names. These are not chosen arbitrarily: for example, Kubuś is a diminutive (of Jakub – James), just like Winnie. It sounds perfectly familiar and friendly to the ear of a Polish child. 'Puchatek', phonetically related to the original 'Pooh', has been developed into a word meaning soft, fluffy and feathery. Together, 'Kubuś Puchatek' works beautifully from a phonetic as well as from a semantic point of view, and is a perfect name for a small teddy bear.[20] On the other hand, it is definitely masculine, thus rendering it impossible to replicate a singular reasoning of Christopher Robin about 'Winnie-*the*-Pooh' in the first chapter of the book. Therefore, Irena Tuwim simply dropped this fragment from the first chapter. Although this drastic intervention into the original text has been often criticized by indignant defenders of rigorous rules of translation, first of all the author of the second Polish *Pooh* translation, in fact, Adamczyk's own version and Italian translations, which all retain the explanation about Winnie's name, sound forced and not really amusing.

The transformation of Winnie-the-Pooh into 'Kubuś Puchatek' is emblematic of Irena Tuwim's translation tactic: similarly, she abbreviated Christopher Robin into 'Krzyś' (the Polish diminutive for Krzysztof – Christopher), she replaced the onomatopoeic Eeyore with a neologism 'Kłapouchy' (Flop-eared) and instead of reproducing mechanically the division of Kangaroo into two names, she created 'Kangurzyca' (female of Kangaroo) and 'Maleństwo' (a diminutive for a very small creature). All these changes should not be dismissed just as a simple domestication: they are clearly dictated by a careful consideration of the morphological and stylistic needs of the Polish language, and are based on a perspicacious analysis of the characters' typology.

This translation strategy is evident throughout the novels. While Tuwim had not altered the plot at any point, she did not hesitate to bring in linguistic alterations every time she felt they were needed for stylistic purposes. A detailed analysis of *Kubuś Puchatek* and *Chatka Puchatka*[21] reveals a number of transformations on syntactic, lexical and phraseological levels. They consist in changing the syntax structure, eliminating words or even entire segments of a given sentence or, on the contrary, adding new elements, absent in the original texts. Meanings of single words and expressions are often shifted or altogether transformed. Therefore, 'Party for me' becomes 'Przyjęcie na moją cześć' ('Party in my honour'), '"All of them," said Owl sulkily.' develops into '– Ich wszystkich i basta – huknęła Sowa ze złością' ('"All of them and that's it" – howled the Owl angrily'), and 'We're going. Only Don't Blame Me.' into 'Chodźmy. Tylko nie miejcie do mnie pretensji, jeśli będzie padał deszcz' ('Let us go. Only don't blame me if it starts raining'). 'Pass it down to silly old Pooh. It's for Pooh.' is in Polish 'Podajcie to najmilszemu, poczciwemu Puchatkowi. To dla niego' ('Pass it down to dearest, good-hearted Pooh. It's for him.'). Despite the fact that these are usually only minor changes, they are so numerous as to give a distinctive Polish character to the style of the entire narrative, which is increased further by the outstanding versions of nursery rhymes that are by far more idiosyncratic of Tuwim than of Milne.

True enough, *Kubuś Puchatek* as a translation is not flawless: a few amusing examples of wordplay have been left out and the author did make some blunders due to the erroneous interpretation of the original novels. However, as a text, this version works beautifully, and if Milne's books managed to captivate Polish children and the adult audience the way they did, it is without doubts due to the merit of Irena Tuwim's linguistic brilliance.

On the other hand, one should not underestimate the possibility that *Kubuś Puchatek*'s triumph in Poland would not have been so overwhelming, had not other, extratextual factors been at work, too. The *Pooh* books became extremely popular during World War II when the serene shelter of Hundred Aker Wood was a way to momentarily forget the horrors of everyday life.[22] The therapeutic role of Milne's books was not to be easily forgotten. But what is more important is that adult readers did not hesitate to talk openly about Pooh and to admit their admiration for Milne's work. The literary status and value of *Kubuś Puchatek* could thus be officially recognized.

Another important factor to be taken into account is the long-delayed entrance of Disney products in Poland. Although Polish children could occasionally watch Disney films in the cinema or on TV, until the 1990s other products of the franchise, such as books, comics, toys or gadgets, were totally absent. The first general reaction in Poland to Disney's massive and aggressive invasion of *Winnie-the-Pooh* was in fact very similar to the British indignation to the 'Massacre in 100 Aker Wood' back in the 1960s, when the first Disney adaptation had appeared (Thwaite 1992, pp. 164–5). Even today, in spite of the extensive exposure to the Disney version of Pooh's adventures, the original novels by Milne still enjoy a great popularity not only among older, nostalgic audiences, but also among new generations of readers. Younger readers often declare that they like both Milne's novels and Disney's films, but, curiously, many of them say that once they have discovered the original novels, they liked them better than their Disney adaptations. Thus, whereas in Italy, 'Quando pensiamo a Winnie-the-Pooh, immaginiamo immediatamente il cartone animato Disney',[23] in Poland one can still say with confidence that 'Kubuś, którego nosimy w głowie, to osobnik, w którym łączą się słowa A. A. Milne'a z rysunkami E. H. Sheparda.'[24]

What conclusions can be drawn from this brief survey of *Winnie-the-Pooh*'s reception in Poland and in Italy? A comparative perspective allows us to notice several interesting points, some of them surely worth being investigated further. First of all, it appears evident that in contrast to what is often believed, the number of translations of a particular work in a given language is not necessarily an indicator of this work's real success in the target language. Second, the comparative failure of Milne's books in Italy raises a number of questions regarding the concept of a canon of children's literature.[25] Whereas the canonical status of *Winnie-the-Pooh* in British culture is indisputable, is it justified to equate an international canon of children's literature with what is essentially a British canon? Despite the fact that 'the need for a canon is now ... becoming evident in children's literary studies, for the purposes of writing the history of the literature and for university teaching' (O'Sullivan 2005, p. 131), the obvious differences between national literary canons for children raise doubts whether such a goal can be accomplished at all.

On the other hand, the amazing success of the *Pooh* books in Poland urges one to consider whether a translation that is faithful to the original children's text and thus confirms its literary status is indeed superior to an adaptation, which is decried as a sign of a paternalistic and purely instrumental approach to children's literature. It is interesting to note that when the first Italian (1936) and Polish (1938) versions of *Winnie-the-Pooh* were created, the original work was already considered a kind of classic and had enjoyed considerable literary prestige. Nonetheless, it is quite clear that this potentially advantageous starting point was of no consequence for the respective success or letdown of the *Pooh* novels in Poland and Italy. The translator seems, in truth, the key figure in the process of a successful transfer of a children's book into a new linguistic and cultural context: probably far more so than in the case of translation of literature written for adults.[26]

But an even more interesting issue related to the Polish success of *Kubuś Puchatek* is the question of the fuzzy distinction between a translation and an adaptation. It is quite difficult to decide whether Irena Tuwim's version should be defined as a liberal translation or if it belongs to the realm of adaptation. To make this distinction is, however, crucial for the purpose of academic study. Classified as a translation, Tuwim's text is deemed to be an object of critical evaluation based on a comparison with the original work. Categorizing *Kubuś Puchatek* as an adaptation, on the other hand, can offer a starting point for a methodological and terminological debate.

However, as crucial as the strategy of linguistic transfer of a children's work into a new cultural context appears to be, it is quite obvious that extratextual circumstances are also powerful and influential factors in the process of assimilation of a given text for children. As far as Italy and Poland are concerned, a fundamental difference lies in the general attitude of the adult readership towards children's texts. In Poland, children's literature came under closer scrutiny of literary critics as early as the nineteenth century, when it was considered an important part of patriotic education and formation of national identity. In 1935, Julian Tuwim, Irena's brother, published his nursery rhymes on the front page of *Wiadomości Literackie*, the most prestigious literary and cultural journal in inter-war Poland. Children's texts were – and still are – reviewed and commented on in newspapers and journals. In other words, they have been always present in the horizon of literary discourse, although not in its mainstream. In Italy, on the contrary, children's writing has been largely excluded from the field of literature proper by the harsh opinion of Benedetto Croce who decreed that 'l'arte 'per bambini' . . . non sarà mai arte vera'.[27] With the exception of Collodi's *Pinocchio* and De Amicis' *Cuore*, children's literature is still struggling to be found worthy of serious academic research in Italy, and is often considered a part of the pedagogical rather than the literary domain. Even more marginal attention is given to the issues of translation for children, taught and researched almost exclusively in English departments of some universities. It is unusual to find reviews, comments or critical discussions about children's books and especially about new translations anywhere in the press or media.[28]

Since adult readership and scholarship have, each in their own way, a major influence on the formation of a given national literary canon, the importance of this lack of interest cannot be underestimated. For a foreign children's book, such as *Winnie-the-Pooh*, to become an integral part of Italian children's literature is always difficult, and the chances of its being nobilitated as part of a general literary canon are remote. This factor seems even more vital than so much amplified Disney influence and should be studied to a greater extent.

The one aspect concerning *Winnie-the-Pooh*'s adaptation to new literary and cultural contexts that has been deliberately left out in this study is the issue of illustration. Ernest H. Shepard's drawings are as a rule considered an integral part of the novels: A. A. Milne himself acknowledged Shepard's contribution to the success of the *Pooh* books and arranged for him to receive a share of the royalties. All Italian and Polish versions of *Winnie-the-Pooh* texts (with the exception of Adamczyk's translation) have been always published with Shepard's illustrations. Nonetheless, the visual charm of Shepard's drawings did not help to captivate the Italian audience. On the other hand, in Russia, where *Winnie-the-Pooh* arrived much later than in Poland (the first translation, by Boris Zakhoder, was published in 1960) the elimination of Shepard's illustrations had been apparently of no consequence to the immense popularity of the books among Russian readers (Tashlitsky p. 6). Successively, the Russians created their own representation of Pooh, distinctly different from Shepard's as well as from Disney's visions, and it became an essential part of their national children's canon. It appears, therefore, that the importance of the visual attractiveness of Shepard's illustrations should not be overestimated, especially when talking about *Winnie-the-Pooh's* successful or unsuccessful transfer into other cultures.

Should children's classics be translated or adapted? In spite of tendencies to distrust adaptations as manipulative and disrespectful of original texts, the history of *Winnie-the-Pooh's* reception in Italy and in Poland suggests that the question must be pondered very carefully. It seems, in fact, that an adaptation-oriented transfer, such as Polish *Kubuś Puchatek*,[29] can be far more effective when it comes to introducing a foreign children classic into the mainstream of a target literature. Even if, from today's point of view, Irena Tuwim was certainly at odds with today's political correctness of translation for children, she achieved something most translators could only dream of: she transformed *Winnie-the-Pooh* into a canonical book of Polish Children's Literature.

# Notes

1  The Editor's decision to order such a high number of copies was inspired by the extraordinary success of Milne's previous book, *When We Were Very Young* (1924).

2  To say 'English-speaking' countries is of course a simplification, as there are – and must be – obvious and significant differences in the status and the perception of Milne's books in the writer's own country and in the United States.

3  Little is known about Lila Jahn except that she was active in the 1930s and 1940s as a translator from English and French and that she was the author of a biography of Maria Bianca Sforza, Duchess of Milan (1941). As for the blatant error of presenting the book as a translation from American, one can only guess that Jahn translated *Winnie-the-Pooh* from an American edition.

4  Elda Zuccaro is an even more anonymous figure than Lila Jahn, the two Milne books being apparently her only translation ever published.

5   In 1953, Genio published yet another *Winnie-the-Pooh*, under the title *Orso di poco cervello* (*A bear of little brain*). This edition is today practically impossible to find, but since the number of pages (156) correspond with Zuccaro's version that was issued before by Genio, too, one can assume that it was, in fact, the same translation.

6   The Italian volume included both *Winnie-the-Pooh* and *The House at Pooh Corner*.

7   Maria Cristina Gaetani, translator of a couple of undistinguished English books, is just as anonymous a figure as the previous Italian translators of *Winnie-the-Pooh*. Ida Omboni (1922–2006) is better known – she was a translator, theatre writer and author of some children's books herself.

8   *Winnie Puh* in 1995 and 2009, *La strada di Puh* in 1997 and 2010.

9   The title could be roughly re-translated in English as *Fluffy Jimbo*.

10  Precise data on Tuwim's translations may be found on N. pag. *Fundacja im. Juliana Tuwima i Ireny Tuwim*. Web http://www.tuwim.org/. 16 January 2012.

11  There are literally dozens Polish websites that list favourite quotations and dialogue from both *Winnie-the-Pooh* books.

12  Fredzia stands for a hypothetical diminutive of the name Winnifred, supposedly the name of the black bear in the London Zoo that was Christopher Robin's inspiration for calling his own teddy bear Winnie. However, the real bear called Winnie in fact got her name from the Canadian city of Winnipeg (Thwaite 1992, p. 34).

13  It does not mean, however, that the Disney Franchise abstained from the policy of aggressive appropriation as far as the Winnie-the-Pooh rights are concerned. New clashes occur continuously (in 2001 the Franchise vetoed a dozen Polish theatrical productions of Pooh's adventures) and there are many bad feelings, especially among adult fans of the original *Pooh* in Poland, concerning what they see as a 'scandalous situation'.

14  In fact, such authors as Lewis Carroll, Rudyard Kipling or Pamela Travers were deemed as unsuitable and harmful for Italian children.

15  This is not the case with all *Winnie-the-Pooh* translations: Boris Zakhoder's acclaimed Russian version (1960) not only reduces extranarrative elements (dedications and the introductory parts of the two books of the cycle) but also modifies the order of events (Papusha 2005).

16  Female proper names end in Italian with -a or -e (Anna, Elena, Alice, Beatrice), and very rarely with -i (Noemi). The desinence with -u is typical of Sicilian variants of male proper names ('Turiddu' for Salvatore, 'Fanu' for Stefano). Only foreign proper names – and almost exclusively male – end with a consonant.

17   Spagnol's idea may have some appeal for adult readers, though, since Isaiah tended to rather gloomy prophecies, just like Eeyore.

18   Adamczyk used the Polish word *Kangurek* – 'small Kangaroo' – and replicated Milne's division of it in two parts.

19   Among the most popular of Tuwim's translations one should mention novels by Pamela Travers, Mary Norton and Edith Nesbit.

20   It also creates a pleasant association with Pimpuś Sadełko, the feline protagonist of a widely popular Polish children's book by Maria Konopnicka.

21   *The House at Pooh's Corner* – another brilliant phonetic and semantic proposal of Tuwim.

22   Characteristically, sales of the *Pooh* books also rose during the war in other countries. American writer Randall Jarrell called them 'the perfect book[s] for the soldier' (Thwaite 1992, p. 141).

23   'When we think about Winnie-the-Pooh, we imagine immediately Disney's animated films' (Gorini 2007, p. 121).

24   'The Winnie-the-Pooh we imagine is the figure that unites words of A. A. Milne with the illustrations of E. H. Shepard' (Mikołajewski 2004, p. 12).

25   It is very telling that in the most complete Italian compendium of children's literature up to date, Pino Boero's *La letteratura per l'infanzia* (1995, revised edition 2009) Milne's name is not even mentioned.

26   There are, in fact, many adult classics that enjoy a canonical position in a given target country in spite of very poor translations: in Italy such was the case, for example, of the Nobel prize winner Henryk Sienkiewicz, whose novel *Quo vadis* became an acclaimed bestseller and definitely a part of the Italian literary canon for many decades, in spite of disastrous translations.

27   'The art "for children" (...) will never be able to be a true art' (Boero 2009, p. 4).

28   For example, since 1984 in *La Repubblica*, one of the two most important Italian newspapers, Milne's *Winnie-the-Pooh* has been mentioned, shortly and very casually, only 12 times. (see: http://www.repubblica.it/2008/04/sezioni/ cronaca/repubblica-ricerca-archivio/repubblica-ricerca-archivio/repubblica- ricerca-archivio.htmlIn). For comparison, in *Gazeta Wyborcza*, one of the most influential Polish newspapers, since 1989, there have been 237 mentions of *Winnie-the-Pooh* books, and at least 30 articles and reviews dealing specifically with their literary and artistic values, new translations, etc. (see: http://szukaj. wyborcza.pl/Archiwum/search?page=1&start=1&bid=fArch&t=iw13szukajp 81101326582213301).

29  It is worth noticing that also in other countries where *Winnie-the-Pooh* acquired the status of a cult book, such as Russia, Estonia or Hungary, the translators chose an adaptation-oriented strategy.

## List of works cited

Adamczyk-Garbowska, Monika (1982), 'Czy Kubuś Puchatek to Winnie-the-Pooh? O potrzebie krytyki przekładu'. *Akcent*, 4.

— (1988a), 'Albo Fredzia Phi-Phi albo Kubuś Puchatek, z M. A-G rozmawia P. Wasilewski'. *Tak i Nie*, 9.

— (1988b), *Polskie tłumaczenia angielskiej literatury dziecięcej. Problemy krytyki przekładu*. Wrocław: Ossolineum.

Boero, Pino and De Luca, Carmine (2009), *La letteratura per l'infanzia*, 2nd edn. Roma, Bari: Laterza.

Connolly, Paula T. (1995), *Winnie-the-Pooh and the House at Pooh Corner: Recovering Arcadia*. New York: Twayne and Macmillan Publishing Co.

— (1999), 'The marketing of romantic childhood: Milne, Disney and a very popular stuffed bear', in James Holt McGavran (ed.), *Literature and the Child: Romantic Continuations, Postmodern Contestations*. Iowa City: University of Iowa Press, pp. 188–207.

Fordoński, Łukasz (2011), 'The art of translation vs. the art of editing'. *Komunikacja Specjalistyczna*, 5.

Gorini, Francesca (2007), 'I *Pooh Books* di A. A. Milne, dalle origini letterarie alla *Disnification*', in Francesca Orestano (ed.), *Tempi moderni nella Children's Literature. Storie, personaggi, strumenti critici*. Milano: CUEM, pp. 121–42.

Mikołajewski, Jarosław (2004), 'Milne, Alan Alexander; Shepard, Ernest Howard: Kubuś Puchate; Chatka Puchatka'. *Gazeta Wyborcza*, 18 November, 12.

Milne, Alan A. (1936), *L'orsachiotto Ninni Puf: Traduzione dall'americano di Lila Jahn*. Milano: Genio.

— (1949), *Uini il Puh. Traduzione di Elda Zuccaro*. Milano: Genio.

— (1960), *Winny-Puh l'orsetto*, Maria Cristina Gaetani and Ida Omboni (trans). Milano: Garzanti.

— (1990, 1986), *Fredzia Phi-Phi*, Monika Adamczyk-Garbowska (trans). Lublin: Wydawnictwo Lubelskie.

— (2004, 1926), *Winnie-the-Pooh*. Egmont: London.

— (2007, 1928), *The House at Pooh Corner*. Egmont: London.

— (2008, 1938), *Kubuś Puchatek*, Irena Tuwim (trans). Warszawa: Nasza Księgarnia.

— (2009, 1993), *Winnie Puh*, Luigi Spagnol (trans). Milano: Salani.

O'Sullivan, Emer (1993), 'The fate of the dual adressee in the translation of children's Literature'. *New Comparison*, 16(Autumn), 109–19.

— (2005), *Comparative Children's Literature*, Anthea Bell (trans). London: Routledge.

Papusha, Olga (2005), 'Translation as adaptation: the winnie-the-pooh stories as children's and adult reading', *LiterNet*, 9 November, viewed 1 April 2012, <http://liternet.bg/publish15/o_papusha/translation.htm>.

Taylor, Aaron (2005), 'Everybody wants a piece of Pooh: Winnie, from adaptation to market Saturation', in Mike Budd and Max H. Kirsch (eds), *Rethinking Disney: Private Control, Public Dimensions*. Middletown, CT: Wesleyan University Press, pp. 181–98.

Tashlitsky, Xenia (no date), 'Lost in Translation: *Winnie-the-Pooh* in Russian and English,' viewed 15 May 2012, <www.international.ucla.edu/cms/files/Tashlitsky.pdf>.

Thwaite, Anne (1991), *A. A. Milne: His Life*. London: Faber.

— (1992), *The Brilliant Career of Winnie-The-Pooh. The Story of A. A. Milne and His Writing for Children*. London: Methuen.

13

# Disney~~Neverland~~'s Tinker Bell

Lisa Rowe Fraustino

'There was another light in the room now, a thousand times brighter than the night-lights, and in the time we have taken to say this, it has been in all the drawers in the nursery, looking for Peter's shadow, rummaged the wardrobe, and turned every pocket inside out. It was not really a light; it made this light by flashing about so quickly, but when it came to rest for a second you saw it was a fairy, no longer than your hand, but still growing. It was a girl called Tinker Bell exquisitely gowned in a skeleton leaf, cut low and square, through which her figure could be seen to best advantage. She was slightly inclined to embonpoint'

(James M. Barrie, *Peter and Wendy* 1911).

'The United Nations today named the Disney animated character Tinker Bell an 'Honorary Ambassador of Green' to help promote environmental awareness among children. The announcement came just prior to a screening at UN Headquarters in New York of the world premiere of the Walt Disney animated film, "Tinker Bell and the Lost Treasure."'

(UN News Centre press release, 25 October 2009)

Peter Pan belongs to no one, and to everyone. *Peter and Wendy*, James M. Barrie's 1911 novelization of his play first produced in 1904, has passed into the public domain. Even during his lifetime, Barrie authorized copyrights to a number of writers who published adaptations, and he himself made frequent changes to the stage version until finalizing a play script for publication in 1928. On the first performance programme, spoof authorship was attributed to the actress who played Liza, the maid. When he finally prepared the script of *Peter Pan or The Boy Who Would Not Grow Up* for posterity, Barrie claimed in his long dedication to the volume, entitled 'To the Five'[1]: 'I have no recollection of having written it' (1995, p. 75). According to Peter Hollindale,

> Barrie's unending revisionism is not just the obsessive tinkering of a perfectionist or indecisive theatrical craftsman; it is the artistic projection of a philosophical stance which was skeptical of a fixed and permanent truth, and convinced of relativity, of circumstantial change, seeing life and art alike as fluid and provisional. (Hollindale 1995, p. xi)

All of this flux from the very start makes *Peter Pan* a fascinating subject of adaptation study. 'Barrie may well be the source of the play', Jacqueline Rose notes in *The Case of Peter Pan or The Impossibility of Children's Fiction*,

> but this constant dispersion of *Peter Pan* challenges any straightforward idea of origin or source. Above all it should caution us against the idea that things can simply be traced back to their beginning, since, in the case of *Peter Pan*, what followed is at least as important as what came before. (Rose 1993, p. 6)

This chapter will explicate the evolution of Tinker Bell, from J. M. Barrie's original conception in the play *Peter Pan or The Boy Who Would Not Grow Up* (1904) and his novelization *Peter and Wendy* (1911), through the appropriation of her figure as a corporate mascot after Walt Disney's animated film adaptation *Peter Pan* (1953), and recently as the most renowned of the 'Disney Fairies', a new franchise designed to rival the 'Disney Princesses' in popularity and profitability. To develop this new brand, the company used its famous synergy, first seeding readers with books by a celebrated author of fairy tale adaptations, Gail Carson Levine. Release of the first Disney Fairies motion picture in 2008 dovetailed with a widespread public service advertisement using Tinker Bell to promote energy conservation, part of an extensive campaign to launch spin-off merchandise, from bibs and preschool backpacks to online games and theme park attractions that extend narrative adaptation into cyberspace. Tinker Bell has become a UN Ambassador of Green and a new temptress into consumption of all things Disney for a new generation of consumers who are not only domestic and feminine but also technological. Besides drawing on Barrie and Disney criticism, this chapter will refer to recent developments in adaptation theory.

## Tinker Bell's public service

Ironically, I was in a Florida airport when I first learnt of Tinker Bell's stunning transformation from Barrie's tinkling ball of light to Disney's spokesmodel for energy conservation. This is ironic on two counts. First, I was a scholar on sabbatical leave at the time to research gender and power ideology in Disney's adaptations of children's literature, but I have never visited Disney World. In March of 2009, I was in Florida visiting my parents who had retired there for the sunshine. Second, I never watch television unless I really cannot escape it, as happened that day in the Jacksonville airport. There was no turning my back to the ubiquitous screens set to Fox News, the volume set high enough to reach the hard of hearing. And so I really could not miss the public service announcement in which Disney's revamped Tinker Bell and her fairy friends flew around giggling and 'switching' nature's seasons while a voiceover said:

> The magical thing about using energy wisely … is that anyone can do it. Use energy saving light bulbs … energy smart power strips … and turn off computers and game systems when not in use. Get together and make a difference. Learn what you can do today at energy.gov/tink/. (U.S. Department of Energy –'EERE Kids')

Frankly, I was astounded to see this. What was Tinker Bell doing in a public service announcement for the U.S. Department of Energy? Was having a licensed character in a public service announcement not tantamount to a government endorsement of the brand? And what had happened to Tinker Bell? Though still recognizable, this was not the same character I knew from Walt Disney's 1953 animated film adaptation of J. M. Barrie's *Peter Pan*, the iconic figure second only to Mickey Mouse in representing the Disney brand. As the tabloids might suggest of any actress of a certain age who suddenly updates her appearance, Tinker Bell must have had a lot of work done. In fact, she looked rather plastic, more like a doll than she had before.

In 'To the Five', his introduction to the published version of his play *Peter Pan*, Barrie himself traced the creation of Tinker Bell:

> It was one evening when we climbed the wood carrying No. 4 to show him what the trail was like by twilight.[2] As our lanterns twinkled among the leaves No. 4 saw a twinkle stand still for a moment and he waved his foot gaily to it, thus creating Tink. (Barrie 1995, p. 84)

She was represented as a bright light on Barrie's stage, a 'fairy of electricity' Murray Pomerance has called her, saying, 'Cast as a fairy, she is, indeed, an embodiment of electric illumination as magical power' (2009, p. 21). However, the public service announcement did not make any reference to Barrie's bright-light Tink at all, and it is doubtful that children raised on the Disney version of *Peter Pan* would draw any connection between her and electricity. There was no obvious reason for Tink to get the public service job as opposed to, say, Kermit the Frog, who really is green, or a character from Sesame Street, which is educational programming on the Public Broadcasting System produced by a non-profit organization. Why did American children have to be indoctrinated by the proprietary corporate icon Tinker Bell? There had to be more to that 30-second spot than met the eye. Disney surely was marketing something besides their wholesome image, and I went online to figure out what.

At http://www.energy.gov/tink, I found the PSA I had seen at the airport. The web page was part of an education campaign conducted by the U.S. Department of Energy programme EERE–Energy Efficiency and Renewable Energy. Besides two animated PSA spots starring Tinker Bell, the page provided links to more information and games not related to Disney. I clicked around until I reached the Web Site Policies. Under Copyright, I found:

> Some materials on this site have been contributed by private individuals, companies, or organizations and include a copyright notice. It is the user's responsibility to contact copyright owners and obtain the written permission required under U.S. copyright law before using these materials. (U.S. Department of Energy –'EERE Kids')

The policy page ends with a Disclaimer: 'Reference herein to any specific commercial product, process, or service by trade name, trademark, manufacturer, or otherwise, does not necessarily constitute or imply its endorsement, recommendation, or favoring by the United States Government or any agency thereof' ('EERE'). So, the U.S. government does not officially endorse, recommend or favour Disney – it just looks that way to the 8- and 9-year-olds identified by the EERE as the target audience.

When I searched online for more information about the relationship between Disney Fairies and the U.S. government, I found a press release from the Ad Council, which describes itself as

> a private, non-profit organization that marshals talent from the advertising and communications industries, the facilities of the media, and the resources of the business and non-profit communities to produce, distribute, and promote public service campaigns on behalf of non-profit organizations and government agencies in issue areas such as improving the quality of life for children, preventive health, education, community well-being, environmental preservation and strengthening families. ('Ad Council' 2008)

As part of a campaign by the Ad Council and the government to educate children about energy efficiency, the PSA that I had seen was one of a series that 'feature characters from Walt Disney Studios Home Entertainment's new DVD and Blu-Ray™ release Tinker Bell'. So there it was. My suspicion was confirmed. Tinker Bell was not just a charitable soul donating her light to the public good; she had her own movie to pitch – no, more than a movie: a whole franchise.

In fact, during the same time the PSAs were running, Disney was also running paid television ads for *Tinker Bell*, the film, whose DVD cover incites viewers to '[j]ourney into the secret world of Pixie Hollow and hear Tinker Bell speak for the very first time as the astonishing story of Disney's most famous fairy is finally revealed in the all-new motion picture *Tinker Bell*' (2008). As John Frost at *The Disney Blog* wrote in September 2008, 'In the biz this is what we call Cause Marketing' (Frost 2008). In its first year, the public service campaign was able to solicit $28 million in donated media including 44,670 TV airings, 430,459 radio spots, 75 million web impressions and over 1,000 prints, according to a report by Linda Silverman, Senior Advisor for Renewable Energy at the Department of Energy. And this was only the beginning.

In October 2009, seven months after I had first seen the PSA in Jacksonville, The Ad Council and the Department of Energy issued another press release announcing a new series of PSAs 'to educate 8–9 year olds on positive energy efficient habits and [featuring] Tinker Bell and other characters from the upcoming film "Tinker Bell and the Lost Treasure"' ('Ad Council' 2009). Disney held its world premiere at the UN Headquarters in New York, where Kiyo Akasaka, Under-Secretary-General for Communications and Public Information, appointed Tinker Bell as an Honorary Ambassador of Green, even though she is a cartoon character and had to send a human actress in a sexy green dress to accept the honour and spread the pixie dust. According to the UN press release, 'Protecting the environment is an underlying theme of the Tinker Bell movies' and 'the Walt Disney Company uses its storytelling to inspire a love of nature and spirit of conservation in its audience' ('UN Casts').

While dozens of news agencies and bloggers disseminated the story faithfully, its spin unquestioned, one scholar of children's new media and literacy, Sara M. Grimes, found the news 'odd, off, and unworthy of the UN' (2009). Grimes further blogged, 'This announcement is much too deeply embedded in the marketing of the film and much too in conformity with Disney's promotional interests to be seen as anything but a new and disturbing form of product placement'. I concur with her opinion.

Janet Wasko analyses the position of animated films within the context of the company as a whole. 'Their aim has been clearly stated', she notes; that is, to 'exploit the most profitable niches and synergies in the franchise' through what she calls 'cross-fertilization' (Wasko 2001, p. 36). The synergy for *Tinker Bell* goes all the way back to *Walt Disney's Peter Pan*, where the company's wildly successful marketing strategies first took root. According to Susan Ohmer,

> [t]he film's release launched the most massive merchandising campaign to date, by a studio already known for its promotional skill. Hundreds of product tie-ins and widespread coverage in various media reveal a company keenly aware of the possibilities of synergy decades before it became a buzzword. (Ohmer 2009, p. 154)

In the weeks and months before the 1953 release of *Peter Pan*, catchy songs from the musical score played widely on radio and television. *Peter Pan* was the first in a series of comic strips, called the Treasury of Classic Tales, that were started to preview forthcoming films in newspapers. Disney had licensing deals with 52 manufacturers of *Peter Pan* merchandise, and Ohmer argues, 'The links its merchandise created between youth and a culture of consumption remains a cornerstone of the company's strategies today' (2009, p. 180).

## The 'timeless' stereotype

According to Jason Surrell, author of a how-to book on writing screenplays for Disney,

> [o]ne of the main reasons Disney animated features have weathered the test of time so well is that the clear majority of them are considered *timeless* as opposed to *timely*. Timeless films often have a fantasy, natural, or even period setting, and, for the most part, don't say or portray anything that might tie them to the time in which they were made. (Surrell 2004, p. 30)

The company aggressively markets this self-perpetuating myth of timelessness through appeal to nostalgia passed along from generation to generation of Disney devotees. 'Disney's popularity or universality is not automatic', says Janet Wasko in *Understanding Disney: The Manufacture of Fantasy*,

> but a result of deliberate, coordinated marketing, advertising and promotional activities. The company has developed its own expertise in marketing its products, both nationally and globally. In the United States, the coordinated efforts

involve advertising and promotion by the company's own outlets, as well as carefully planned tie-ins with other companies and public relations campaigns (Wasko 2001, p. 102)

– including, now, government sponsored public service announcements.

Part of buying Disney products is buying into the image Disney sells so successfully: wholesome, clean, good, fun, magical and, most of all, timeless entertainment no child should be without. In fact, Walt Disney's animated films and the books based on them are not the least bit timeless but instead are drenched in the culturally defined attitudes of the men that produced them. As Susan Ohmer states in 'Disney's *Peter Pan*: Gender, Fantasy, and Industrial Production', the film 'bears the marks of these industrial, economic, and social changes' (2009, p. 153). A close reading of adapted details makes this obvious. For instance, Disney's masculine boy is in the throes of puberty voiced by 15-year-old Bobby Driscoll instead of a child who still has baby teeth in Barrie, and indeed the PR disseminated by the Studio bragged that 'Peter, for the first time, is all boy ... outlined in angular, masculine gesture and action' ('He Lives'). Susan Ohmer, granted permission to visit Disney's archives and study their files (unlike me) found the reason for this: 'From the first storyboard meetings, the senior animators expressed concern that Peter not be "sissy". Later they congratulate one another for making him "less effeminate"' (Ohmer 2009, p. 174).

This upping of machismo happens in numerous adaptations to Barrie's source, these among them: Disney's Peter Pan comes to the nursery to hear stories about himself instead of Cinderella, as in Barrie; he frequently swoops in to rescue damsels in distress; he says things like 'Girls talk too much' instead of 'Wendy, one girl is more use than twenty boys' (Barrie p. 91). Disney adds a male Indian Chief to take charge, whereas the tribe was ably led by Tiger Lily in Barrie's version. As for our Tink, along with Murray Pomerance,

> We might ask what sort of femininity she represents in this production. Sexual availability and desire are supplanted by the willingness to compete against another woman for possession of a male, which is a stark reaffirmation of masculinity – masculine embodiment and masculine presence – as a central and shared value; in short, the movie becomes an advertisement for patriarchy. (Pomerance 2009, p. 35)

Disney's supposed universality was rather a product of traditional sexist attitudes that dominated the Studio and much of American culture during the post-war period. But as long as consumers continue to greet the onslaught of studio updates and reissues every time a new format or technology provides fresh profit potential, the gender stereotypes of the *Peter Pan* patriarchal order will be a long time with us. Janet Wasko wisely points out, 'Unless the corporate context in which Disney operates is taken into consideration, we are left with readings of individual Disney texts that mostly just apply the latest method of textual analysis to a wider range of products' (2001, p. 152).

## Disney fairy synergy

Various branches of Disney began seeding the market for the new Disney Fairies franchise years in advance. Their Disney Publishing Worldwide (DPW) overview for 2005 promised that in September,

> the secret, tiny world of Tinker Bell and her fairy friends will be discovered by young girls around the world with the launch of an illustrated novel from DPW, *Fairy Dust and the Quest for the Egg*, by renowned author Gail Carson Levine. The novel will be followed by an extensive, multi-titled book and merchandise launch that will be the foundation of a new long-term property, Disney Fairies. ('Overview' 2005)

As the popular author of a beloved and critically acclaimed Newbery Honour book, the Cinderella adaptation *Ella Enchanted*, Gail Carson Levine brought serious literary stature as well as a large audience of loyal readers who would not necessarily be drawn to a typical Disneyfication. 'But – then again – how could Ms. Levine's novel not be a success?' Jim Hill blogged in May of 2006. 'Given that Disney Publishing Worldwide launched "Fairy Dust and the Quest for the Egg" in 51 countries and in 32 different languages and was backed by both a million dollar marketing campaign as well as Gail's global tour' (Hill 2006).

In the early stages of my research for this chapter, I asked Gail Carson Levine a few questions about writing for Disney (2010). She told me James M. Barrie's *Peter Pan* had been her favourite story as a child and that she was basing her adaptation on his novel. She did not grow up on the Disney version and in fact could not remember ever seeing the animated cartoon. She went about writing these books as she does all of her fairy tale adaptations, not just copying from the prior sources but imagining new ways to fill in the gaps or explain inconsistencies. For one thing, Levine thought Wendy was a fool ever to leave Never Land, the greatest place on earth. Levine dedicated *Fairy Dust and the Quest for the Egg* (2005), her first Disney Fairies book, 'To James M. Barrie and my first boyfriend, Peter Pan'. This despite the fact that Levine wound up hating Peter for his arrogance and, most of all, for his heartless forgetting of his old adventures in the final chapter of Barrie's book. Peter does not remember Captain Hook; 'I forget them after I kill them', he tells Wendy when he returns after a year to get her for spring cleaning. And when Wendy mentions Tinker Bell, he asks, 'Who is Tinker Bell'? Wendy, shocked, explains to him, but still 'he could not remember' and of fairies he says, 'There are such a lot of them... I expect she is no more'. Barrie's narrator in *Peter and Wendy* tells us in response to Peter's words, 'I expect he was right, for fairies don't live long, but they are so little that a short time means a good while to them' (Barrie 1991, p. 219). In contrast, Disney's franchise resuscitates Tinker Bell from the dead and imagines a back story that Barrie neglected to tell us.

'Tink was not all bad', Barrie's narrator explains,

> or, rather, she was all bad just now, but, on the other hand, sometimes she was all good. Fairies have to be one thing or the other, because being so small they unfortunately have room for one feeling at a time. (Barrie 1991, p. 111)

The one feeling that Walt Disney emphasized most of the time in his 1953 adaptation was Tinker Bell's jealousy, which becomes both a major plot point and a source of misogynist humour. 'There's trouble brewing on the island – woman trouble', says Walt Disney's Smee. 'Ah, yes, a jealous female can be tricked into anything. The wench may chart our course to a certain hiding place', says Walt Disney's Hook (Geronimi 1997). Whereas Barrie's Hook discovers the home of the Lost Boys on his own, Walt Disney's Hook manipulates Tinker Bell into revealing the location on a map:

> Rumor has it she has come between you... the way of a man with a maid, taking the best years of her life and then casting her aside like an old glove. Mustn't be too harsh on Peter. Wendy is to blame. (Geronimi 1997)

In *Fairy Haven and the Quest for the Egg*, Gail Carson Levine develops an inner life for our fairy along with a more complex and sympathetic personality. No longer does Tink say 'You silly ass' (Barrie 1995, p. 94) and fly around pinching people like in Barrie's novel. Instead, she helps the new fairy Prilla find her talent, watches over the injured Mother Dove (who is the source of pixie dust in the new mythology) and carries a sense of grief over Peter's betrayal. '"If he really thought I was the best, why did he bring over the Wendy?" She collapsed on the sand, still sobbing. "Why did he spend all his time with her?"' (Levine 2005,

p. 125). No longer does Tink need an inhabitant from Never Land to translate her bell tones into human language. Now she and all the fairies in Pixie Hollow can speak the tongue of any country where Disney publishes.

## The adaptation of Tinker Bell: From Never Land to Pixie Hollow

Upon the launch of Levine's book, the fairy 'home world' of Pixie Hollow was immediately open to visitors at the Disney website. Fairy dolls hit the Disney Stores in January 2006, a new Disney Fairies magazine was published in Germany and Japan, and a series of Random House chapter books were shipped all over the place, picking up on some of Gail Carson Levine's characters and introducing 'a new circle of enchanting fairy friends' who with Tink are the mainstays of the franchise, 'Fawn, Iridessa, Rosetta and Silvermist – each with an incredibly diverse talent, personality and look', according to a press release to *Business Wire*. The same source indicated in October of 2009 that

> over 575 Disney Fairies books and over 125 Tinker Bell movie books have published worldwide in 60 countries and 35 languages, selling nearly 18 million copies; Disney Fairies magazines have sold over 7.5 million copies in 28 copies and an array of products from apparel and toys to electronics, home décor and stationery has extended storylines into many girls' homes across the globe. ('Tinker Bell and Friends')

And what is the storyline all this merchandise is extending, exactly? The gloss on the back of the DVD begins, 'Have you ever wondered how nature gets its glow – who gives it light and color as the seasons come and go'? (2008). Turns out Disney Fairies are responsible for that! Who knew?

The blurb goes on,

> Enter a land of adventure and mystery as Tinker Bell and her four best fairy friends turn winter into spring and, with the power of faith, trust, and a little bit of pixie dust, learn the importance of being true to yourself. (2008)

In the film, Tinker Bell discovers on the day of her birth (from a baby's first laugh, as Barrie had it) that she is a Tinker Talent, destined to live her days in Never Land making pots and kettles for fairies while her friends with more prestigious talents get to make forces of nature and change the seasons on the mainland. 'Tinkers are uneducated, accented, and overweight', Alaine Martaus has noted, while 'Other fairies are elegant, well-spoken, and lithe' (2010). The plot revolves around Tinker Bell's resistance to this lower-class destiny in menial labour and her final acceptance when she realizes her talent allows her to make wonderful inventions out of broken things and lost trinkets. In the end she invents the machinery to increase the productivity of all the nature talents, and she gets to join the upper classes bringing spring to the mainland after all; her magical American corporate dream has come true.

At the same time as the U.S. government and the Ad Council launched the second round of public service announcements to coincide with the premiere of the second film and the naming of Tinker Bell as a UN ambassador, Disney released another tie-in to the franchise, its second Nintendo game for wannabe fairies (the first Nintendo game, naturally, had been released to tie in with the first film). 'The video game sequel allows players to mix creativity with gameplay, recreates memorable film moments and gives players more ways to connect with the online world of Pixie Hollow, the center of the Web-based universe for Disney Fairies', according to the *Business Wire* press release ('Tinker Bell and Friends'). Of course, 'gives' is a generous word since you have to pay $5.95 per month, $29.95 semi-annually or $57.95 annually to become a member and truly belong as a fairy avatar in Pixie Hollow.

On their interactive website, Disney's synergy expands to social networking between characters and consumers of their adapted texts. What could be cooler than being a fairy in a chat with other fairies? Of course, children have always loved role playing, and that is part of what *Peter Pan* has always been about too, with the Darling children playing at being Mother and Father in the first scene of Barrie's play or John and Michael playing at being Peter Pan and Captain Hook in the Walt Disney version, so in a certain respect, the extension of the Never Land characters into virtual reality seems an appropriate and even natural adaptation. In fact, Tinker Bell has already appeared in other video games on Playstation, Nintendo, Atari, Game Boy and others dating back to at least 1991.[3] If not for the crass commercialization and the limited choice menus at Disney's free area, I might even be tempted to suggest that the net narrative could be described as what Söke Dinkla calls a 'floating work of art', which is 'mobile and dynamic and therefore only recognizes temporary hierarchies. Its uniqueness lies precisely in the fact that it is recreated with every moment of perception' (Dinkla 2002, p. 38). The virtual reality at http://www.DisneyFairies.com, sadly, does not live up to that potential because it is so narrowly programmed, its hierarchies built in to predefined choices.

Still, in some ways, Tinker Bell's evolution in cyberspace does remain true to the spirit of organic adaptation in which narrative adapts to sociocultural context, an inevitable evolution from her beginnings in Barrie's ever-changing versions to our global, technological age. In fact, Barrie's ball-of-light Tinker Bell can be viewed as existing as a direct result of change. Tracy C. Davis in '"Do You Believe in Fairies?": The hiss of dramatic license' discusses Tinker Bell as representing 'the epic struggle between fairies and modernity' (2005, p. 80). Barrie gave stage spectators a choice: 'They vote on the existence of fairies – long said to be all dying out or leaving the British Isles altogether – as well as the proper custodians for belief in fairies, and thus the status of folklore in modernity' (Davis 2005, p. 70). Murray Pomerance also looks back at our fairy's beginnings in a liminal space:

> Tinker Bell was born at a particular historical moment, which is to say, there is a certain cultural, scientific, and artistic necessity that undergirds her curious domestic, fantastic, electrical nature. Toward the end of the nineteenth century gas lighting gradually gave way to electrical light, and European civilization (and the particular neo-European civilization that was America) changed forever. (Pomerance 2009, p. 24)

In the past decade, we have changed forever again with the seeming magic of the electronic media. Fairies can live again, children will believe. Barrie would surely like that. Perhaps technology is the ideal habitat for them. Except… these are not folkloric fairies or even Never Land fairies. They are Disney Fairies™.

Anyone who has ever tried to deconstruct the Disney canon in a college classroom has encountered the arguments for its defence. It is entertainment. It brings pleasure. It is just for children. What is the harm? For that matter, what is wrong with making a lot of money? As Jacqueline Rose points out, *Peter Pan* also made a lot of money for J. M. Barrie and his estate's beneficiary, the Great Ormond Street Hospital Children's Charity:

> One look at the extent of the commercialisation of *Peter Pan* is enough to establish that we do not really know what we are talking about when we refer to *Peter Pan*. In its history to date, *Peter Pan* has stood for, or been converted into, almost every conceivable (and some inconceivable) material forms: toys, crackers, posters, a Golf Club, Ladies League, stained glass window in St James's Church (Rose 1993, p. 103)

and she goes on with a long list that includes 'Animated Cartoon Rights'. Similar defences can be extended to the recent political appropriation of Tinker Bell. Why should the Department of Energy not take advantage of the Disney magic for an important cause, anyway? Why should the United Nations not name Tinker Bell an Honorary Ambassador of Green? What better way to get an important, positive message across to young people who are sure to fall in love with the franchise? There is certainly no harm on the surface of those good intentions. As many young people as possible should learn to make smart energy decisions, and it makes sense to communicate where the target audience is already paying attention. However, given that by definition the primary mission of any capitalist corporation in the United States is to profit shareholders, it behoves cultural critics to look beneath the surface intentions of Disney's contributions to public service. These ads, as sure as the films themselves, carry excess meanings.

Disney's fairies, like their princesses, appeal primarily to young girls; hence it is girls aged 8 and 9 who are targeted to receive messages about conserving energy in the home. This (inadvertently, I hope) reinforces the default position of the place of women in patriarchy, the domestic realm, looking after men and children. Media messages are targeted according to audience gender all the time, but there is no parallel energy awareness campaign of PSAs for boys. When I wrote to the Ad Council to ask if there was a reason they had chosen to target girls over boys, their contact person responded with an evasive answer:

> The strategy behind the work is to create a movement and, as you mention above, an energy ethic for future generations. What we found in the research, especially among the younger girls, was that they really sparked to the idea of banding together for a cause. Therefore, the Tinker Bell partnership was a perfect fit. (Shanley 2009)

Girls in third and fourth grade will definitely spark and band together for a cause – we call such bands *cliques* – and we can try to steer them towards using peer pressure for forces of good. But again, what kind of role models do the Disney fairies provide little girls in the films that the PSAs will inevitably draw audiences towards? Reversing real biology, a baby's first laugh immediately births the body of a voluptuous woman. Tinker Bell is a born sex symbol. Her friends, Silvermist the water talent, Rosetta the garden talent, Iridessa the light fairy, and Fawn the animal talent, all have hourglass figures, beautiful faces, great hair and nice clothes. As Alaine Martaus has pointed out,

> Disney, in creating and maintaining the thin, dancer model[4] for the new crop of fairies, despite what the voice models look like in real life, abandons the *embonpoint* Tinker Bell of Barrie's text and reinforces a more troublesome and controversial body image. (Martaus 2010)

These heroines banter sarcastically like girls in high school when they are not busy doing their life's work bringing spring to the mainland. Granted, as a franchise, fairies with Talents are a huge step up from princesses, but they still market a stereotyped femininity. They still do women's work: They reproduce nature.

# Conclusion

Disney Fairies look like pin-ups, behave like adolescents and may well appeal to 8- and 9- year-old girls, while in reality, the synergy campaign aims much younger. Disney starts marketing to expectant parents, selling bedding, furniture and other baby supplies to create a new generation of Disney consumers from birth. Early conditioning continues with Disney-branded bottles, diapers and spoons. For most Americans, their first fairy tales for three generations have been the abridged Disney versions, their first films Disney animations, their family vacations often Disney-themed as well. Mickey, Pooh and princess characters have been long-time favourites, and now they are being joined by themed baby showers featuring the Tinker Bell Diaper Cake. Toddlers can learn to feed off Disney Fairy tableware, toilet train with Disney Fairy potties and panties, carry a Disney Fairy backpack to preschool and eventually graduate into a Tinker Bell training bra. Adults can pay for all this out of their Tinker Bell debit card holders and checkbook covers. Fairy-licensed merchandise extends Disney's favourite storyline of all, the annual report to shareholders.

Adaptation should, ideally, work through what Linda Hutcheon calls 'natural selection', which is

> both conservative and dynamic; it involves both stabilizing and mutating. In short, it is all about propagating genes into future generations, identical in part, yet different. So too with cultural selection in the form of narrative adaptation – defined as theme and variation, repetition and modification.... Each newly indigenized version of a story competes – as do genes – but this time for audience attention, for time on radio or television or for space on bookshelves. But each adapts to its new environment and exploits it, and the story lives on, through its "offspring" – the same and yet not. (Hutcheon 2006, p. 167)

The Disney brand of adaptation fits Hutcheon's description quite neatly except for one caveat. The biological term 'natural selection' perhaps does not account adequately for the artificial selection carefully controlled by capitalist human ideologies. Disney uses its marketing synergies and aggressively exploits proprietary rights to effect corporate dominance and hold still its own genetic variations. Jack Zipes has written extensively about 'Disney's great talent for holding antiquated views of society *still* through animation and his use of the latest technological developments in cinema to his advantage' (1995, p. 39). The company that bears Walt Disney's name and markets a mythology of his genius continues to use new technologies to sell 'timeless' – that is, antiquated – patriarchal and colonializing views of society. Any story or character appropriated by the Disney Studios must bend to share the qualities of other films or characters in their 'timeless' canon because that is what they sell. Once Disney has made a film adaptation, their version often becomes the new site of canonical authority, not the prior text. As Richard Schickel said so famously in his seminal book *The Disney Version: The Life, Times, Art and Commerce of Walt Disney*, 'In fact, when it came to billing, J. M. Barrie's *Peter Pan* somehow became Walt Disney's *Peter Pan...*' (1997, p. 296).

From my experiences of teaching children's literature to college students at a public liberal arts university in the north-eastern United States, I have come to understand first-hand the extent to which Disney has branded the culture that American children are born into. The majority of students resist efforts to deconstruct themes of gender, race and power, preferring to view the company's products as innocent, harmless, wholesome entertainment, exactly as advertised. When it comes to critical thinking about all a fairy can signify – whether the 1953 animated Tinker Bell is stuck in a keyhole because her hips are too big or her 2008 update is switching off lights as a public service targeted to girls – people immersed in hegemonic marketing synergies from an early age are at a disadvantage. They have been cast as characters in Disney's greatest adaptation, producing lifelong consumers where once upon a time there were imaginative audiences actively participating in the natural selection of adaptation.

## Notes

1  The five were the sons of Sylvia and Arthur Llewelyn Davies. Barrie's relationship with the family and their role in the story of *Peter Pan* is best described by Andrew Birkin in *J. M. Barrie and the Lost Boys: The Real Story Behind Peter Pan*.

2  Michael Llewelyn Davies, who was born in 1900.

3  Details are described by Cathlena Martin and Laurie Taylor in 'Playing in
   Neverland: Peter Pan Video Game Revision' (2006).
4  Dancer Margaret Kelly played Tinker Bell in the live-action sequences film
   as models for the animation. For an interesting discussion of the influence
   of ballet in the early films, see Elizabeth Bell's 'Somatexts at the Disney Shop:
   Constructing the Pentimentos of Women's Animated Bodies' (1995).

## List of works cited

Barrie, J. M. (1991), 'Peter and Wendy', in Peter Hollindale (ed.), *Peter Pan in Kensington Gardens and Peter and Wendy*. New York: Oxford University Press, pp. 67–226.
— (1995), 'Peter Pan or The Boy Who Would Not Grow Up', in Peter Hollindale (ed.), *Peter Pan and Other Plays*. New York: Oxford University Press, pp. 73–163.
Bell, Elizabeth (1995), 'Somatexts at the Disney shop: constructing the pentimentos of women's animated bodies', in Elizabeth Bell, Lynda Haas, and Laura Sells (eds), *From Mouse to Mermaid: The Politics of Film, Gender, and Culture*. Indianapolis: Indiana University Press, pp. 107–24.
Birkin, Andrew (2003), *J. M. Barrie and the Lost Boys: The Real Story Behind Peter Pan*. 1979. New Haven, CT: Yale University Press.
Bradley Raymond (dir) (2008), *Tinker Bell*, DVD, Walt Disney Home Entertainment.
Davis, Tracy C. (2005), '"Do You Believe in Fairies?": the hiss of dramatic license'. *Theater Journal*, 57: 57–81.
Dinkla, Sőke (2002), 'The art of narrative: towards the *Floating Work of Art*', in M. Rieser and A. Zapp (eds), *New ScreenMedia: Cinema/Art/Narrative*. London: British Film Institute, pp. 27–41.
'Disney Fairies – The Official International Gateway', *DisneyFairies*, viewed 22 March 2009, <www.disneyfairies.com>.
Frost, John (2008), 'tinker-bell-friends-want-you-to-save-energy', *The Disney Blog*, 14 September, viewed 22 March 2009, <http://thedisneyblog.com>.
Geronimi, Clyde et al. (dir) (1997, 1953), *Peter Pan*, Video, Walt Disney Home Video.
Grimes, Sara M. (2009), 'Transmedia Expansions from Fairies to Fairy Godmothers', *Gamine Expedition*, 2 November, viewed 17 July 2010, <http://gamineexpedition.blogspot.com>.
'He Lives in Neverland'. Richard G. Hubler Collection. Gotlieb Archival Research Center, Boston University. Box 27, Folder 108.
Hill, Jim (2006), '"Disney Fairies" Franchise Gets Ready to Take Flight', *Jim Hill Media*, 30 May, viewed 22 March 2009, <http://jimhillmedia.com>.
Hollindale, Peter (1995), 'Introduction', in Peter Holindale (ed.), *Peter Pan and Other Plays*. New York: Oxford University Press, pp. vii–xxv.
Hutcheon, Linda (2006), *A Theory of Adaptation*. New York: Routledge.

Levine, Gail Carson (2005), *Fairy Dust and the Quest for the Egg.* New York: Disney Press.
— (2010), Personal Interview, 7 May. Willimantic, CT: Eastern Connecticut State University.
Martaus, Alaine (2010), 'The Many Faces of Tink: Disney's Once-Size-Fits-All Pop Culture Icon'. Conference presentation. International Conference on the Fantastic in the Arts. Orlando, Florida. [Unpublished manuscript.]
Martin, Cathlena and Taylor, Laurie (2006), 'Playing in Neverland: Peter Pan Video Game Revisions', in Donna R.White and C. Anita Tarr (eds), *J. M. Barrie's Peter Pan In and Out of Time, A Children's Classic at 100.* Children's Literature Association Centennial Studies no. 4. Lanham, MD: Scarecrow, pp. 173–93.
Ohmer, Susan (2009), 'Disney's Peter Pan: gender, fantasy, and industrial production', in Allison B. Kavey and Lester D. Friedman (eds), *Second Star to the Right: Peter Pan in the Popular Imagination.* New Brunswick, NJ: Rutgers University Press, pp. 151–87.
'Overview – Publishing' (no date), Publishing – Disney Consumer Products, viewed 24 March 2009, <http://dcpcareers.disney>.
'Pixie Hollow' (no date), *Disney Fairies,* viewed 15 July 2010, <www.pixiehollow.go.com>.
Pomerance, Murray (2009), 'Tinker Bell, the Fairy of Electricity', in Allison B. Kavey and Lester D. Friedman (eds), *Second Star to the Right: Peter Pan in the Popular Imagination.* New Brunswick, NJ: Rutgers University Press, pp. 13–49.
Rose, Jacqueline (1993, 1984), *The Case of Peter Pan or The Impossibility of Children's Fiction.* Philadelphia: University of Pennsylvania Press.
Schickel, Richard (1997, 1968), *The Disney Version: The Life, Times, Art and Commerce of Walt Disney.* Chicago, IL: Ivan R. Dee.
Shanley, Beth. 'RE: Questions about energy.gov/tink'. Email Correspondence. 23 March 2009.
Silverman, Linda (2009), 'DOE Energy Efficiency Marketing Campaigns – Trying to Build Sustainable Energy Behavior', U.S. Department of Energy – Energy Efficiency & Renewable Energy. Viewed 17 July 2010. PowerPoint.
Surrell, Jason (2004), *Screenplay by Disney: Tips and Techniques to Bring Magic to Your Moviemaking.* New York: Disney Editions.
The Ad Council and the U.S. Department of Energy (2008), 'The Advertising Council and U.S. Department of Energy Launch New PSAs to Help Create an Energy Ethic for Future Generations', 12 September, viewed 23 March 2009, <www.adcouncil.org>.
— (2009), 'The Advertising Council and U.S. Department of Energy Launch New PSAs to Help Create an Energy Ethic for Future Generations', 2 October, viewed 17 July 2010, <www.adcouncil.org>.
'Tinker Bell and Friends Return to Nintendo DS™ in Disney Fairies: Tinker Bell and the Lost Treasure' (2009), *Business Wire,* 27 October, viewed 17 July 2010, <www.businesswire.com>.
UN News Service (2009), 'UN Casts Disney's Tinker Bell to Raise Environmental Awareness Among Children', 25 October, viewed 17 July 2010, <www.un.org>.

U.S. Department of Energy (2008), 'DOE and Ad Council Launch Energy Efficiency Campaign for Youth: Campaign Encourages Wise Energy Choices', 12 September, viewed 22 March 2009, <www.energy.gov>.

U.S. Department of Energy – Energy Efficiency and Renewable Energy (2008a), 'EERE Kids Saving Energy: Magic Video (Text Version)', 19 September, viewed 22 March 2009, <http://.energy.gov>.

— (2008b), 'Web Site Policies', 14 April, viewed 22 March 2009, <www.energy.gov>.

U.S. Department of Energy – Energy Efficiency and Renewable Energy, 'energy.gov/tink', viewed 22 March 2009. [Note: this site now redirects to <http://www.eere.energy.gov/kids/>]

Wasko, Janet (2001), *Understanding Disney: The Manufacture of Fantasy*. Malden, MA: Polity.

'"What's Your Excuse?" Energy Efficiency Campaign: Talking Points' (2008), *State of Louisiana*, 12 September, viewed 23 March 2009, <dnr.louisiana.gov>.

Zipes, Jack (1995), 'Breaking the Disney spell', in E. Bell, L. Haas, and L. Sells (eds), *From Mouse to Mermaid: The Politics of Film, Gender, and Culture*. Bloomington, IN: Indiana University Press, pp. 21–42.

# Index

Lightning Source UK Ltd.
Milton Keynes UK
UKOW04f0511020914

237875UK00003B/31/P